Church and Israel
After Christendom

Church and Israel After Christendom

THE POLITICS OF ELECTION

Scott Bader-Saye

Wipf & Stock
PUBLISHERS
Eugene, Oregon

To
Karen Nolan Saye

Wipf and Stock Publishers
199 W 8th Ave, Suite 3
Eugene, OR 97401

Church and Israel After Christendom
The Politics of Election
By Bader-Saye, Scott
Copyright©1999 by Bader-Saye, Scott
ISBN: 1-59752-078-0
Publication date 1/31/2005
Previously published by Westview Press, 1999

Contents

5 Trinitarian Election   95

6 The Freedom of Election   117

7 The Peace of Election   135

Acknowledgments

If I have learned anything while writing this book, it is that my life is not my own, and thus neither are my achievements. I have been sustained both personally and academically by a host of friends and family who have proved to be the very hands of God enfolding my life and work. Anything I could say here to thank them would be too little, though I welcome the opportunity to name these debts as the gifts they are. First, it must be said that without the encouragement and prayers of my community at University Presbyterian Church in Chapel Hill, this project would never have gotten off the ground. Likewise, the friendship and support of classmates at Duke, especially John David Ramsey and Wendy and Dan Shenk-Evans, graced the long days of writing with times of much-needed refreshment.

Jim Fodor, a consummate close-reader, provided some very helpful comments on material in Chapter 4, and Oliver O'Donovan graciously critiqued my treatment of his work with a seriousness and extensiveness that I hardly deserved but gladly accepted. Kendall Soulen has not only furnished a challenging response to my critiques but has become a partner in dialogue on a variety of related topics where we find ourselves engaged in common pursuits. His writings as well as our conversations have stretched me in ways I could not have predicted but could not have done without.

The members of my dissertation committee—Richard Hays, David Novak, Ken Surin, and Geoffrey Wainwright—gave me the intellectual nourishment and critical feedback necessary not only to produce the earlier dissertation version of this work but also to press on with the task of crafting and honing the argument into its present form. My dissertation director, Stanley Hauerwas, has been for me an adviser, mentor, teacher, and friend. I would be hard-pressed to return thanks enough for the ways in which he has nurtured my thinking and enriched my living in these last years. I have had my vision expanded and sharpened by our many conversations, for which he always seemed to have time, even in the midst of a multitude of other commitments. He has been a friend to me in the best Aristotelian sense, and I have learned from his example what it means to embody a theological stance—which is to say, he lives what he writes.

Ray Barfield has been my most committed and long-lasting intellectual sparring partner, always reminding me that thinking can be a joyous exercise and that good conversation is food for the soul. My own work would surely be less interesting had it not been again and again leavened by delightful arguments with this man. My mother, Karen, is not only my link to the people of Israel but a source of strength and gladness in my life. If I know anything about the unmerited grace of election, it is because she has loved me with such love. Finally, my wife, Demery, has lived more closely with this project than anyone, and she has borne patiently and with good faith my periods of preoccupation with it. Her presence in my life is a constant reminder that God's providence upholds us and carries us toward *shalom,* even when such a destination lies hidden in an unknown future. Demery's gift of hopefulness rescues me time and again from my cynicism, and her passion for life makes my own life more joyful than I could have ever expected.

Scott Bader-Saye

Church and Israel
After Christendom

Introduction

The day I discovered my grandfather was a Jew, I knew I had learned something important, but I did not know quite what it was. I was already an adult, my mother's father having made his Jewishness largely invisible to his grandchildren. Not unlike other Jewish immigrants, he and his brothers, after fleeing to the United States from Russia, had changed their name—from Ominski to Nolan—in an attempt to Americanize, to assimilate, to avoid the persecution that had driven the family from its home. I imagine their flight as something like the final scene of *Fiddler on the Roof*—a parade of Jewish families exiled from their land wandering down a muddy road, their faces a mixture of fear and hope as they journey to Poland, to Jerusalem, to America. I hold a single memory of talking to my grandfather about his Jewish identity. Once during our Christmas celebration (oddly enough), he told me of his bar mitzvah. With tears in his eyes, he described the experience of holding the Torah scroll for the first time as he read from the holy text. I knew then that his Jewishness, though not often visible, was rooted deeply in his bones. I began to wonder, as a Christian, what it meant that I stood at the edges of that chosen people, at the border of the holy land. It was the growing realization that *all* Christians share a link to the people of Israel that first put me on the path to writing this book, but it was only as I began to reflect on the ecclesiological crises of the post-Christendom world that I understood why this truth is so important.

To shift from the personal to the political, two seismic events in this century have made this book both possible and necessary. The first is the demise of the Christendom paradigm, in which the church was positioned as the spiritual sponsor of Western civilization. Although this paradigm has been in its death throes for some time, it is arguably only in the latter half of the twentieth century that it has passed from the American scene. For many, this disestablishment has been perceived as a loss, as a diminishment of Christian relevance to the dominant culture. However, it may just as well be an opportunity for rethinking faithful forms of ecclesial existence now that the church is no longer expected to prop up an alien politics.

The second event is the Holocaust, the Shoah, the systematic attempt by a "Christian nation" to eradicate the Jews. In the decades after the Holocaust, both Roman Catholic and Protestant churches have widely repudiated the teachings and attitudes that undergirded the dark history of Jewish persecution. In a watershed statement, which today seems still too deeply infused with the assumptions of supersessionism,[1] the Vatican II document *Nostra Aetate* professed that all Christ's faithful, who as men of faith are sons of Abraham (cf. Gal. 3:7), are included in the same patriarch's call and that the salvation of the church is mystically prefigured in the exodus of God's chosen people from the land of bondage. On this account the Church cannot forget that she received the revelation of the Old Testament by way of that people with whom God in his inexpressible mercy established the ancient covenant. Nor can she forget that she draws nourishment from that good olive tree onto which the wild olive branches of the Gentiles have been grafted (cf. Rom. 11:17–24). . . . It is true that the Church is the new people of God, yet the Jews should not be spoken of as rejected or accursed as if this followed from holy Scripture.[2]

More recently, Pope John Paul II, speaking in 1980 before Jewish representatives in Mainz, Germany, made explicit what was not necessarily so in *Nostra Aetate,* that is, that the covenant with Israel "has never been revoked by God (cf. Rom 11:29)."[3]

The Presbyterian Church (USA) put forth in 1987 a powerful and theologically challenging statement on Christians and Jews, affirming explicitly "that the church, elected in Jesus Christ, has been engrafted into the people of God established by the covenant with Abraham, Isaac, and Jacob. Therefore, Christians have not replaced Jews."[4] In light of this affirmation of a common covenant and a common calling, the statement adds, "We acknowledge in repentance the church's long and deep complicity in the proliferation of anti-Jewish attitudes and actions through its 'teaching of contempt' for the Jews. Such teaching we now repudiate, together with the acts and attitudes which it generates."[5] These statements reflect a fundamental shift in the way the Christian churches in the West conceive of their relation to Israel and Israel's relation to God.[6] This change in the church's view of Israel requires Christians to rethink their own doctrines and practices just to the extent that these were built upon and thus reproduced the church's prior conviction that it had replaced Israel in God's plan. Ecclesiology is one of the doctrines most affected by this change in posture toward Israel, yet little has been done so far to ask how the church's own life and witness are impacted by the conviction that the church's identity is grounded in Israel's election.

The theologies that are now being produced in the West must take both of the above shifts into account. We can no longer write theology as if the Holocaust never happened, nor can we write theology as if Christianity still maintained its cultural hegemony in America or in Europe. The goal of the present work is to ask how a renewed theology of Israel can provide resources to envision a faithful post-Christendom ecclesiology.

The subtitle of this work, *The Politics of Election,* calls attention to the fact that the political language associated with the election of Israel and the church's ingathering ("holy nation," "commonwealth of Israel," "citizens with the saints," "citizens of heaven") is not accidental. If the church is understood as that body of people grafted into and thus carrying forward Israel's covenantal politics (alongside the Jews), then this means we can no longer read the New Testament as superseding the social concerns of the Old Testament.[7] We cannot divide the Christian community from the explicitly political identity of Israel. The church, as much as the Jews, exists within the one covenant of God, which leaves no arena of life unaccounted for, including politics. This means that attending to Israel as a way to rethink ecclesiology will mean resisting the depoliticizing of the church. Such depoliticizing of ecclesiology has both internal and external roots. Internally, the church has lost its political witness because of its inadequate understanding of election, which sought to leave the Jews and their materiality behind. Externally, the churches in the West have been depoliticized by accepting their place in a modern liberal polity that renders them largely irrelevant to the public square.[8]

The doctrine of election is the linchpin by which I bring together my reflections on Israel and my proposal for the post-Christendom church. This doctrine has fallen on hard times in modern theological thought, for it bumps up against modern conceptions of freedom and autonomy, it calls into question explanations of the world as a closed system, and its unabashed particularity makes it troubling to the universalist aspirations of the Enlightenment. Election thus has become an embarrassing doctrine to those who wish to commend Christianity to modern consciousness. Apart from some Calvinists, who have continued to talk about election because they simply could not stop, Christian theologians in the modern era have tended to ignore the doctrine or radically reinterpret it so as to render it inoffensive. Its exit from the heart of theological debate, however, has left Christian theology unable to account for the biblical and premodern theological emphasis on election as a central description of God's economy.[9]

And this is not just a Christian problem. Jews have no less relativized the doctrine. David Novak describes his project in *The Election of Israel* as a "retrieval" of the biblical-rabbinic understanding of election.[10] Such a retrieval has become necessary because modern Jewish thinking has pushed election to the margins in two related ways. On the one hand, Spinoza and his followers rejected God's special election of Israel in favor of Israel's election of a universal, monistic God. In this formulation, Spinoza retains God's universality but relinquishes Israel's uniqueness. In short, Spinoza "opted . . . for God over Israel." Modern Jewish secularists, on the other hand, have opted for Israel over God—holding fast to Jewish particularity but grounding this identity not in God's election but in biology, culture, and history.[11]

In part this modern shift away from election is understandable, at least on the Christian side, given the transformation of the doctrine from its Jewish roots in community and vocation to its Christian focus on the predestining of the individual soul for eternal salvation or damnation. What is needed now in Christian theology is a reconsideration of this doctrine, a rereading of scripture, and a recovery of Israel in ecclesiology. Ironically, we will discover in the process that a *nonsupersessionist* doctrine of election also leads to a more fully *trinitarian* doctrine of election. My hope is that this project goes some way toward answering the call "to ponder with Jews the mystery of God's election of both Jews and Christians to be a light to the nations."[12]

1

Aristotle or Abraham?

"Now in these dread latter days of the old violent beloved U.S.A. and of the Christ-forgetting Christ-haunted death-dealing Western world I came to myself in a grove of young pines and the question came to me: has it happened at last?"[1] So the Roman Catholic writer Walker Percy opens his apocalyptic novel *Love in the Ruins*, aptly subtitled *The Adventures of a Bad Catholic at a Time Near the End of the World*. The echo of Dante's *Inferno* rings clearly in these opening words, and they indeed foreshadow a descent into hell. But the hell Percy portrays is the end of the American dream come to the suburban enclave of "Paradise Estates." "Has it happened at last?" Has the American experiment finally collapsed? Has God removed the blessing long assumed to be the special prerogative of America—God's new chosen people? These questions haunt the protagonist and narrator of the novel, Tom More, a decidedly unsaintly character who nonetheless finds himself indelibly marked by the faith of his namesake.

As the novel progresses, the deeper question turns out to be not whether the American project is coming to an end, but whether it was doomed from the beginning. "The poor U.S.A.!" More laments, "Even now, late as it is, nobody can really believe that it didn't work after all. The U.S.A. didn't work! Is it even possible that from the beginning it never did work? that the thing always had a flaw in it, a place where it would shear, and that all this time we were not really different from Ecuador and Bosnia-Herzegovina, just richer."[2] He traces this fault line back to the act of primal violence that inaugurated the American project—the enslavement of African people. It was America's "one little test." "Flunked! Christendom down the drain. The dream over."[3] And although Tom More the scientist thinks his new invention might yet save America, an undercurrent in the novel suggests that it is only through another people, and another story, that salvation will come.

That story, it turns out, is the story of the church, or more specifically, a tiny Roman Catholic remnant worshiping in the run-down chapel of the old slave quarters near the swamp. The question Percy never fully answers and with which we are left to wrestle is how this remnant will sustain itself in these "last days." How will it re-envision its life and work and witness after the collapse of

Christendom, the fall from Paradise? This is not just the fanciful question of an apocalyptic novelist; it is the question that churches in America are increasingly having to face. The decline in membership and influence of the churches (especially the so-called mainline churches), combined with widespread cultural fragmentation, has led to a range of proposals, from the church-growth movement to contemporary spiritualities to political retrenchment, for how Christians might shape a new identity and mission in the post-Christendom world. If Percy is right in his cultural critique, and I think he is, then he may well be right in suggesting that a tiny Catholic enclave in the swamp could be the unpredictable form God's work will take in this new day.

One particularly engaging proposal for reforming ecclesiology along these lines has been the recovery of the Greek model of the polis and the life of virtue as a way of recalling Christians to the peculiar politics and practice of being church. Theologians such as John Milbank and Stanley Hauerwas have in various ways turned to Aristotle and the Greeks to recover a discourse about politics and character that contrasts with the dominant discourse of modern liberalism. This recovery has fruitfully challenged the church in the West to rethink its mission in the wake of disestablishment, but it has done so by appropriating a political and moral discourse from outside the church's biblical idiom. Although such a move is not foreign to the history of Christian theology, it nonetheless bears the burden of proof concerning its faithfulness to Christian belief and practice. My conviction is that although these proposals have been invaluable in their diagnosis of the problems, their constructive moves have at times missed the mark precisely insofar as they have sought to recover Aristotle at the expense of Abraham.

Voluntarism and Violence

In the first chapter of *After Virtue,* Alasdair MacIntyre presents his own apocalyptic vision to describe the state of moral discourse in modernity.[4] Imagine a time, he asks us, when a series of natural disasters occurs and is blamed on scientists. A reign of terror ensues in which physicists are lynched, laboratories destroyed, and textbooks burned. What might be left and discovered by a later generation would be mere fragments—charred chapters from books, single pages from articles, portions of the periodic table. This, he argues, mirrors the state of moral and political discourse in modernity. Western liberal social thought is composed largely of fragmented vestiges of earlier, more coherent, frameworks. Abstracted from these, our discourse has been reduced to assertions of will (voluntarism) and our politics reduced to a struggle for power (violence). MacIntyre argues that the only alternatives left in these latter days are Nietzsche or Aristotle—the nihilistic end of modernity or a recovery of a premodern moral and social vision.[5] Following MacIntyre, I want to suggest that *voluntarism* and *violence* name the two central features of the modern social, political, and moral landscape. Under these two rubrics I summarize the critiques of modernity that make the return to the Greeks (or a variation on the Greeks) such an attractive political and ecclesiological position.[6] Yet unlike MacIntyre, I argue that the real question is not "Nietzsche or Aristotle?" but "Aristotle or Abraham?"

"Voluntarism" names the triumph of freedom as choice. In morality and politics this term refers to the primacy of the will (*voluntas*), that is, the primacy of individual assertions of desire. The issue of what *ought* to be desired or what choices *ought* to be made is privatized in modern liberal democracies as a way of removing such volatile discussions from the public arena. A certain kind of peace results from making any substantive determinations about the good or the right a matter of private decision. Yet such a peace only serves to hide our deep disagreements, and thus it excludes the possibility of constructive confrontation. Whether the issue is abortion, physician-assisted suicide, or nuclear weapons, in the end such debates devolve into assertions of will and appeals to feeling—all parties claiming to be right because they have chosen certain "values" that make their position right. MacIntyre labels such claims "emotivist," that is, "the doctrine that all evaluative judgments and more specifically all moral judgments are *nothing but* expressions of preference, expressions of attitude or feeling, insofar as they are moral or evaluative in character."[7] He goes on to point out the weakness of such claims: "The terminus of justification is thus always, on this view, a not further to be justified choice, a choice unguided by criteria. Each individual implicitly or explicitly has to adopt his or her own first principles on the basis of such a choice. The utterance of any universal principle is in the end an expression of the preferences of an individual will and for that will its principles have and can have only such authority as it chooses to confer upon them by adopting them."[8] So on the one hand, no one need be persuaded by another's position since it is but an expression of preference, and on the other hand one's own decisions are never binding, since one can always choose different principles or authorities (or indeed choose to have none at all!).

Modern liberal politics mirrors the voluntarism of our moral discourse by striving to create a social space in which agreement on the goods and ends of life is unnecessary. Liberal democracy names that polity in which people can decide for themselves what constitutes "the good life" and pursue it as they wish, so long as they do not infringe on others. In this way the state seeks to maintain unity apart from any shared story or ethos. Or rather its only story is that it has no story and its only ethos that it has no ethos.[9] Story, ethos, and a shared vision of the good are replaced by a bureaucratic system designed to maximize personal choice, within limits, about the goods and ends of life.[10] The system itself claims to be neutral with respect to such overarching determinations. Yet the very ubiquity of the appeal to "freedom of choice" suggests that there is in fact a single determining good in liberal society that is unavoidable: the good of choice itself. Liberal claims to neutrality are thus spurious, since certain ways of conceiving the political project are ruled out of court from the beginning. As Ronald Beiner writes, "To forego a substantive theory of the human good in favor of consumer

freedom is already to exclude an entire way of life postulated upon noncon-
sumerist conceptions of human fulfillment, and so to favor a particular vision of
the human good, thereby contradicting the neutralist presumption. Thus, paradoxically, to say there is no need to adjudicate between rival conceptions of the
good is already to yield, by default, to a particular vision of personal and political good, namely that of consumerist liberalism."[11] In other words, "choice in itself is the highest good."[12]

Liberal politics turns out to be the perfect handmaid of a capitalist economy.
Not only are "goods" produced and distributed according to a free market, but political decisions are likewise driven by consumer preference. Bargaining between
individual interests replaces rational debate about goods and ends.[13] Interest
groups emerge as ways of collectively asserting individual preferences and vying
for the power to pursue these preferences over against the conflicting interests of
others. Citizens who have more money or influence thereby wield inordinate
leverage in the bargaining game. Not long ago U.S. president Bill Clinton came
under attack for accepting foreign campaign contributions as well as for "reward-
ing" contributions with photo sessions, coffees, and even nights in the White
House. The possibility that political influence is being bought, though it may dis-
turb us, should not surprise us. Insofar as political decisions have come to be understood on the model of bargaining in the marketplace, it is no great leap to assume that with more money one will be able to buy more favorable decisions.
Apart from some agreement on substantive common goods, bargaining for interests can hardly be avoided as the dominant mode of political decisionmaking.

The voluntarism of the moral and political arenas correlates in liberal societies
with the construction of the "individual," by whom the right of free choice can be
exercised. One of the hallmarks of modern society is that the individual constitutes the primary political unit. The state, or even the local community, exists not
as a political entity in itself prior to the individual but precisely as an aggregate of
individuals. Thus, the role of the state becomes the bureaucratic management of
the inevitable conflict between individuals seeking to assert their wills through free
choice. Yet in such a polity, as Robert Bellah nicely articulates, "freedom turns out
to mean being left alone by others. . . . What it is that one might do with that freedom is much more difficult for Americans to define. And if the entire social world
is made up of individuals, each endowed with the right to be free of others' demands, it becomes hard to forge bonds of attachment to, or cooperation with,
other people, since such bonds would imply obligations that necessarily impinge
on one's freedom."[14] Freedom is purchased at the price of isolation.

As the individual's assertion of free choice has come to be the only real grounding of morality and politics, Friedrich Nietzsche's dark vision has proven
prophetic. It was Nietzsche who unmasked the Enlightenment antinomy between
the affirmation of individual freedom as the highest good and the concurrent attempt to hold on to traditional (Christian) morality. Taken to its logical end, he
argued, voluntarism swallows up morality whole, reducing it to a matter of indi-

vidual preference. Therefore, he proclaimed, throw off the shackles of "slave morality" (Judaism and Christianity) and reaffirm classical heroism, by which the good is defined by the noble, the strong, the powerful.[15] The new humanity is self-created, "We . . . *want to become those we are*—human beings who are new, unique, incomparable, who give themselves laws, who create themselves."[16] The struggle for self-creation evolves through the assertion of "will to power" whereby the necessity of violence is embraced by the strong and the heroic.[17] Thus, the other shoe falls and we uncover the intrinsic connection between voluntarism and violence. Assertion of will (voluntarism) as a good in itself opens the door for violence as a justifiable act in the service of personal or national interest (i.e., the personal or national will).

Despite its clear acceptance of the primacy of choice or volition, the modern age has been ambivalent in its response to Nietzsche's call to throw off its supposedly objective, traditional morality and embrace the violent struggle for dominion. Although Nietzsche hoped this would resurrect the glory of the classical contest for honor (in the person of the *Übermensch,* the superman), others denied this frightening fruit of the modern project. These Nietzsche scornfully dubbed "the last men," who, instead of reaching for the glory of dominance and self-creation, take refuge in empty sentimentality.[18] The twin perils of sentimentality and violence continue to haunt the modern project.

Three hundred years before Nietzsche, Thomas Hobbes articulated the myth of primal violence in his *Leviathan,* one of the founding documents of modern political thought. Hobbes described the human condition before the advent of the state not as a golden age now lost but as a time in which the struggle between individual wills was without restraint. He argued that outside of the restraint imposed by civil states, "*there is always war of every one against every one.* Hereby it is manifest, that during the time men live without a common power to keep them all in awe, they are in that condition which is called war: and such a war, as is of every man, against every man. For WAR, consisteth not in battle only, or the act of fighting; but in a tract of time, wherein the will to contend by battle is sufficiently known."[19] Unless and until individuals agree together to a social contract, thus placing above themselves a sufficient power to enforce "peace," this state of fear and violence holds sway, making life "solitary, poor, nasty, brutish, and short."[20] Yet even such a peace is only a temporary constraint on the more fundamental and thus always threatening violence. Peace can only be the use of ample force to limit the violence inherent in the human condition; thus, only the threat of violence can hold the war of each against each in check. In this modern political vision, there seems to be no alternative to a fundamentally violent social order.[21]

Nietzsche or Aristotle?

It was just such an analysis of modernity's voluntarism and violence that set up MacIntyre's famous alternative, "Nietzsche or Aristotle?"[22] Drawing on Aristotle's political and ethical vision and the development of this tradition through Augustine and Aquinas, MacIntyre seeks to direct us toward "the construction of local forms of community within which civility and the intellectual and moral life can be sustained through the new dark ages which are already upon us." He adds, "And if the tradition of the virtues was able to survive the horrors of the last dark ages, we are not entirely without grounds for hope."[23] It is this tradition of the virtues that he argues provides the most rationally defensible alternative to the modern liberal tradition.

In contrast to the voluntarism of modernity, MacIntyre returns to the language of virtue, where the focus is not on particular decisions and unguided choices but on the quality of a complete human life. The virtues are habits of character that enable one to pursue and achieve those goods internal to practices as well as the good end of human life as a whole.[24] As such, virtues cannot be understood apart from a correlative set of practices and narratives that are carried forward within a tradition.[25] The life of virtue (ethics), therefore, requires training and initiation into a distinct way of life (politics).

MacIntyre begins with the idea of a practice, which he defines as "any coherent and complex form of socially established cooperative human activity through which goods internal to that form of activity are realized in the course of trying to achieve those standards of excellence which are appropriate to, and partially definitive of, that form of activity, with the result that human powers to achieve excellence, and human conceptions of the ends and goods involved, are systematically extended."[26] Parsing this complex definition leads one deeply into the interconnections of virtues, practices, narratives, and traditions. For MacIntyre, the kinds of activities that count as practices include such things as baseball, architecture, and farming. They do not include batting, bricklaying, or planting turnips. The latter are particular skills that are necessary to the practice but that do not constitute practices themselves.[27] Practices produce internal goods; for instance, the activity of chess produces the goods of "analytical skill, strategic imagination, and competitive intensity."[28] The virtues are the qualities of character, such as patience and practical intelligence, that make possible the achievement of these goods, while simultaneously participation in the practices leads to the development of the virtues.

To think of virtues, however, simply as ways of achieving the goods internal to practices would be insufficient. Virtues are about shaping one's character so as to participate in the larger good of human life itself. Here MacIntyre discusses the role of narratives.[29] Although there are many ways in which narrative is an important concept for MacIntyre, I am interested in his construal of the unity of a human life in narrative terms, specifically, the human life understood as a quest for the good. MacIntyre contrasts his narrative view of the self with the liberal individual. He observes, "From the standpoint of individualism I am what I myself choose to be. I can always, if I wish to, put in question what are taken to be the merely contingent social features of my existence." But such a person is fated to be "a self that can have no history."[30] "Having a history" means recognizing that one is "born with a past," born into a social context and a network of relationships that will always be part of one's identity. Although one is not destined to live within the limitations of that particular world, one must know one's starting point in order to move forward in the search for the good.[31]

Such a storied self appears threatening to those shaped by the American story, for they continue to assume that being embedded in a narrative and a web of relations can only mean the loss of freedom. But as MacIntyre so aptly puts it, without a story people are left as "unscripted, anxious stutterers in their actions as in their words."[32] In contrast, the life of virtue provides the constancy of character necessary to tell one's story as a unified whole in a quest for the good. That is, virtues make integrity possible, and such integrity, or narrative unity, proves to be the foundation for truly free actions.

Only as one is able to understand one's life as a quest for the good will one be able to discern and develop the virtues necessary for the journey. But MacIntyre is less than helpful when it comes to defining what the good end of a well-lived life actually is. He believes it is the role of a tradition to name that good, but because he attempts to give a general account of virtue, he does not claim to speak out of any *particular* tradition himself.[33] This leads to an account of the good life, toward which the virtues are supposed to lead, that is disappointingly abstract and circular: "The good life for man is the life spent in seeking for the good life for man, and the virtues necessary for the seeking are those which will enable us to understand what more and what else the good life for man is."[34] To give a more explicit depiction of the good end of human life and the virtues that, in part, comprise that good end, MacIntyre would have had to draw on a *particular* set of stories within a *particular* tradition of knowledge. But because he wishes to give a general account, his description of the ancient alternative on this point remains only suggestive and vague.

Nonetheless, he does make clear that just as liberal "emotivism" presupposes a certain social context in which such a life could be pursued, so the virtue tradition brings with it a certain social world that is the necessary context in which virtues can be developed and sustained. Just as Aristotle's account of the virtues required the context of the Greek polis, so MacIntyre's account requires at least something like a polis. He writes,

> If the conception of a good has to be expounded in terms of such notions as those of a practice, of the narrative unity of a human life and of a moral tradition, then goods, and with them the only grounds for the authority of laws and virtues, can only be discovered by entering into those relationships which constitute communities whose central bond is a shared vision of and understanding of goods. To cut oneself off from shared activity in which one has initially to learn obediently as an apprentice learns, to isolate oneself from the communities which find their point and purpose in such activities, will be to debar oneself from finding any good outside of oneself. It will be to condemn oneself to that moral solipsism which constitutes Nietzschean greatness.[35]

A political community that shares a common vision of the good is necessary in order to name the good end of human life and thus to encourage the practices and virtues by which such a goal could be achieved. Such a political body, however, is a far cry from modern Western politics. Here we are back to MacIntyre's either-or: Nietzsche or Aristotle?—either a fragmented politics in which appeals to "pluralism" hide a deep and debilitating lack of consensus and an ongoing internal struggle for power and interests, or a political recovery of the virtue tradition along with the forms of life necessary for its practice.

The Church as Voluntary Association?

The church in America today finds itself implicated in these ongoing debates about modernity, politics, and ethics. For just as the ethos of Western liberalism is being challenged, so the church, which has largely defined itself in terms of this culture, finds its own life and work called into question. The debate between the ancients and the moderns has become for Christians a debate about the identity of the church and its relation to the dominant politics of the West. In short, do Christians have a stake in maintaining the liberal order, within which the church has been situated as a "voluntary association"? Or do Christians have a stake in the recovery of a politics of the polis, which suggests an alternative ecclesiological model set in stark contrast to the liberal order?

Returning to *Love in the Ruins,* we find that Percy questions not only the future of the American project but the future of the American church. With his usual mix of sympathetic insight and ruthless critique, he imagines a time in which the church's capitulation to "Americanism" reduces Christian practice to absurdity. "Our Catholic church here split into three pieces: (1) the American Catholic Church whose new Rome is Cicero, Illinois; (2) the Dutch schismatics who believe in relevance but not God; (3) the Roman Catholic remnant, a tiny scattered flock with no place to go. The American Catholic Church, which emphasizes property rights and the integrity of neighborhoods, retained the Latin mass and plays *the Star-Spangled Banner* at the elevation."[36] He goes on to add, "Property Rights Sunday is a major feast day in the A.C.C. [American Catholic Church]. A blue banner beside the crucifix shows Christ holding the American home, which has a picket fence, in his two hands."[37] The edge in Percy's satire comes, of course, from the vague uneasiness that such a thing is just almost imaginable.[38]

Yet what becomes of such a church when individual autonomy, property rights, and the American way are called into question? What becomes of such a church if the end goal of American liberalism turns out to be not prosperity and happiness but fragmentation, emptiness, and conflict? These questions are becoming an unsettling chorus for the churches in America, and they strike at the heart of the long-held conviction that being a Christian and being an American are complementary, if not identical.

With the rise of the modern nation-state and liberal political philosophy, the church was given the dubious honor of a protected place within the culture. But such protection has turned out to be equally a containment.[39] Christianity is protected as a *private* belief system but is contained insofar as these beliefs cannot challenge the *public* realm; that is, they cannot translate into actions that are in conflict with the interests of the nation-state. As William Cavanaugh has insightfully displayed, the so-called wars of religion in the sixteenth and seventeenth centuries were less the *result* of religion than the *creation* of religion: "What is at issue behind these wars is the creation of 'religion' as a set of beliefs which is defined as personal conviction and which can exist separately from one's public loyalty to the State. The creation of religion, and thus the privatization of the Church, is correlative to the rise of the State."[40] Religion comes to be understood as a "belief system" that is separable from the bodily practices of the church. Thus, the soul is kept for religion but "the body is handed over to the State."[41] As a "religion," Christianity finds itself both protected and contained—given a place but kept in its place. Its role is to explain or engage that which is inexplicable within the prevailing social system. Religion is therefore granted dominion over the mysterious and the marginal, whereas those issues at the center of the society's life are shielded from religious interference. Religion and the church are "saved," but only "at the price . . . of a total emptying of [their] concrete practical content."[42]

The name given to such a socially domesticated entity is "voluntary association"—a place where people who happen to share similar beliefs can come together to discuss those beliefs and encourage one another. As a "voluntary" gathering, the church exists because of the free choice of individuals who decide to be a part of it. As an "association," the church is a place where people congregate to pursue their interests and meet their needs by associating with like-minded people. As John Locke put it back in 1685, "A Church, then, I take to be a voluntary society of men, joining themselves together of their own accord in order to the public worshiping of God. . . . Some enter into company for trade and profit: others, for want of business, have their clubs for claret. Neighbourhood joins some, and religion others."[43] Being subsumed under the category of "voluntary association," the church shares a common status with the Kiwanis and the Masons, the garden club and the country club. It is reduced to a gathering that can be no threat to a polity based on the primacy of individual choice.

Positioned in this way, the church can hardly resist becoming just another consumer commodity. We read books on marketing the church; we hire consultants to plan our capital campaigns; we sell the church as a provider of spiritual goods. Once the church is captured and placed by the liberal polity, the only logical way to conceive of its mission will be in terms the culture understands—the free market. In such an orientation, mission is turned in on the self so that "the church exists to serve our needs."[44] That the practice of "church-shopping" does not strike us as odd only confirms the extent to which the church as voluntary association has become the church as consumer commodity.

As a player in the religious market, church is reduced to, in Bellah's words, a "lifestyle enclave"—a homogenous gathering of people linked by common habits of leisure and consumption.[45] This "enclave" is segmented in two ways. First, it engages only a certain segment of the individual's life, the private areas of leisure and consumption. There is no claim on the whole person. Second, it is segmented off from people of other "lifestyles," who are at best tolerated but are in fact the necessary "other" over against whose habits of consumption each enclave defines itself.[46] Within a polity dominated politically and economically by the rights of individual preference, the church is tolerated and even supported, so long as it agrees to its particular role in service to the wider social vision. Once the church allows itself to become such a lifestyle enclave, the distinctiveness of Christian identity is reduced to distinctive consumptive patterns. "Hence, in American culture 'christians' are those who consume 'christian' commodities, thus making it possible for people to discern who they are; they are the ones buying christian music, jewelry, books, games, bumper stickers, and wall hangings, and the ones going to christian concerts, workshops, and conferences. By consuming these christian products, they set themselves apart in one of the few ways they know how to."[47]

Within a liberal polity that prizes individual choice above all else, the church can maintain a place in the culture only by acquiescing in its own demise. Once the church allows itself to be named as a voluntary association, a social entity moved into and out of at will by the consuming public, it loses its grounding in the story of God's calling and choosing a people to be a witness to God's reign. Of course the churches in America cannot simply decide to step out of the ubiquitous liberal polity that surrounds them, nor need they seek to overthrow it in order to substitute another variety of modern nationalism. For better or worse, this is where they find themselves called to live and bear witness. Yet churches in America can refuse to be placed by the current principalities and powers. They can seek to embody an alternative to the modern creation, protection, and containment of religion. It is just such an alternative that some have found in the politics of the polis, and this is what makes the return to the Greeks so powerfully attractive as an ecclesiological paradigm.

The Church as Polis?

If MacIntyre is right, then the future belongs to local, polislike, communities bound together by shared stories and a common vision of the good. In such communities lives of virtue could be nurtured and a tradition of rational debate concerning the goods of life could be carried forward. Such might indeed be a prescription for the church in the postmodern world. MacIntyre himself ends *After Virtue* with a call for a new (and different) St. Benedict.[48] Yet does this alternative model of the polis, arising out of Aristotle, provide the church with the communal and conceptual resources to live its own story more faithfully?

Both Milbank and Hauerwas draw on the Greeks to construct a polislike ecclesiology. However, neither of them does this uncritically, and each is more than willing to name the ways in which the polis is, in itself, an insufficient model for the radical life and witness of the church. Milbank, for instance, points out the ways in which the language of virtue can tend toward an individualized conception of happiness and "the good life," which fails to challenge modern voluntarism effectively. He asks, "Is the main goal for Christian ethics the achievement of a certain state of individual character, according to the role which society prescribes for us?"[49] He answers negatively, affirming rather that it is the formation of peaceful communities of forgiveness. "Augustine asserts that, for us, the approach to divine perfection cannot be by any achieved excellence of virtue, but only through forgiveness. . . . Augustine's real and astounding point is this: virtue cannot properly operate except when collectively possessed."[50] Milbank here points out one of the problems of classical accounts of virtue. They do not see that virtue must be held in common, rather than being the possession, the habit (from *habere*, "to have, hold") of the individual.

In the polis happiness can be achieved by some (well-born men of property), while others are necessarily excluded (women, slaves, and the sufferers of ill fortune). In the church, Milbank argues, the good end of life is reached not by leaving anyone behind but by properly sharing in common the diversity of gifts that each person brings to the body through the grace of the Holy Spirit. The very language of "the body of Christ" suggests that if there is to be virtue in the church it is the virtue of this common body—one might call it a collective habit. To the extent, however, that the discourse of "virtue" threatens to turn the conversation away from the good end of the whole community back toward the character of the single human being, it remains an insufficiently communal way of describing the goal of Christian life.

Milbank also charges that as in the modern nation-state, an element of violent struggle is intrinsic both to the Greek polis and to the life of virtue. For instance, Aristotle's "magnanimous man," whose life sums up the virtues, is characterized as beneficent toward others in need while self-sufficient in the face of his own needs. His desire to be honored as an independent benefactor, however, "implies a competition for limited economic resources," and the calculating nature of his munificence "shows that Aristotle's ideal of virtue is not perfectly separable from a heroic pursuit of honour. Excellence is still in some measure 'effectiveness', which can emerge only from engagement in an *agon* [struggle, fight]."[51] The greatness of the virtuous stands in a relation of necessary opposition to those who are "inferior," those without honor and without the means of indebting others to themselves. The attainment of virtue turns out to be a competition for virtue, since there must always be those over against whom one's honor is defined.

Hauerwas, too, writing with Charles Pinches, acknowledges the intrinsic violence in the Greek understanding of virtue and polis. "A full scale return to Greek virtue cannot but involve a return to a pre-Enlightenment/pre-Christian world of war. Consequently, the liberal suspicion of the return to virtue is not to be dismissed."[52] A church conceived of as a kind of polis would thus have to be extremely cautious not simply to replicate in a new form the exclusion and violence of the Greeks. Hauerwas and Pinches thus note there is a great difference between the Greek polis and their own understanding of the church, "for as Christians repudiate the idea there will always be unruly passions in the human soul which reason must police by means of the virtues, so they refuse to live on the assumption that the barbarians perpetually reign in the dark regions beyond the city wall, whom the heroes of the city must always be prepared to battle."[53]

Despite these critiques of the polis and the virtues, both Milbank and Hauerwas continue to appropriate the concepts of polis and virtue in their own ecclesiological descriptions. In so doing, however, they fall prey to some of the very critiques they level.

John Milbank

As we have seen, Milbank unmasks both the violence of the modern nation-state and the agonistic politics of the ancient polis. Neither of these models of social life could in itself provide a proper vision for rethinking ecclesiology. What is needed is an alternative city, one that is not the Greek polis yet still something *like* a polis.[54] Milbank wants to envision and call forth a church that embodies the peaceful harmony of the divine self-giving in creation. To do this he employs the concepts of virtue, polis, *oikos*, and ontology—noting all the while that these must be fundamentally transformed to apply to the peaceful communion of the church.

For this conceptual transformation, Milbank relies heavily on Augustine, and especially his *City of God*, which unmasks pagan virtue as "hopelessly contaminated by a celebration of violence" (288). Milbank calls upon the church to reject both ancient and modern forms of the ontology of violence that makes such conflict appear necessary. In its place he sets forth an ontology of peace, displayed most concretely in the practice of forgiveness. Unlike the modern nation-state, with its primal vision of a war of all against all, and unlike the Greek polis, driven by the *agon* of opposing dualisms (intellect/passion; polis/*oikos*; Greek/barbarian), "the Christian social ontology, linked to the idea of an emanative procession of all reality from a single divine source, abolishes this duality [between whole and part] which supports the idea of an ineradicable ontological violence" (410).

Milbank begins his constructive account of "the other city" by distancing his position from the postliberal theology of George Lindbeck. He offers two main critiques: First, Lindbeck's "cultural-linguistic" theory of religion does not sufficiently account for the propositional content of doctrine (and thus does not give ontology its rightful place); and second, his construal of the biblical narratives as paradigms removes them from historical development and thus leaves his theology trapped in a Kantian formalism (382–387). In contrast to this Milbank calls for a return to both ontology and history à la Hegel—"one has to pass from

Lindbeck's 'Kantian' narrative epistemology of scheme and content to a 'Hegelian' metanarrative which is a 'philosophy of history', though based on faith, not reason" (387). He argues that any narrative and the correlative history of the performance of that narrative requires a description of the "permanent 'setting'" in which the story takes place (383). Christian ontology is the doctrinal description of this setting. Milbank sees such a description as a necessary speculative moment that resolves the "interpretive doubts" and the "interpretive undecidability" that arise in the reading and performance of the biblical narratives. Doctrine, as ontological speculation, seeks to "secure" what is only implicit in the text; it "emphatically pronounces with regard to doubts that narrative and practice do not clearly decide" (383–384). Milbank's ontology, then, serves two functions. First, it strives for an interpretive stability of setting that the church's narratives and practices alone cannot give. Second, it makes peaceful difference thinkable as an alternative to an ontology that would make violence the necessary correlate of difference.

This peaceful difference is grounded in creation ex nihilo, which is the emanation of a pattern of harmonic difference (Augustine, *De Musica*) from the God who is understood as "superabundant Being . . . not a Plotinian unity beyond Being and difference," and who is also "a power within Being which is more than Being." This creator is "the infinite series of differences" (423ff.), "infinite Being, as difference in harmony" (430). When creation and the creator are understood in this way, difference need not be feared, for it does not necessitate violence; rather, difference holds together as beauty and thus as peace. In true Hegelian style, such continuing creation ex nihilo is understood by Milbank as "God's infinite self-realization," that is, "the divine self-realization in finitude" (429), since God's infinite giving of difference means that even God does not foresee the ultimate pattern of Being. "The unity, harmony and beauty of the emanation of difference cannot, in consequence, be anticipated in advance, even for God himself" (428).

Milbank concludes that over against the ancient-modern ontology of violence "should be set not a revived Platonism or Aristotelianism, including their Christianized versions (viz. MacIntyre) . . . , but rather the Christian critique and transformation of neo-Platonism (although a vital Aristotelian influence is necessarily involved here)" (428). Unity, in such a Christianized Neoplatonism, no longer exists over against difference but precisely as the subjective perception of the harmony of difference. The center of the historical unfolding of this ontology is located in the story of Jesus as fleshed out and continued in the life of the church (387).[55] The church is the polis that "is no longer exactly a *polis*" (369) in that it is the site of the realization of the perfect practice of peace through the forgiveness of sins and the proliferation of harmonious difference. In the *ecclesia* the violence of difference found in the polis is overcome by the embodiment of the peaceful practices instituted by Christ. The proper and peaceful relation of whole and part is the central distinction of the church as an alternative polis.

This short summary of Milbank's position is enough to reveal the nature of his project—to redefine the church as a kind of polis that embodies the permanent metaphysical setting of ontological peace. This vision is undeniably attractive, as Milbank lifts the church out of its containment in Western liberalism and calls it to embody for the world an alternative politics of peace. Nonetheless, by seeking to guarantee peace through a form of Neoplatonic ontology he ironically pushes peace to the edges of history, while simultaneously writing Israel out of any determinative role in God's story. These two failings prove to be interrelated, since it is only as the church takes the risk of waiting for the peace of Israel that it is able to embody peace in the present.

The central problem is that Milbank's turn to metaphysics does not so much *stabilize* the church's story (as he claims, 383ff.) as it does *replace* it with another story, an ontological metanarrative. This metanarrative is the story of the eternal emanation of creation out of the divine Being, the fall into violence, the overcoming of violence in the exemplary practice of Jesus Christ, and the rise of the church as the community of peaceful forgiveness—the salvific telos of the proper ordering of the difference of Being. The problem with this metanarrative is that it presents an ontological "setting" in which the story of Israel could not have taken place. Specifically, within Milbank's ontology Israel cannot be the chosen people they claim to be, and God cannot be the electing God. The people of Israel are pushed to the margin; they are the ambiguous supplement, the embarrassing relatives whose pictures are left out of the family album. The inn is crowded with ontological difference, but there is no room for the Jews. For in this time between the times they continue to live a story that is in some sense "other" than the Christian story. Yet for Milbank there is no way to recognize their "otherness" as having ongoing significance in God's plan, since, for one thing, it is not at all clear that Milbank's God can *have* a plan and, for another, the turn to ontology is so totalizing that there is no place for true difference. Ironically, infinite harmonic difference turns out to make all differences alike, and thus Israel can no longer profess to be *the* difference that makes a difference for all creation. Their claim to be an elect people, set apart from all others, becomes unintelligible, since ontologically they can represent nothing more than one difference among many. The only concern for Milbank is whether their difference can be brought into peaceful harmony with other differences. Oddly enough, such an ontology mirrors liberal pluralism, in which differences can be multiplied infinitely with the one provision that all differences are relativized. No difference can make *the* difference for the whole (be it a political order or an ontology), since the whole is the condition of possibility for difference itself.

Thus, in this alternative metanarrative, "Being" substitutes for "covenant" as a way of naming God's fundamental relation to the world. Milbank argues, in fact, that theology is complicit in the rise of secularism precisely because "by abandoning participation in Being and Unity for a 'covenantal bond' between God and men, it provided a model for human interrelationships as 'contractual' ones"

(15). Surely covenant *can be* perverted into contract, but the language of "covenantal bond" does not *of necessity* lead to "contractual" relations. To critique the former because of its misuse in the latter is a mistake. Milbank attempts to foreclose the possibility of a falling away from covenant to contract by taking refuge in ontology—Being and Unity—rather than risking the perilous historical enactment of covenant life. In the process, however, he reduces "covenant" (and thus Israel) to a theological error.

If one listens closely, one hears in the background echoes of Spinoza, whose influence may illumine Milbank's displacement of the Jews. Indeed at one point Milbank writes that in Augustine's

> deferral of all that is finite to a "supernatural end" . . . we do not really have to do with a "transcendence" of the material, social world—for the Christian understanding of "creation", there is no "spiritual" aspect of the world that in any way transcends our created (and I would want to say material, social and linguistic) condition. So acknowledging God is not like diverting our corporeal resources to another "goal": instead it means, as Spinoza most cogently intimated, never foreclosing the material, social body which preserves itself (or better, non-identically repeats itself, to modify Spinoza with Kierkegaard) through time, but instead seeking to gain through and for this social body the widest possible "perspective" upon things, a ceaselessly renewed vision of nature and history.[56]

This is a gesture in the direction of what Milbank calls "an important project for postmodern theology," that is, to "'Spinozize' Augustine, so as to make him more materialist."[57] Yet in drawing on Spinoza (the first "modern" Jew) in this way, Milbank also takes up his radical deconstruction of Judaism. Not that Milbank does this explicitly (or even intentionally), but just to the extent that Spinoza envisioned a God who, as the nonvolitional unity of Being, could not be the electing God of Israel, so Milbank's God turns out to have little in common with the God of Abraham, Isaac, and Jacob.

The God of Spinoza (and Milbank) cannot be the God of election since election, along with the concomitant relationship of covenant and promise of redemption, "requires an ontology that can constitute possibility, mutual relationship, and purpose. All three of these modes, however are precluded from the ontology of Spinoza. All of them as external relations intend transcendence, something that Spinoza's immanence of internal relations cannot bear."[58] To the extent that Milbank gives us a Spinoza-like picture of a God who "is simply all that there eternally 'is,'"[59] he fails to give us a God who can elect Israel. Thus, Milbank's metanarrative of the eternal emanation of peaceful difference in Being conflicts with some of the most basic claims of the biblical story. The Jews (and to a lesser extent that particular Jew, Jesus) are displaced from any decisive role in God's relation to the world (if indeed we can talk of such a "relation" at all).

One can hardly fault the goal of Milbank's ontology, which is to secure peace. Yet in seeking to guarantee the peaceful resolution of the world's story, he proves unwilling to await the eschatological fulfillment of God's peace in Israel. Just as he retreats from historical particularity, then, he also retreats from peace. For, as it turns out, he holds that coercion exerted by the church, though tragic, may prove necessary (418). This is in contrast to God, who cannot be coercive because it is against God's nature. For if God is the peaceful difference of all Being, then God could never stand over against any particular being in coercion or punishment (420). We find here an ironic reversal of Paul's logic in Romans, "Bless those who persecute you; bless and do not curse them. . . . Do not repay anyone evil for evil. . . . Beloved never avenge yourselves, but leave room for the wrath of God; for it is written, 'Vengeance is mine, I will repay, says the Lord'" (Rom. 12:14–19). For Paul, the command to renounce violence is tied to the conviction that God will bring justice. But in Milbank, since God is ontologically constrained not to punish, it becomes the role of the church to wield coercive power when necessary. Seeking to guarantee peace, Milbank ontologizes it, yet in the very effort to secure it, he loses it.

The peace of Israel, however, contingently located in the rough ground of the covenant, is a peace that must come through God's continued engagement with history and God's people. As Michael Wyschogrod writes,

> The futurity of Judaism is not a natural futurity. The future that Jews expect is a historic future. This future is not assured by the nature of things, as is the future of process philosophers. The Jewish future hinges on, and is derived from, the promise of God. It is not embedded in creation. When the prophet speaks of the messianic future in which the lion will lie down with the lamb (and in which both and not only one will rise) he is indeed foreseeing a transformation of nature, but this transformation is not an evolutionary but an apocalyptic one. It is a transformation that is discontinuous with nature as it has been. It envisages a break with the autonomy of nature brought about by God's intervention and not by the working itself out of the *telos* of nature.[60]

As found in the Gospel witness to Christ as the Messiah of Israel, such peace, historically mediated through a person and a people, has begun to be realized.[61] The power of the Christian call to peace results from God's active engagement in history rather than from an abstract ontological claim. When Milbank's ontology retreats from the soil of the covenant, it takes with it any conclusive call for nonviolence, and a window for coercion opens again. In contrast, the messianic peace of Israel, inaugurated through Christ, makes peace both possible and normative for God's community.

Though he draws heavily on Augustine's *City of God,* Milbank does not appropriate Augustine's emphasis on the biblical narrative as the fundamental description of the *altera civitas*. Whereas *City of God* displays the character of the *altera civitas* through the story of God's chosen people (church as Israel) on their journey toward the New Jerusalem and the eternal Sabbath, in Milbank this people is replaced by a new people (church as polis) on a journey to the harmonious difference of Being. Milbank's attempt to think of church as a kind of polis thus fails in what I have shown are two interrelated ways: It does not adequately provide an alternative to the violence of modernity, and it continues the church's supersessionistic posture toward Israel by denying the Jews their place in God's story.

Stanley Hauerwas

In contrast to Milbank, Hauerwas does not attempt to construct an ontology to overcome the violence of ancient and modern politics. He does, however, proffer a vision of the church as a certain kind of polis and of the Christian life as a life of virtue. Indeed, in the titles of two recent books he highlights these themes: *In Good Company: Church as Polis* and *Christians Among the Virtues* (coauthored with Charles Pinches). Like Milbank, Hauerwas is not unaware of the ways in which the concepts of virtue and polis must be thoroughly transformed in order to be Christianly appropriate. In *Christians Among the Virtues,* for instance, Hauerwas and Pinches are clear about the dangers involved in using the language of polis and virtue to describe the church's life and work. "We cannot, then, begin with Aristotle's virtues and fill in the gaps with Christianity, nor can we, as Christians, defend virtue first and Christianity later, the strategy we find prevalent in MacIntyre." They go on to add:

> We need not, however, leave off discussion of virtue altogether, nor need we deny the link between Greek virtue and Christian virtue, between Aristotle and Aquinas. . . . We are convinced that the insights about virtue offered by Aristotle and other ancient Greeks are indispensable in any true and subtle treatment of Socrates's fundamental question regarding how one should live. Yet as we believe the great Christian thinkers such as Saint Paul and Saint Thomas meant to teach us, Greek accounts of the virtues are there to be *used* by Christians, not *built upon*. These name two entirely different things. To use requires that one apply a thing within a framework significantly other than the one in which it originally appeared, which is precisely what Christianity requires in so far as it refounds human life on the life, death and resurrection of Jesus Christ, God made flesh. As founded on Christ, Christian virtue cannot but be teleologically ordered to peace, just as Greek virtue cannot but be ordered to war.[62]

Hauerwas and Pinches are surely right in their conviction that the language of virtue can be "used" by Christians but not "built upon." Yet it is significant that their argument for listening to Aristotle on these matters is that he helps us answer *Socrates'* question.[63] But who decided that Socrates got to ask the question? This is important, of course, because the nature of the question always to some extent predetermines what answers might be given. By giving the Socratic query such a privileged place, Hauerwas and Pinches are in danger of allowing their account of Christian life and practice to be located within the Socratic story rather than vice versa. They risk letting Socrates set the framework, and thus they risk "building upon" rather than "using" the tools of the Greeks. Granted, "How should one live?" is not a bad place to start, even for Christian ethical reflection. But there are dangers in this simple formulation. Most obviously problematic is the little word "one," for it asks us to think about ethics *impersonally* and in the *singular*. Who is the "one" to whom this question is addressed? The Socratic question is posed in general but can be answered only in particular. Further, it is posed in the singular, but for Christians can be answered only in the plural. So why not ask, "How should *we* live?" or even better, "What does it look like to be the people of God?"

I am not suggesting by this that Hauerwas and Pinches are giving an account of an abstract and individualistic ethic. Far from it. They are determined at every turn to ask what is distinctively *Christian* about their account of virtue and to affirm the centrality of the Christian community. Nonetheless, their failure to problematize the framework of the Socratic question threatens to exert a subtle pull toward an individualized account of the telos of human life and a generalized account of the virtues. Thus their description of the Christian life may lack the resources necessary to challenge modern voluntarism. For instance, Hauerwas argues that the question of character, "What ought I to be?" is prior to and more determinative than the Kantian question, "What ought I to do?"[64] Yet although the former may indeed be more compatible with the church's life, stories, and practices, it remains as abstract and individualized as its Kantian counterpart.

In another example Hauerwas makes a typical assertion: "'Virtue as its own reward' is a reminder that we choose to be virtuous for no other reason than that to be so is the only condition under which we would desire to survive. Only by so embodying the virtues have we the power to make our lives our own."[65] Such a determination to make our lives our own is a common theme in Hauerwas's discussion of virtue and constancy. Yet this goal of self-possession, achieved as it is by choosing to be virtuous, echoes the self-sufficiency of Aristotle's "magnanimous man," in contrast with the witness of the elect people whose lives are not their own because they belong to God.[66] I suspect it is a similar observation that lies behind Gregory Jones's critique that "Hauerwas at times locates continuity in the 'self' rather than in the God who continually calls people's 'selves' into question."[67]

Although Hauerwas clearly has little time for or interest in something called "individual salvation," his emphasis on virtue and character at times pushes his thinking in that direction. That is, salvation for Hauerwas does seem to imply becoming a particular kind of person who is shaped as such by the practices of the church. The danger is that the ecclesial practices threaten to become instrumental to the larger goal of the formation of the individual person.[68] In contrast to this, "the biblical story," as Richard Hays reminds us, "focuses on God's design for forming a covenant *people*. Thus, the primary sphere of moral concern is not the character of the individual but the corporate obedience of the church."[69] Hauerwas is obviously as concerned as anyone about the corporate life of the church, yet it is not always clear how he holds this together with the highly personal language of virtue. His indebtedness to Aristotelian patterns of thought sometimes leads him in directions that conflict with his own better insights.[70] My concern is not that Hauerwas (or Pinches) has failed to give an adequately Christian display of the virtues but rather that such a project faces certain dangers if it does not first give a decisive account of the "significantly other framework" within which talk of the virtues can be *used* but not *built upon*. This is why it is only after unfolding the character of God's covenant with Israel and the in-gathering of the Gentiles that one can begin such conversations with other voices.

I have so far focused on Hauerwas's account of virtue rather than his understanding of the church as polis. This is primarily because he in fact talks so little about the polis, and when he does so it is often to critique it. Indeed, I would suggest that despite Hauerwas's occasional use of the language, the model of the Greek polis does very little actual work in his theology. For instance, even in the book subtitled, *Church as Polis,* the term "polis" comes up just six times, and each time in either a quotation from or discussion of someone else.[71] In addition, two of these references explicitly suggest the *inadequacy* of church as polis in ways that I have already explored above. In the end, for Hauerwas, polis seems to name only the conviction that the production of people of a certain character requires political communities commensurate with that task. This, however, is a quite formal use of "polis." In many material ways Hauerwas eschews the politics of the Greek polis, most notably its inherent violence.[72]

I would argue that Hauerwas's work in fact points more determinatively toward Jerusalem than Athens. Indeed, Hauerwas concludes the first, programmatic essay of *In Good Company* with a discussion of "why the 'body of Christ' Does not 'exist' except as Jewish and eucharistic."[73] He writes,

> Any ecclesiology remains seriously deficient that is not explicated in relation to Israel and the ongoing existence and witness of the Jewish people. This is surely the "sociology" required for any account of what it means for the church to be the body of Christ. . . . The body that the church becomes, resurrected though it is, cannot be less than the body of Israel, since our Christ is of this body. No doubt the body that is the church is different than the body that is Israel; however, gathered as the latter is from out of the nations, it can be no less physical.[74]

What Hauerwas has not given us, however, is any serious account of this Jewish "sociology," much less how it relates to other emphases in his work. As in the above quotation, "Israel" often seems in danger of becoming a cipher for materiality.[75] It remains unclear how Hauerwas's convictions about church and Israel hold together with his continued use of the language and concepts of polis and virtue. The point is not that they cannot be held together but that Hauerwas has not yet shown us how they cohere in his own work.

The danger, of course, is that the people of Israel will be marginalized in Hauerwas's thinking, just as they are in MacIntyre's and Milbank's, as a result of reading the church's moral and political life as a continuation of and/or answer to the traditions of the Greeks. In MacIntyre, for instance, Christianity becomes part of the larger dialectical movement of Greek history. "Crucial to his project is the possibility that the Christian account of the virtues can be successfully grafted onto the Greek heritage."[76] Yet what MacIntyre fails to see is that Christians have always believed they were grafted onto Israel (Rom. 11:17ff.). And if the story one tells is really as determinative as MacIntyre, Milbank, and Hauerwas all agree it is, then Christians must say, quite simply, that the story of Israel must provide the framework from which any account of virtue or polis is judged.

I do not wish to imply that Christian conversation with the Greek traditions cannot be fruitful, for of course it can be. Rather, the question that must stand before any such task is whether the church comes to the conversation clothed in the life and story of the covenant people or whether it comes seeking a new polity, having left Israel behind and thus finding itself "underdressed politically."[77] It may well be true that the model of the polis, at least as Hauerwas and Pinches describe it, shares much more with what I call the "politics of election" than does modern liberalism. Nonetheless, if the polis begins to define the parameters of the conversation, it poses no less a threat to the church's identity than the liberal temptation to become a "voluntary association." Both models fail ecclesiologically precisely insofar as they tempt the church to make the Jews irrelevant to the church's life and mission.

Why Abraham?

At the end of *Love in the Ruins*, a remnant church—"a tiny scattered flock with no place to go"—muddles along, bearing witness to the possibility of a hopeful alternative. This remnant is led by a befuddled, perhaps even mad, priest named Father Smith. On Christmas Eve he offers absolution to a reluctant Tom More and proceeds to celebrate the mass, assisted by an African American seminarian. Here the violent rupture that undid the American project appears healed. Here in the swamp, in a run-down old church, peace erupts—Protestants and Catholics, black and white, share the Eucharist.[78] This remains, however, a church constantly in danger of being accommodated to, indeed subsumed by, the dominant culture. After the mass the children gather around outside shooting off fireworks and shouting, "Hurrah for Jesus Christ! Hurrah for the United States!" The superimposition of the Fourth of July onto Christmas leaves the reader uneasy about the future of this remnant people.

Nonetheless, Percy drops hints throughout the novel that the church can and must bear witness as a faithful alternative community, not by virtue of its participation in American dream but because of its connection to the Jews. Tom More knows this; for despite his inability to sustain a moral life, he never stops believing "in the Holy Catholic Apostolic and Roman Church, in God the Father, in the election of the Jews, in Jesus Christ His Son our Lord, who founded the Church on Peter his first vicar, which will last until the end of the world."[79] Percy, via Tom More, interjects into the traditional credal confessions an affirmation of faith in the election of the people of Israel.[80] Father Smith (the madman who, like demons in the Gospels and fools in Shakespeare, speaks the truth) has to remind More later, "Salvation comes from the Jews, as holy scripture tells us. They remain the beloved, originally chosen people of God"; Christians, he exclaims, are simply "a Jewish sect."[81] In Percy's fiction the church, despite its regular capitulation to the dominant culture, remains the point of hope precisely in this connection to the people of Israel. Everything depends, then, on retaining this connection. The Jews endure as a "sign" of God in the world; indeed, they are for Percy a *sacramental* people. "Since the Jews were the original chosen people of God, a tribe of people who are still here," Father Smith continues, "they are a sign of God's presence which cannot be evacuated."[82] That is, they are the one sign that cannot cease to signify. To the extent that the church participates in this people, it participates in this sacramental mission.

Percy's relentless satire delivers a wake-up call for the accommodated American church, while at the same time seeking to bend this people toward Israel. This, I want to suggest, is the direction we must turn in seeking to envision and embody Christian existence more faithfully today. Yet it is important that the Jews not be seen simply as a particularly interesting example of "community," nor simply as a model for successfully negotiating the vicissitudes of time and history. Granted, they are both of these things, and Christians in the United States surely must be attentive to any group that models community well and maintains its identity in the face of great threats and temptations. Yet to look to the Jews to teach us something about community or identity is to risk reducing Israel to an example of some more determinative reality. For Christians, however, Israel *is* that reality. The church looks to the Jews not just because they embody something that the church wants to imitate but more importantly because the church's own life and story are unintelligible apart from this people and their God. Thus, the true ecclesial alternative to being subsumed by late-twentieth-century liberalism is not a recovery of the polis, but a return to Israel, into whose election the church has been graciously grafted.

This proposal may seem to fly in the face of history, for Christians have long sought to distance themselves from Jews, claiming to be the new and true chosen people. With the conversion of Constantine and the elevation of Christianity to the official religion of the empire, the church hitched its wagon to Rome, having successfully unhitched itself from Israel.[83] For centuries thereafter, the church's triumphalistic posture toward the Jews was given teeth by its alliance with the sword of Caesar. But the twentieth century has seen both the collapse of the remnants of Christendom and the darkest turn in the long history of Christian and Western anti-Judaism. Supersessionism bore its poisoned fruit in the Holocaust, and Christendom drew its last breath.[84] In the wake of these extraordinary alterations of the political and ecclesial landscape, an opportunity is opened up for rethinking the church's relation both to the people of Israel and to Western politics. Lindbeck calls on us to grasp this opportunity by recovering an early church, "people-of-God" ecclesiology based on the model of Israel:

> There are a number of familiar ways in which the present period is becoming more like the Christian beginnings than the intervening ages. Christendom is passing and Christians are becoming a diaspora. The antagonism of the church to the synagogue has been unmasked (we hope definitively) for the horror it always was. . . . Some of the reasons for distorting and then rejecting the scriptural people-of-God ecclesiology are disappearing, and perhaps its original version is again applicable.
>
> Certainly there are reasons for wanting to apply it. For it, there is no church except the empirical churches, and this emphasis is badly needed. The empirical churches are losing the loyalty and devotion of their members. Special-interest enclaves are replacing comprehensive communities as the locus of whatever shreds of communal identity the isolated individuals of our society retain. The conviction that the churches even in their crass concreteness have a crucial place in God's plan has weakened. All these considerations call for a return to Israel's story as a template which helps shape Christian communities.[85]

If Lindbeck is right, and I think he is, then the demise of the last remnants of Christendom in the West and the repudiation of anti-Judaism combine to present a unique opportunity to recover the significance of Israel for ecclesiology.

This recovery begins with the recognition of the fact that Christians worship the God of Israel. The New Testament witness makes clear that the life, death, and resurrection of Christ; the outpouring of the Holy Spirit; and the life of the church redound to the glory of Israel's God. And even as the early church grew and changed in the following centuries, it showed again by its repudiation of Marcion that the church's God is Israel's God and the church's story is necessarily related to Israel's story. Does this mean that Israel's God has given up on the Jews and turned to another people instead? "By no means" (Rom. 3:4). For if the God of Israel has not remained faithful to the covenant with the Jews, how could Christians believe God would be faithful to a replacement people? Paul addresses this crucial question most directly in his Epistle to the Romans. "The driving question in Romans," Hays explains, "is not, 'How can I find a gracious God?' but 'How can we trust in this allegedly gracious God if he abandons his promises to Israel?'"[86] God's faithfulness to the church is predicated on God's faithfulness to Israel, and thus the church's own place in the covenant is secure only if Israel remains part of the covenant. The limbs are no sturdier than the trunk that upholds them.

Thus, if Christians are to worship and follow Israel's God, they must not ignore or reject God's Israel. Although this is not a logical imperative (one could conceivably worship the God of Israel while repudiating the people of Israel), it is a *theo*logical imperative based on Christian scripture and tradition. In the election of Israel, Christ, and church, God has chosen to be known in and with humanity and thus not in abstraction from God's chosen ones. To know God is to know God through those in whom God has been revealed. To gloss John Calvin, true knowledge of God is always correlated with knowledge of God's people. To ignore those with whom God has joined God's self is to close one's eyes to the ways in which God has chosen to be present in the world. Paul van Buren, using a slightly different metaphor, makes this point nicely: "The church has turned a deaf ear to Jewish voices for so long, that unless it learns to listen explicitly to living Israel, it may be tempted to try to hear Israel's God apart from his chosen witness Israel. Not hearing him as he elected to be heard means not hearing him as he is."[87] In contrast to either Nietzsche and the moderns or Aristotle and the ancients, Abraham and the people of Israel exert an intrinsic claim on the church's life and thought. As such, this people should be the first place Christians turn to help us construct an alternative ecclesiology in the wake of contemporary social and political change.

Finally, and perhaps most important, the church's political witness depends on a recovery of its relation to Israel. As noted above, the dissolution of the lingering remnants of Christendom has left the church unsure of its calling in the political arena. Should it accept its relativizing as a voluntary association, should it press its interests in the public square, or should it seek to embody another political alternative altogether? Attentiveness to Israel reveals a people chosen and formed by God into a distinct political community. That this community has proven itself able to maintain its politics while in diaspora gives hope to Christians seeking to retain their communal identity in the wake of disestablishment.

Whether or not these turn out to be the "dread latter days of the old violent beloved U.S.A. and of the Christ-forgetting Christ-haunted death-dealing Western world," it is nonetheless the case that the church in America is at a crossroads that requires faithful reflection on its identity and mission, especially in relation to the dominant politics of the West. In this context the election of Israel turns out to be the most fundamental political and ecclesiological claim the church can make. Because of this, the church needs desperately to recover and re-Judaize its doctrine of election.

2

The Election of Israel

The conversation that is more vital for Christians today than that between the liberals and the virtue theorists is the one going on among Jewish scholars who are seeking to reclaim the theological and political significance of election for Jewish life. David Novak and Michael Wyschogrod in particular have made persuasive cases for a retrieval of a biblical-rabbinic doctrine of election as the determinative description of Israel's identity. In so doing, they present a challenge to the modern liberal inversion of election in which God's choice of Israel has been replaced by the more palatable belief in Israel's choice of God.[1]

Their radical retrieval of election stands within a particularly interesting and growing movement in Jewish theology and philosophy that has been variously identified as "aftermodern," "postmodern," or "postcritical." More recently the term "textual reasoning" has been used to describe these Jewish thinkers whose modes of thought arise out of a rigorous recovery of Jewish tradition and who therefore resist the modernist impulse to present an a priori justification for their theological claims.[2]

Both Novak and Wyschogrod see the doctrine of election as a central pillar of this radical traditionalism, for election challenges the universalizing epistemologies of modernity as well as the political priority of individual autonomy. This Jewish *ressourcement,* especially as undertaken by two Jewish thinkers who have been in dialogue with Christianity, offers a summons and a blessing to Christians who are seeking to understand the church's calling in the postliberal world.[3]

The aim of this chapter is to listen in on this Jewish conversation about election. Such listening has historically proven difficult for Christians, since the temptation has always been to construct a Christian concept of Israel without regard to whether this picture is recognizable to Jews themselves. Of course, Christians *must* understand Israel differently than do Jews precisely to the extent that Christians believe Jesus of Nazareth to be Israel's Messiah. Nonetheless, this does not relieve Christians of the call to hear the witness of Israel *post Christum,* since the Jews remain God's chosen people and thus remain the vessel through whom God has promised to be known.

Which Israel?

Listening to the witness of Israel becomes a complex task once one begins to ask "Which Israel?"—for there seem to be many, both politically and theologically. Are we referring to the Israel of the Jewish Bible or the modern State of Israel? The tribal confederacy under the judges, the united kingdom under Solomon, the holy remnant in Exile, the Jews of the Second Temple period? The Zealots, the Pharisees, the Essenes, or the Sadducees? Do we mean the Israel found in Christian readings of the Old Testament or another "true Israel" constituted by belief in Christ? Is this a biological Israel made up of all people born of a Jewish mother? Or perhaps all those who practice the religion of Judaism faithfully? The question of what constitutes "Israel" corresponds to the equally vexing question, Who is a Jew?

Novak has suggested three levels on which this question might be answered—the legal, the essential, and the existential.[4] These three levels correspond to the discourses of the ethical, the political, and the theological.[5] As Novak makes clear, the three questions and their concomitant fields of discourse cannot be understood apart from each other: "The ethical question of 'who is a Jew?' cannot be answered adequately unless the prior political question 'what is the Jewish people?' is answered." This question, in turn raises the further theological question: "How are Jews to be related to God?"[6] The ethical, political, and theological are indissolubly bound in a Jewish theology of Israel.

Thus, in answer to the question "Who is a Jew?" one might respond, "Someone who either (1) is born of a Jewish mother or (2) has been properly converted to Judaism."[7] This has sufficed as a *legal* answer for more than 2,000 years, but Novak suggests this is not a *sufficient* answer. Although it may speak to the status of the person before me, it does not address the deeper question, the essential question, of what it means to be a Jew. Here one might attempt an answer either on natural-biological grounds or on historical-cultural grounds. Noting that the natural-biological way of defining the Jews is unsatisfactory insofar as it "seems to lead straight into the pseudo-biology that justifies modern racism,"[8] Novak suggests instead that Jewish identity must be understood as a historical reality and thus as a *social and political* identity. This leads, then, to the third level of the identity question: the *existential*. Novak's use of the term "existential" does not carry with it any hints of an individualistic inward gaze; rather, the existential is for Novak necessarily social, and thus the existential identity question is, "*With whom are the Jews what they are?*"[9] Identity is never a private matter, but a question of one's participation in a people and ultimately one's relation to God. Here again, there are two possible ways to answer the question of what makes this historical people a people. Secular Jews have argued that the claim to peoplehood is a cultural claim based on a common language and customs. This cultural defense, however, provides an inadequate warrant for the survival of the Jewish people, since peoples and cultures naturally wax and wane. Given this natural process, on

cultural grounds alone there would be no sufficient basis for secular Jews to resist assimilation if this furthered their individual survival.[10]

Novak argues instead for a theological answer to the question of Jewish identity.
He writes, "It is the only complete answer to the existential question: *With whom
do the Jews live their life in the world*, and *how* does this coexistence make them
what they are and are to be? It answers that God elects Israel, that God chooses the
Jewish people for a continuing covenantal relationship with himself for which he
gave them the Torah."[11] What it means to be a Jew is to be one who participates
with the Jewish people in the history of God's election and covenant. In so defining the identity of the Jew, Novak helps us answer the question of "Which Israel?"
For there is, if he is right, only one Israel.[12] This one Israel from which Christians
can and must hear a witness is not reducible to any one particular historical embodiment of Jewish polity (though none is excluded from view) but rather en-
compasses the whole of God's chosen people who are the historically elected descendants of Abraham and Sarah and whose common life is shaped by their
covenant relationship with God.[13] It is an Israel theologically determined and socially embodied, and for Christians it is an Israel paradigmatically characterized by
the Old Testament narratives of election and covenant (though Israel's life and
identity are by no means exhaustively portrayed in this biblical witness).

What can be said about the identity of the Jews in all their different social instantiations is that being Jewish means being a particular historical people who
are constituted as such by their election and covenant with God. This entails in
turn Israel's calling to live a communal life that contrasts with that of the nations
and thus brings glory to God's name. That this is a basic assumption of what it
means to be Israel is exhibited in the blessing recited before the reading of Torah
in daily study and in the synagogue service: "Blessed are You Lord our God, king
of the world, who has chosen us from among all peoples (*asher bahar banu mi-
kol ha'amim*) and who has given us his Torah (*ve-natan lanu et torato*)."[14] Novak
comments that "the basic logical relations" in this blessing are: "(1) Israel is related to God because of God's election of her; (2) Israel is related to God because
of God's revelation of the Torah to her; (3) Israel is disjunct from the nations of
the world because of God's election of her."[15] Israel's identity as God's people involves both a *calling into* a life with God through the Torah and also a *calling out*
from among the nations. It is this Israel—the elected and covenanting people
called out from the nations—that is the focus throughout this work. It is an Israel
that combines a distinct theological description with a historically locatable presence and an implicit (if not always explicit) distinction from the Gentiles.

Election

Novak presents an analysis of election in relation to covenant and redemption
that serves as a helpful framework for understanding the richness of this doctrine.

Election is the choice by one person of another person out of a range of possible candidates. This choice then establishes a mutual relationship between the elector and the elected, in biblical terms a "covenant" (*berit*). Election also promises its ultimate purpose will be fulfilled, which is to bring the whole world finally into the covenant, that is, "redemption" (*ge'ulah*). Election is much more fundamental than just freedom of choice in the ordinary sense, where a free person chooses to do one act from a range of possible acts. Instead, the elector chooses another person *with whom* he or she will both act and elicit responses, and then establishes the community *in which* these acts are to be done, and then promises that *for which* the election has occurred. The content of these practical choices is governed by law (*Torah*), but there could be no such coherent standards of action without the prior context of election, the establishment of covenantal community, and the promise of ultimate purpose.[16]

Election proper is the choice God made of Israel to be God's people (the "with whom" of election). *Covenant* is the form of the communal relationship thereby established (the "in which" of election). *Redemption* is the goal, the promise, the ultimate purpose toward which election and covenant move (the "for which" of election). The three are related such that election founds the covenant community in God's choice and redemption extends the covenant community to include all the world. Any discussion of Israel's election must take all three of these features into account.[17]

The first of these, election, might be explicated as follows: *Election is the communal and carnal, eternal and unconditional choosing of Israel by God, through which Israel is constituted as a people who will embody a politics of blessing.* Israel's election is *communal*. God does not choose individuals and then make them part of the community, but rather God chooses a people, a family, and within that family lays claim to all who are a part of it. Thus God said to Abraham: "I will maintain My covenant between Me and you, and your offspring to come, as an everlasting covenant through the ages, to be God to you and to your offspring to come. . . . I will be their God" (Gen. 17:7–8, cf. 12:1–7).[18] God is the God of all the descendants in the line of Abraham and Sarah, since the election of the community precedes and thus already includes even those who do not yet exist.[19] Personal election can make sense only as a correlate of communal election. The psalmist assumes this priority of the chosen community when he writes,

> Be mindful of me, O Lord, when You favor Your people;
> take note of me when You deliver them,
> that I may enjoy the prosperity of Your chosen ones,
> share the joy of Your nation,
> glory in Your very own people. (Ps. 106:4)

The deliverance, prosperity, joy, and glory of the particular Jew is found in participation with the deliverance, prosperity, joy, and glory of the people. The logic of election moves from the communal to the personal. The goods of election are enjoyed only within the gathered people.

This priority of communal identity places the Jewish doctrine of election at odds with the powerful individualizing tides of modernity. Wyschogrod laments, "Assimilation has seriously eroded a proper understanding of Jewish communal existence. Because the liberal stresses the individual, he sees all communities as voluntary associations into which and out of which the individual moves at will. But that is not true of a family and it is not true of the house of Israel."[20] The community of Israel *precedes* the individual Jew, giving one an identity and a people prior to one's choice of associations. One can neither opt in nor opt out of Israel's election at will.

The Deuteronomic renewal of the covenant, for instance, presupposes the communal solidarity of God's people across both time and space. Moses addresses the gathering, "I make this covenant, with its sanctions, not with you alone, but both with those who are standing here with us this day before the Lord our God and with those who are not with us here this day" (Deut. 29:13–14). No part of the community is elected alone or covenants alone. And correlatively, no part of the community sins alone. The rabbis called attention to the mutual responsibility and accountability laid on each Israelite because of their constitution as *one* people: "'Israel is a scattered sheep' (Jer. L, 17, A.V.). Why are the Israelites compared to a sheep? Just as if you strike a sheep on its head, or on one of its limbs, all its limbs feel it, so, if one Israelite sins, all Israelites feel it. R. Simeon b. Yohai said: It is like as if there are men in a boat, and one man takes an auger, and begins to bore a hole beneath him. His companions say, 'What are you doing?' He replies, 'What business is it of yours? Am I not boring under myself?' They answer, 'It *is* our business, because the water will come in, and swamp the boat with us in it.'"[21] Both Israel's election and Israel's sin are communal matters, for they share a common ship and thus a common destination.

It is said that a Hasidic master asked God to show him heaven and hell. In hell he discovered that the people were starving despite a surfeit of food. They were unable to bend their arms and thus were unable to carry food from the table to their mouths. In heaven everything was the same, except that each person fed another and thus all enjoyed the bounty of God's provision and were satisfied. Wyschogrod comments on this story, "God has set human beings in communities. And among these, the community of Israel is central. It is the community elected by God for his service. . . . The Jew must, therefore, more than anyone else avoid narcissism. He must place himself in his community. He must live in it. Its tribulations must become his tribulations, its joys, his joys."[22]

Israel's election is a communal election, and as such it is also a *carnal* election. Wyschogrod especially challenges us to keep this corporeality in view. Indeed, in *The Body of Faith* each chapter, each new topic, turns out to be a different voicing of the one fundamental conviction that Israel's election is not based on belief or virtue but rather on God's gracious choice of a people *in the flesh*. It therefore cannot be shaken. "The election of the people of Israel as the people of God constitutes the sanctification of a natural family. God could have chosen a spiritual criterion: the election of all those who have faith or who obey God's commandments. The liberal mind would find such an election far more congenial. But God did not choose this path. He chose the seed of Abraham, Isaac, and Jacob.... The election of Israel is therefore a corporeal election. One result of this is that a Jew cannot resign his election."[23] Israel's election is based not on a human decision to follow God but on God's decision to be for Israel. God decided for a corporeal election. Thus, participation in the chosen people is not a gathering of like-minded or mutually interested people but rather a sharing of Jewish flesh.

Just as Israel's election is communal and carnal, it is also *eternal* and *unconditional*. It neither requires a prior worthiness on the part of Israel nor relies on Israel's faithfulness for its preservation. "Even though [the Jews] are unclean, the Divine Presence is among them" (*Sifra* on Lev. 16:16).[24] Since the election of Israel is not based on the faith or even the faithfulness of the chosen ones but on the faithfulness of the one who chooses, "the bond between Hashem and Israel is eternal and cannot be severed by the deeds of Israel.... Israel's election is a gift of Hashem and since Hashem is a faithful God, it will never be canceled."[25] Novak speaks with the same conviction when he writes, "Because [the covenant] is founded by God's promise, it is ... interminable. 'My covenant of peace shall never depart, says the Lord who loves you' (Isaiah 54:10)."[26]

Rabbinic thought on the unconditional nature of God's election asserted that no sin could threaten Israel's status before God. Since the covenant was not based on obedience, disobedience could not overturn it. "R. Me'ir said: Even though the Israelites are full of blemishes, they are still called 'His sons' (Deut. XXXII, 5).... If they are called 'sons' when corrupt, how much more would they be His sons did they not act corruptly! Jeremiah calls them 'sons, wise to do evil' (Jer. IV, 22). If they did good, how much more would they be his sons! Beloved are Israel, for whether they do God's will or not, they are called His sons" (M&L, 103). The classic statement of this conviction is found in B. Sanhedrin 43b–44a: "'Israel sinned' (*hata yisra'el*—Joshua 7:11): even though they have sinned, they are still Israel (*af-al-pi she-hata yisra'el hu*)."[27] Largely because of its use by the great French commentator Rashi in the eleventh century, this affirmation became a slogan of great halakhic importance during the First Crusade. As Jews were being converted at sword point by Christians, the question of the status of the apostate became critical. Would Jews who converted to save their lives still be considered Jews? It was ruled that they were, since "even though they have sinned, they are still Israel."[28] This maxim became a weapon against the oppressor, for it affirmed that even if the sheer power of the crusaders forced Jews into renunciation of their God and people, this could not prevail against the unbreakable seal of God's election. God's covenant would not be shaken either by human weakness or human power.[29]

The biblical prophets return often to the theme of God's enduring covenant. Jeremiah even compares it to the permanence of creation. As long as the created order remains in place, says Jeremiah, so long will God be faithful to Israel. God's electing grace extends to the limits of existence itself.

> Thus said the Lord,
> Who established the sun for light by day,
> The laws of moon and stars for light by night,
> Who stirs up the sea into roaring waves,
> Whose name is the Lord of Hosts:
> If these laws should ever be annulled by Me
> —declares the Lord—
> Only then would the offspring of Israel cease
> To be a nation before Me for all time. (Jer. 31:35–36)

As long as the world exists, God will remain faithful to Israel. Life and covenant are coextensive.[30] Isaiah stretches the comparison beyond Jeremiah to affirm that God's faithfulness is not only as steadfast as the creation itself but is in fact even *more* abiding. "For the mountains may move and the hills be shaken, but my loyalty shall never move from you, nor My covenant of friendship be shaken—said the Lord, who takes you back in love" (Isa. 54:10).

Even in those biblical passages where it seems election is made conditional on Israel's obedience, such as Lev. 26, the reader's initial expectations are surprisingly upended by God's grace. The "if . . . then" structure of the chapter sets up the typical pattern of blessing and curse: If you obey, you will be blessed; if you do not, you will be cursed. "If you follow My laws and faithfully observe My commandments," then God will bring good upon Israel, blessing the land with bounty and the people with peace (26:3–10). "I will be ever present in your midst: I will be your God, and you shall be my people" (26:12). The promise that "I will be your God, and you shall be my people" seems in these verses to be predicated on the preceding clause, "If you follow My laws and faithfully observe My commandments." That is, God will be Israel's God on the *condition* of their obedience. In what follows, God delineates the punishments for disobedience: "But if you do not obey Me and do not observe all these commandments and you break My covenant," then God promises to bring destruction on the land and on the people and to turn them over to their enemies. One expects at this point to hear that if Israel does not obey, they will be rejected as God's people, but this predictable quid pro quo is transposed by God's enduring election. "Even then, when they are in the land of their enemies, I will not reject them or spurn them so as to destroy them, annulling My covenant with them: for I the Lord am their God. I will remember in their favor the covenant with the ancients, whom I freed from the land of Egypt in the sight of the nations to be their God: I, the Lord" (Lev. 26:43–45).[31] God's faithfulness proves able to sustain Israel's election even in the face of its sin, for "even though they have sinned, they are still Israel." And as this passage would add, even though they have sinned, the Lord is still God. The covenant is the condition of possibility for blessing and curse alike, and thus it undergirds even Israel's unfaithfulness.

The unconditionality of election reflects simply the conviction that election is *God's* work. "In the Bible, it is not Abraham who moves toward God but God who turns to Abraham with an election that is not explained because it is an act of love that requires no explanation."[32] Unlike the modern anthropocentric turn, in which election comes to be understood as the rational human choice of God, the biblical-rabbinic doctrine knows election to be *God's* choice.[33] As Novak reminds us, "The fact of election designated by the word 'covenant' (*berit*) is not a bilateral pact jointly initiated by both God and Israel together. It is, rather, a historical reality created by God to be accepted by Israel." He adds, "It is a relationship . . . they cannot finally refuse. Sooner or later they are convinced to accept it."[34] God's election is God's irresistible work. Without Israel's decision to live in accordance with its election, however, God's work would remain de facto irrelevant in history despite being de jure a reality. The decision of each Israelite, then, is not whether to be a *part* of God's chosen ones, for this is determined by God alone, but rather whether to be *faithful* to the covenant. Election itself is God's work and God's choice, and Israel, faithful or not, lives with both the blessing and the burden of being the chosen ones.

The election of Israel is communal and carnal, eternal and unconditional—it is the pure grace of the irresistible and loving choice of God. In and by this election God *constitutes* the Jews as a people. Israel did not arise out of a collection of autonomous individuals who agreed that their self-interest would be furthered by entering into a political alliance. Nor did the people qua people exist as a prior political entity which God then elected as God's own. Rather, Israel became a people by God's action and remains a people by God's continually welcoming new generations into the covenant of their ancestors. Chosenness *calls forth* existence.[35] The Jewish doctrine of election reminds us that Israel's peoplehood is a product, not a precondition, of God's choosing. For the Jews, there is no ground outside of the holy ground of God's election.

Because God's election is the ground of Israel as a people, the Jews have been able to sustain their political identity apart from place. That is, though land is promised to Abraham's and Sarah's descendants, it is not a prerequisite for Israel to be a people. Israel's peoplehood is constituted by election rather than territory, and thus God's presence with them as well as God's jurisdiction over them extends beyond any boundaries. It should not be forgotten that ancient Near Eastern gods were territorial gods and thus were thought to have no authority outside their realm. "For the average non-Jew, to continue to worship a god after one had left his territory would be as strange as it would be for a modern man to insist that the jurisdiction of one state extended beyond its borders into another state."[36] In contrast, Hashem's rule had no borders, and thus Israel was prohibited from worshiping the gods of the lands in which they sojourned.

The way in which being such a "placeless people" has contributed to Israel's ability to survive is not lost on Wyschogrod:

Hashem was the God of Israel before either a Tabernacle or a Temple existed. The people Israel becomes a people before it has a land, a location. Abraham is sent out from his place of birth and told to go to a place that God will show him, not a specified place but an unspecified, indefinite one. While this people has a land because Hashem ultimately gives it a land and dwells in it, its peoplehood is not coextensive with the land, as is the peoplehood of others, who cannot survive as a people once they are separated from their land.[37]

This detachment from place is what made possible the sustaining of Israel as a people after the destruction of the Second Temple in 70 A.D. When the Day of Atonement came and there was no temple in which to make a sacrifice for sin, Rabbi Akiba reminded the people of Israel that they were purified by God's presence with them.[38] Their peoplehood and their purity depended finally on the determination of Hashem to be the God of Israel, rather than on the possession of land or temple. Because Israel did not require place to be a people, they could sustain their peoplehood in diaspora.

This allows us to make sense of the unusual fact that the Jews continue to remember a time when their land belonged to someone else. Other nations do not do this, because such a memory is always a threat to those whose existence is based on a territorial claim. "The national identities of other nations are land-bound identities. The nation is defined by the territory it occupies. But Israel comes into national existence before it occupies the land. It becomes a nation on the basis of a promise delivered to it when it is a stranger in the land of others. This awareness of being a stranger is burned into Jewish consciousness. The God of Israel is not a God whose jurisdiction is defined by territorial boundaries."[39] Israel's politics of election thus differs fundamentally from the politics of the nations. The remarkable ability of the Jews to remain a people while scattered and landless is but a witness to God's ability to form a people for whom place is a gift to be received rather than a status to be defended.

In Abraham God determined to create a new kind of nation, a placeless people whose identity was grounded in blessing rather than belligerence. From the time that humanity began to multiply, the powers of evil bred violence in its midst—first between Cain and Abel and then throughout the world. Finally, because "the earth was filled with violence" (Gen. 6:11, 13), God unleashed the waters of chaos, uncreating the world's inhabitants but saving Noah and his family. Yet just after Noah's family returns to dry ground, in a hungover fury, Noah curses Ham and his Canaanite descendants and sets Shem against them (Gen. 6:25–26). Humankind is again, so quickly, divided in conflict. The nations spread among the lands and the stage is set for a war of all against all. But God does a new thing. Or rather God takes a new step in the same eternal plan that infused creation itself, the plan to form a people of God's own. God calls Abraham and promises him, "I will make of you a great nation . . . and in you all the families of the earth shall be blessed" (Gen. 12:3, NRSV). Rather than becoming one nation among many struggling for power against each other, Abraham is to become a nation characterized by peaceful blessing. This did not forestall the effects of Noah's curse. The children of Shem did struggle and rage against the children of Ham. Yet God's words to Abraham continued to ring out as an eschatological hope that was never lost from sight. The time would come when the people of Israel would extend their blessing throughout the earth. This vocation to embody a unique politics is why God resists Israel's determination to be like the nations in 1 Sam. 8:4–22. The monarchy constitutes a fundamental rejection of the divine rule; God's ways are not like those of the nations. God's people are not to have kings who claim power and place and sustain themselves through violence. Rather, they are to be a people of blessing.

Novak reads the story of Abraham's defense of the righteous in Sodom and Gomorrah as an instance of "blessing the nations."

> Abraham's relationship with God is correlative to his relationship with the world. And the precise presentation of that correlation is found in Abraham's dialogue with God over the judgment of the cities of Sodom and Gomorrah. God justifies including Abraham in this dialogue as follows:
>
> > How can I conceal what I am doing from Abraham? And Abraham shall surely become a great and important (*atsum*) nation, in whom all the nations of the earth shall be blessed. For I know him, so that (*le-ma'an*) he will command his children and his household after him to keep the way of the Lord to do what is right (*tsedaqah*) and just (*mishpat*). (Genesis 18:17–19)
>
> The question now is to determine the connection of the blessing of the nations of the earth to Abraham and his people keeping the way of the Lord to do what is right and just.[40]

The people of Israel are called to imitate God's relationship with the world both in terms of *tsedaqah*—God's transcendent graciousness toward creation—and *mishpat*—God's immanent ordering of the cosmos, conformity to which is justice.[41] So as this passage suggests, blessing the nations is one and the same with Israel's faithfulness to its election. When Abraham argues with God for the sake of Sodom and Gomorrah, he imitates God's own *tsedaqah* and *mishpat*. "His response to being known-and-chosen by God is to want to imitate in microcosm the way God relates to the whole world in macrocosm."[42] Abraham blesses the nations by standing with them and taking their side, which is to say, standing "*with* God *in* and *for* the world."[43] Such a politics is a radical departure from the usual ways of the nations, whose oppositional identities incline them always to see others as potential threats to their existence and prosperity.

Covenant

Covenant is the correlate of election that, through Torah and the land, determines the material and political shape of Israel's free and holy life in mutual relation to God. Although election per se involves the choice of another for relationship, covenant names the establishing of a communal context for that relationship, that is, the establishing of a community within which God will "act and elicit responses."[44] Election is merely the prelude to the formation of a people who will reflect God's holiness. "You are, as He promised you, His treasured people," and "you shall be, as He promised, a holy people to the Lord your God" (Deut. 26:18–19). God treasures those whom God has elected and promises to make them holy—which is a way of saying they will imitate God's own ways: "You shall be holy, for I, the Lord your God, am holy" (Lev. 19:2). The origin and the telos of election, its beginning and its ending, is the formation of a people for God. This is why one cannot talk about election without talking about covenant.

This people-making activity, unlike the act of election itself, requires a relationship of *mutuality* between God and Israel. In the covenant God calls Israel to *respond* to its election. Here Israel's freedom becomes important—not to initiate a relationship with God but to respond to God's choice and thus to live in accordance with God's ways. It is here that the rabbis are most helpful, because they address the danger that election alone can come to sound like coercion. The question is how to avoid describing the covenant as compulsion or domination, while at the same time refusing to turn it into a contract between autonomous subjects. The rabbis answered by emphasizing the human side of the covenant without rejecting the priority of God's election. They did not dispute the basic biblical understanding of the election of Israel, yet within this framework they highlighted the role Israel *did* play in the covenant—stretching beyond the biblical picture at times, but "without . . . concluding that the covenant itself is essentially contingent upon Israel's choice."[45] The importance of Israel's response to God is brought out in a favorite story of the rabbis in which the Torah is offered to all the nations but only Israel will accept its demands: "When God determined to give the Law, none of the nations except Israel would receive it. . . . So when God revealed himself upon Mount Sinai, there was not a nation at whose doors He did not knock, but they would not accept the Law and keep it. But when he came to Israel, they said, 'All that the Lord has spoken we will do, and we will hearken'" (M&L, 121).[46] In this legend Israel's *response* to God and the Torah is given a central place in establishing the covenant. God does not unilaterally create the relationship through inexorable force, but rather invites and enables response from the other.

Israel's relationship with God, then, should be seen less as "an offer they could not refuse"[47] than as a proffered love that evokes reciprocity.[48] The language of love is particularly appropriate here since it denotes a dialectical and free mutuality that is nonetheless driven and evoked by forces that belie any simplistic descriptions of "free choice." The love between God and Israel is not some general and disinterested agape, but full-blooded eros. "The heavens to their uttermost reaches belong to the Lord your God, the earth and all that is on it. Yet it was to your fathers that the Lord was drawn in His love for them, so that He chose you, their lineal descendants, from among all peoples" (Deut. 10:14–15). God's love for

Israel is passionately interested and particular. As Wyschogrod makes clear, it is this eros that makes possible a love with God that is not coercive. "The *eros* element in God's love for Israel is . . . the element that maintains the separateness of the people of Israel from God, without which God's love would simply absorb into his being that which he loves."[49] Because God loves the particularity of the other, God creates the distance necessary for this other to exist in its particularity separate from God. The undifferentiated love of agape, Wyschogrod argues, does not see the uniqueness of the beloved and thus fails to be a truly personal love. It remains distant and invulnerable. It remains abstract and all-encompassing. In contrast,

> the divine love is concrete. It is a genuine encounter with man in his individuality and must therefore be exclusive. Any real love encounter . . . is exclusive because it is genuinely directed to the uniqueness of the other and it therefore follows that each such relationship is different from all others. . . . The election of Israel is thus a sign of the humanity of God. Had he so willed it, he could have played a more godly role, refusing favorites and loving all his creatures impartially. His love would then have been a far less vulnerable one because impartiality signifies a certain remoteness, the absence of that consuming passion that is a sign of the need of the other. Herein resides the inhumanity of *agape* and the humanity of *eros*.[50]

Election and covenant create a mutual love between God and Israel that recognizes the full particularity of each. This mutual love prohibits coercion, for rather than overwhelming Israel with invulnerable power, God risks the vulnerable love of eros. Yet eros carries with it the experience of inevitability, of being drawn into a love that is beyond choice alone. Thus, neither party is purely active or purely passive. Each experiences the passivity of "falling in love" and the activity of extending love. This mutuality, this give and take between God and Israel is evident in the passionate tenderness of this rabbinic reflection:

> The Israelites say, "Hear O Israel, the Lord thy God, the Lord is One" (*ehad*). And the Holy Spirit calls from heaven and says, "Who is like unto thee, O Israel, a people unique (*ehad*) upon the earth?" (I Chron. XVII, 21). The Israelites say, "Who is like unto thee, O Lord, among the gods?" (Exod. XV, 11). And the Holy Spirit calls from heaven and says, "Happy art thou, O Israel, who is like thee?" (Deut. XXXIII, 29). The Israelites say, "Who is like the Lord, who answers us whenever we call upon Him?" (Deut. IV, 7), and the Holy Spirit cries out and says, "What nation has God near it like Israel?" (*ib.*). The Israelites say, "Thou art the glory of their strength" (Ps. LXXXIX, 17), and the Holy Spirit cries out and says, "Israel, in thee I will be glorified" (Isa. XLIX, 3). (M&L, 101)

This is the language of lovers, of mutual adoration. And it reflects not only loving reciprocity but also Israel's imitation of God. "Who is like thee?" God asks of Israel; "Who is like thee?" Israel asks of God. Israel is unique (*ehad*) because Israel has been chosen and loved by the God who is one (*ehad*). The mutuality of love yields a commonality of character between God and the chosen people. To love is to become like the beloved. Such love is not coercion, though one may find oneself drawn irresistibly to the other and changed in ways that one never expected.

In short there is both freedom and choice on the part of both God and Israel, but the terms are at best used analogically, if not equivocally, in these two instances. God's freedom and choice are rooted in God's identity as creator. For God's creative actions, there is neither cause nor necessity. God's freedom does not exist within a predefined realm of options but rather creates the possibility of possibility. The covenant with Israel is likewise grounded in the divine creative freedom. Human choice, however, is limited to the possibilities set in place by God. The people of Israel are free to respond to the covenant or not, but they are not free to establish or annul that which God has created. "There is an essential difference between freedom of response and freedom of initiation. . . . Humans can accept the covenant or reject it, but cannot escape it."[51]

Israel's "choice" to love the beloved, then, is never rightly understood if it is thought of in relation to the "other options" available. Yet Novak acknowledges that the question is common and understandable, "If the covenant requires human compliance, why doesn't Israel have any other real option?" To think in such a way, however, is to misunderstand the call of eros and to replace the mutuality of lovers with the sterility of the contract. "For all the language of choice that characterizes covenant texts, the Hebrew Bible never regards choice to decline covenant as legitimate. The fact that a choice is given does not make the alternative good or even acceptable, as a proponent of a purely contractual ethic might wish."[52] The people of Israel never stand in a position of neutrality, from which they could equally say yes or no to God's covenant call. The call evokes a corresponding response, yet failure to affirm the covenant is not to annul it but only to stand against it. The covenant does not require Israel's response to make it a reality, but it does elicit a response as one lover elicits the love of another.[53]

Although it is a helpful way to describe the free response of Israel to God's election, the analogy of lovers does break down. The love in a marriage relationship requires and creates an equality that does not characterize Israel's relationship with God. "Marriage is both initiated and sustained by the natural necessity of eros in both partners. In the covenant, conversely . . . the divine partner is not bound by any necessity at all." Novak continues, suggesting a different metaphor, "The relationship between God and Israel is often more political than familial. That is why, it seems to me, the model of God as king is more often used in rabbinic teaching."[54]

Novak properly reminds us that the *political* nature of the covenant can never be lost from sight; thus neither can the *materiality* of the covenant. The peoplehood of Israel is established neither as an abstract entity in the heavens nor as an eschatological hope at the end of time. This is neither a *spiritual* covenant floating above earthly engagements nor a *formal* covenant lacking substantive content. Rather, God's covenant with Israel is almost embarrassingly material and political—at least to the modern person who is used to tamed and circumscribed religion. It is concerned with rulers and enemies, pots and pans, genitals and off-spring. This covenant matters because it lays claim to matter and refuses to be rel-egated to the nonmaterial realm. It is not up in the heavens or out across the sea where it cannot be found much less practiced, but it is "very close to you, in your mouth and in your heart, to observe it" (Deut. 30:14). Israel's covenant with God lies close to home, close to the mouth and heart, close to the everyday things.

In light of this a notion such as the separation of religion and politics makes little intrinsic sense within the logic of the covenant. Quite simply, within the covenant religion and politics are not conceptualized as separable entities. Theology, politics, and ethics are all tied up in one package, as Novak never lets us forget. "More than anything else the covenant is a political idea and a political reality. By 'political' I mean the whole range of human communal existence and its place in the very nature of things, the overall kind of political philosophy sug-gested by such earlier modern thinkers as Leo Strauss and Eric Voegelin and now being carried on by such contemporary thinkers as Alasdair MacIntyre and Charles Taylor. It is only within Jewish political theology that the questions of ethics entailed by emphasis of the covenant can be properly treated."[55] Nonetheless, modern thought, at least from Spinoza forward, posited a political sphere outside of the covenant and within which the covenant had to be made in-telligible. Israel's worship and practices had to be justified on alien soil. Politics and ethics, as secular descriptions of human action, were given conceptual prior-ity and thus became the context into which covenant life had to fit.

Conversely, in classical Jewish understandings of the covenant, politics and morals derived their intelligibility from their place in an overarching covenant life.[56] The modern question inverted the traditional structure, asking how covenant life can serve the political project of the state, rather than how poli-tics can further the production and enjoyment of the goods of the covenant. In biblical-rabbinic thinking, no sphere of life extended beyond or evaded the au-thority of the covenant. Covenant named for Israel the very playing field and the ground rules within which all other activities were carried out. The partic-ular politics of the covenant resists both nationalism and the primacy of self-interest, seeking instead the glorification of God's name through the produc-tion of a holy people. This is not to say that covenant status has never been perverted into a nationalist or self-interested claim. But the cure for this was not the separation of politics from religion; it was the sanctification of poli-tics.[57] Election names a political vocation to holiness rather than a privileged individual or national status.[58]

By wedding the activities of choosing, *bahar,* and forming, *yatsar,* Deutero-Isaiah deftly highlights this connection between election and vocation. God both chooses Israel (41:8, 9; 43:10, 20; 44:1, 2; 48:10; 49:7) and fashions Israel into a people (43:1, 7, 21; 44:2, 21, 24; 45:11; 49:8) who will "declare [God's] praise" (43:21), "teach the true way to the nations" (42:1), "establish the true way on earth" (42:4), and be "a light of nations" (42:6). Israel is to God

> My chosen [*bahar*] people,
> The people I formed [*yatsar*] for Myself
> That they might declare my praise. (Isa. 43:20–21)

In contrast, the nations "choose" (*bahar*) and "fashion" (*yatsar*) idols in self-glorifying opposition to God. The woodworker chooses (*bahar*) the wood (40:20) from which he fashions (*yatsar*) a god (44:10,12)—using the remainder of the wood to roast meat and stay warm (44:16). The idol is then chosen (*bahar*) by human beings to be their god (41:24). The production and worship of the idol, the presumption that humans can choose and form God, reflects a precise reversal of God's activity. For to be able to *choose* one's god is necessarily to be choosing an idol, for only an idol could be objectified before the courts of human preference.

God, in turn, reverses this reversal, claiming the role of the maker and purging Israel of its complicity in idolatry.

> See, I refine you, but not as silver;
> I test [*yatsar*] you in the furnace of affliction. (48:10)

Israel is lowered into the blacksmith's furnace; its iron neck and bronze forehead (48:4) are shaped by the divine craftsman under the scorching heat of affliction. God reclaims the role of creator by laying hold of Israel and creating in this chosen people an instrument of God's salvation (49:6).

The material and political nature of the covenant, the formation of God's holy people, is grounded in the giving of the Torah. Torah is at the heart of the covenant because it names the ways in which Israel is to be set apart in its life of holiness. If election and covenant name God's people-making activity, then Torah names the kind of people God is forming. Novak observes, "The law [is the means] through which the separateness of the Jewish people that their election involves is concretized by specific repeatable acts."[59] Election is given its material content in the Torah, and thus talk of Israel's being formed into God's people must center on the revelation of God's will on Sinai. Torah observance shapes the people by developing habits of holiness and creating a distinct way of life.

It must be recognized that Torah is concerned not only with what we might call "ethical" issues but also with housekeeping, eating, hygiene, illness, worship, economics, politics, sex, birth, festivals, work, and play. In the practice of Torah, the lines between "ritual," "ethics," "culture," and "politics" break down. Although, as Novak remarks, "the life of the covenant itself largely consists of an elaborate system of acts that we today would call 'ritual,'" this term "is hardly adequate to describe what Jewish tradition has designated as 'what is between humans and God' (*bein adam la-maqom*)."[60] He suggests that the word "ritual" be used of Torah only in the most basic, introductory way, since its use in modernity already presupposes a split between "mere ritual" and something more determinative called "reality." The Torah itself calls this kind of split into question by its refusal to divide the discourses of worship and politics.

Torah is much bigger than "ritual" and it is also much bigger than "law." For Torah includes also the formative narratives of Israel. As Wyschogrod reminds us, "Whatever prominence legal codes later assumed in Judaism, the Torah is not only a legal code. It is well known that it was when the Hebrew word *Torah* was translated into the Greek *nomos* that Torah became law. The correct translation of Torah is teaching. It is the story of God's encounter with Israel and of his will expressed in the context of that encounter."[61] Torah includes both the stories of Israel and the practices that correspond to these stories—practices that make it possible for the Jews to live in the world these stories create.[62] Which is to say the practices set the people of Israel free to live their story faithfully.

Performing the Torah, therefore, cannot be reduced to a memorial of prior events or a means to desired consequences. The goods of Torah are intrinsic to the practices themselves. So Novak writes, "More than what God has done for us, the good is what God enables us to do with him here and now, namely, practice the commandments. Thus it is not that the Jews are to observe the commandments in return for what God did when he 'took us out of the land of Egypt, out of the house of slavery' (Exodus 20:2), but rather God's taking Israel out of Egypt is the beginning of the good we now experience in keeping his commandments."[63] Celebrating the Passover, for instance, is not simply a way of remembering the liberation from Egypt, but rather such liberation is a way of making possible the celebration of the Passover.[64] Torah practices must never be confused with "memorials," since the events of Israel's history are finally for the sake of the practices and not vice versa.

Similarly, the observance of Torah can never be understood rightly in utilitarian terms. One does not keep the Sabbath in order to provide rest from work; instead, one rests from work in order to keep the Sabbath. One does not worship God in order to bring justice; instead, "justice is to be practiced in order that the people can dwell with the true God in covenantal intimacy."[65] Becoming a holy people, a people who live Torah-shaped lives, is the goal of the covenant, for only such a people can be capable of dwelling with God in joy. Thus, Torah obedience is not in opposition to freedom (a point Christians have long misunderstood) but rather is the ground of freedom. Freedom is the result of being trained by the practices of Torah. Such formation results in the freedom to be faithful to the covenant and thus to the community's truest identity. The goal, then, is for Israel to become the incarnation of Torah, the embodiment of divine teaching, and thus freely to be who God created them to be.[66]

None of this is meant to imply, however, that Israel is always or even usually obedient to the Torah. Christian theology has tended to overemphasize Jewish sin, and thus the temptation now is to overcompensate, to downplay or ignore it. But one must be careful not to romanticize Israel. As Wyschogrod notes, "The history of Israel was, like the history of man, from the beginning, a history of disobedience. . . . The special attention paid to Israel, while not without some effect, still left a deeply disobedient chosen people. Israel thus turned out to be more like the rest of humanity than envisaged."[67] The difference in Israel is that its sin becomes an opportunity for God to display faithfulness to the covenant. Despite their disobedience, God will not cast the Jews away, for God's election is trustworthy.

In addition to the Torah, the promised land constitutes a distinct material component of the covenant. As we have seen, the peoplehood of Israel does not *depend* on the land; nonetheless, the promise of a place set apart for covenant life was from the beginning intrinsic to Abraham's election. "The Lord said to Abram, 'Go forth from your native land and from your father's house to the land that I will show you'" (Gen. 12:1). This promise of a land, despite the ever shifting horizon of its fulfillment, remained a constant hope for this sojourning people. "When I said, 'I the Lord am your God,' that same day I swore to them to take them out of the land of Egypt into a land flowing with milk and honey, a land which I had sought out for them, the fairest of all lands" (Ezek. 20:5–6). Although Israel can and does remain God's chosen people even apart from the land, "no Jew is ever permanently away from Israel. The exile is temporary. In our deepest unconscious, the land of Israel is our home from which we are temporarily parted."[68]

The deep connection between the people and the land comes out in the symbiotic relationship between Israel's faithfulness and the fruitfulness of the land (Deut. 11:13–17; Lev. 26). The land suffered when Israel disobeyed God (Num. 35:33–34; Jer. 12:4). The land cried out in protest and stood in judgment at Israel's failure to keep the covenant (Lev. 18:28; Mic. 6:1–2). The land prospered when the people followed God's ways (Deut. 28:4, 11–12). Just as the Jews were chosen from among the people of the earth, so the land was chosen for them. The land itself is an "elect" land for the elect people.[69] This land continues to remind Israel of God's intention to give the descendants of Abraham a particular place for their covenant life. It continues to be a focal point for Israel's hope of redemption.

Redemption

The promised redemption of Israel and the inclusion of all creation in God's reign of peace is the unseen political and historical horizon of God's election. In addition to choosing a people (election), and establishing a community (covenant), God also promises to fulfill the purposes of election. The precise content of this redemption, however, is seen only dimly on the horizon. Generally, Jewish tradition has affirmed that redemption will include Israel's deliverance from exile and oppression and will be ushered in with the coming of the Messiah, who will establish God's kingdom of peace.[70] Beyond this the character of redemption is hidden in God's future. Novak tries to sum up what can be said about this eschatological event: "All that can be known about the final redemption . . . is that the estrangement between God and Israel will be ultimately overcome, and that God's redemption of Israel will be central in his redemption of all his creation—that

the Lord will be king of Israel together with his being king over all the earth."[71]
Granted that Israel's redemption is a hope shrouded in darkness, a dim outline of
this hope can be seen in the prophetic witness of Zechariah.

"Thus says the Lord of hosts: I will save my people from the east country and
from the west country" (Zech. 8:7). In response to the tragic scattering and oppression of God's people, redemption comes to name first the regathering of
Israel from its exile among the nations. To be redeemed is to be joined once again
as one people, no longer splintered by the violent hands of the enemy. Deutero-
Isaiah also witnesses to the hope that God's creation of Israel as a people and formation of that people will be brought to its fulfillment in God's restoration of
that people.

> But now thus said the Lord—
> Who created you, O Jacob,
> Who formed [*yatsar*] you, O Israel:
> Fear not, for I will redeem [*ge'ulah*] you;
> I have singled you out by name,
> You are Mine. (Isa. 43:1)

> For you, O Israel, are My servant,
> I fashioned [*yatsar*] you, you are My servant—
> O Israel, never forget Me.
> I wipe away your sins like a cloud,
> your transgressions like mist—
> Come back to Me, for I redeem [*ge'ulah*] you.

Israel's sin will be wiped away, its transgressions forgiven. In election this final
determination of God's people for holiness is made certain, even if only in the eschatological future.

Second, redemption means the restoration of the land, where Israel will live
under the rule of God alone: "I will bring them to live in Jerusalem. They shall be
my people and I will be their God, in faithfulness and in righteousness" (Zech.
8:7–8). The hope for the land is pervasive, and it reminds us that redemption is
not only historical and temporal; it is tangible, political, and spatial. Redemption
will occur in a very particular *place*. But as Zechariah points out, the redeemed
city of God, the restored Jerusalem, will be a city without walls, for the multitudes
of both people and animals will be too great to be contained.[72] The holy space
will be marked only by the presence of God—glory within the city and fire surrounding it (Zech 2:4–5). Because of this connection to a real people and a real
place, Israel's redemption has always rebounded from efforts to spiritualize it.
Redemption "takes place publicly, on the stage of history," Gershom Scholem asserts. "It is an occurrence which takes place in the visible world and which cannot be conceived of apart from such visible appearance."[73]

In addition to naming the gathering of God's people and the restoration of the land, redemption names the peace and plenty of dwelling in Israel: "There shall be a sowing of peace; the vine shall yield its fruit, the ground shall give its produce, and the skies shall give their dew" (Zech. 8:12). The messianic reign is seen as a time when a "peaceable ruler" will establish "peace without limit" (Isa. 9:6, 7); the nations will beat their swords into plowshares and will know war no more (Mic. 4:3). Humans and animals together will live at peace, no longer sustaining their lives at the expense of one another (Isa. 2:1–4; 11:6–9). There will be no struggle for sustenance, as this will be "a land flowing with milk and honey" (Ex. 3:8).

Such an existence of plentiful peace is not only the goal of all God's working; it is the basis of all creation, as the rabbis understood. "Great is peace, for it is equal to everything, as it is said, 'He makes peace and creates all' (Isa. XLV, 7)" (M&L, 534). Peace is the fullness of blessing: "R. Simeon b. Yohai said: Great is peace, for all blessings are contained in it, as it says, 'The Lord will bless His people with peace' (Ps. XXIX, 11)" (M&L, 533). Peace is the hope for Jerusalem: "God comforts Jerusalem only with peace, as it is said, 'And my people shall dwell in a habitation of peace' (Isa. XXXIII, 18) (M&L, 533–534). Indeed, peace is the very name of God: "R. Yudan b. R. Jose said: Great is peace for God's name is peace, as it is said, 'And he called it Jehovah-Shalom'" (Judges VI, 24) (M&L, 533).

Fourth, and finally, redemption includes the ingathering of the Gentiles to share the blessings of the peaceable kingdom:

> Thus says the Lord of hosts: People shall yet come, the inhabitants of many cities; the inhabitants of one city shall go to another, saying, "Come, let us go to entreat the favor of the Lord, and to seek the Lord of hosts; I myself am going." Many peoples and strong nations shall come to seek the Lord of hosts in Jerusalem, and to entreat the favor of the Lord. Thus says the Lord of hosts: in those days ten men from nations of every language shall take hold of a Jew, grasping his garment and saying, "Let us go with you, for we have heard that God is with you." (Zech. 8:20–23)

As we have seen, from the start the election of Israel was not set off dualistically against a rejection of the Gentiles. Rather it was an election that would bless the Gentiles, an election that would eventually reach out and welcome all people into God's covenant. Thus, the redemption of Israel is not only the redemption of Israel, since to the restored Jerusalem will come "all the nations and tongues," indeed "all flesh," to worship God (Isa. 66:17, 23; Mic. 4:1–2). Israel's redemption is both a result and a means of God's creation of a new heaven and a new earth (Isa. 65:17; 66:22). As Wyschogrod poetically envisions in the final lines of his book, "The circumcised body of Israel is the dark, carnal presence through which the redemption makes its way into history. Salvation is of the Jews because the flesh of Israel is the abode of divine presence in the world. It is the carnal anchor that God has sunk into the soil of creation."[74]

In the messianic age, all of humankind is to be drawn into God's future with Israel. Novak defines "redemption" (*ge'ulah*) as God's plan "to bring the whole world finally into the covenant."[75] There will be, one could say, a "judaizing of humanity."[76] Again, Israel's election is not to be understood as contrasted with God's rejection of others. For it is precisely *through* the elect people that God works to bring redemption to all. There is no intrinsic opposition set up between the elect and the nonelect in Jewish thought. "The separateness of Israel has never implied that the purpose of Israel's election is only Israel's redemption. The redemption leaves out no member of the human family."[77] God's redemption reaches to all, though it moves first to and then through the chosen ones out toward the world. "The prophetic picture of the end of days envisages a reconciliation among the peoples of the world, so that the redemption of Israel is also the redemption of humanity. The election of Israel and the biblical focus on the history of Israel are therefore, in a sense, the means chosen by Hashem for the redemption of humanity."[78] Redemption is thus the fulfillment of election. It is God's reaching out to restore Israel and through Israel to extend covenantal peace to the world.

But again it must be stressed that the precise nature and character of God's redemption is hidden; it lies in the darkness of God's future. It is unrealized and unpredictable. "The future remains dark, even if it is not totally dark," observes Wyschogrod. "The shadows that can be glimpsed in it are seen very imperfectly and can therefore be thoroughly misinterpreted. The darkness of the future predominates over its light."[79] Israel knows that its election was for a purpose and that the sanctifying of a people for God through the covenant points in some way toward God's coming reign of peace. The relation, however, between the present form of the covenant people and the coming redemption is not clear. Redemption cannot be understood as a simple, mechanical projection of election and covenant into the future. Nonetheless, Israel's current existence leans already into the unknowable future of God's fulfillment. What *is* certain is that Israel will be a part of this future.

Both Novak and Wyschogrod embrace an "apocalyptic," or "maximalist," eschatology as opposed to the "extensive," or "minimalist," view that some in the Jewish tradition have held.[80] In the extensive view the redemptive future looks like an extension of the present. It is thus a predictable future. The nature and content of covenant life and communal faithfulness will not change. What will change are Israel's political conditions, making possible a Torah-based life and politics free from foreign domination. Other nations will either convert or be subordinated to Israel's rule as the authority of Torah is extended over all people. On this view, classically expressed by Maimonides, the redeemed future will be only quantitatively, not qualitatively, different from the present.[81]

In contrast, the apocalyptic position of Novak and Wyschogrod expects God's redemptive work to bring qualitative changes, which will extend even to the Torah itself.[82] As Jeremiah makes clear, God will transform the heart of Israel, so that the Torah will be known immediately, carved into the character of the House of

Israel.[83] "See, a time is coming—declares the Lord—when I will make a new covenant with the House of Israel and the House of Judah. . . . I will put My Teaching into their inmost being, and inscribe it upon their hearts. Then I will be their God and they shall be My people. No longer will they need to teach one another and say to one another, 'Heed the Lord'; for all of them, from the least of them to the greatest, shall heed Me—declares the Lord" (Jer. 31:31–34). The form of the Torah will change from spoken command to habit of life. In addition, the referent and context for covenantal life will shift from the Exodus to the eschatological gathering of Israel. "Assuredly a time is coming—declares the Lord—when it shall no more be said, 'As the Lord lives, who brought the Israelites out of the land of Egypt,' but rather, 'As the Lord lives, who brought out and led the offspring of the House of Israel from the northland and from all the lands to which I have banished them'" (Jer. 23:7–8).[84] Further, the very content of the Torah will be altered, since there will be "many cultic commandments that would no longer be within the range of Jewish observance because of the absence of their necessary preconditions."[85]

Such a change in the actual content of the Torah is expected in this rabbinic reflection: "'The Lord permits the forbidden' (Ps. CXLVI,7) (A.V. and R.V. 'looses the prisoner'; the word 'forbidden' is got by a pun). What does this mean? Some say that in the time to come all the animals which are unclean in this world God will declare to be clean, as they were in the days before Noah. And why did God forbid them [i.e., make them unclean]? To see who would accept His bidding and who would not; but in the time to come He will permit all that He has forbidden" (M&L, 583). In the apocalyptic view the form, the narrative referent, and even the actual content of the Torah will be changed in God's redeemed future. Nonetheless, the people of Israel will not change. Whatever Jeremiah's "new covenant" looks like, it will still be a covenant with Israel.[86]

In either its apocalyptic or its extensive forms, Jewish understandings of redemption are permeated by political and historical concerns. "In Judaism, redemption is a religious-political concept. During the first century, this meant the throwing off of the Roman yoke in favor of a genuinely independent Jewish commonwealth. The hoped-for Messiah was therefore inevitably a religious-political figure who could not avoid being a threat to Roman rule."[87] Likewise today, in Judaism redemption is not simply about a future life of the spirit (though such a view is not entirely absent from the tradition), but more about material changes in history and politics. Redemption means Israel's political sovereignty; it means being ruled by God alone; it means peace.[88] But again, redemption is not just about Israel's politics but about world politics, not just about Israel's peace but about world peace. Despite R. Judah's assessment that Israel's enemies Doeg and Ahithophel shall "have no share in the world to come" (M&L, 604–605), "It is said that even Doeg and Ahithophel shall have a part in the life to come. The angels of the Service say, 'If David complains of this, what wilt thou do?' God replies, 'It is my business to make them friends with one another'" (M&L, 587). Israel's peace will extend even to enemies. Israel's redeemed politics will water the wounded soil of history.

This understanding of the politics of redemption has implications for how the Jews live even now in expectation of God's coming reign. For Novak, the present implications are purely negative. Because redemption has not arrived, even partially, Israel witnesses in its common life only to the *absence* of redemption:

> Now our testimony to the nations of the world is not positive but negative. It is to remind them by our very vulnerable and incomplete life that God is not present in the world, that redemption is not to be expected by human criteria, that redemption will only come when God decides by his own mysterious criteria that the time is right for us and for them along with us. And so our testimony is to belie those who say that the world is redeemed and to insist that the world wait with Israel for her and its redeemer.[89]

Jewish social ethics, then, must always take into account the "finitude, mortality, and fallibility" of human subjects.[90] There is, thus, a tentative quality to all moral decisions. When Elijah comes at the end of history, he will bring a divine eschatological judgment to prove finally what is right and good. He will make right those human decisions distorted by unredeemed fallibility. Presently, one cannot know which of one's judgments will eventually be overturned before Elijah's court.[91] This leads to a certain humility that rejects utopianism or pseudomessianism—movements that claim to be able to embody the redeemed life in the present. Rather, over against these movements, "Judaism's greater sobriety teaches us that frequently all we can do is the lesser evil. This is our more modest task."[92] Elijah stands at the edge of history with an ethic that cannot be lived, or even known, in the present by a finite, fallible, unredeemed Israel. To attempt to do so would be both arrogant and unrealistic. Novak therefore calls for a healthy realism in ethics and politics, based on Israel's unredeemed state and the apocalyptic gap between the present world and God's future.[93]

Although Wyschogrod holds to a similarly apocalyptic view of eschatology, he does have, at least in one area, a conviction that the messianic future is beginning to be embodied already among the Jews—that is, the peace of God's redeemed future is proleptically present among the people of Israel:

> If large-scale, organized violence between groups of Jews is possible, if war is possible among Jews, then the Jewish people is not one. I do not believe such violence is possible. . . . In spite of all the irritations and tensions that exist among Jews, were the possibility of war among Jews to arise, I am convinced that the bond that unites Jews would reassert itself and prevent such war. If this is so, then the messianic vision of the abolition of war is already realized in the community of Israel. But none of this can be taken for granted. It must be constantly cultivated and deepened.[94]

Wyschogrod sees that the seeds of messianic peace lie planted firmly in Jewish election. He holds out the possibility that the people of Israel can already begin to make a political witness to that messianic peace in their own life together. Here, at least, the redeemed future has begun to break in on the present.

The Jewish No

Because of how Jews have traditionally viewed election, covenant, and redemption, they have said no to any attempts to spiritualize election or to locate God's redemption as a present reality. In both of these ways, Jewish life and thought continue to stand as a critique of Christian theology and practice.[95] First, to Jewish eyes, Christianity represents a flight from the material into the spiritual. Throughout *The Body of Faith*, Wyschogrod relentlessly emphasizes this difference between Jews and Christians. He interprets Jesus as a figure detached from the world and its concerns, as one who preached a transcendent spiritual gospel that blew through the things of earth as if they were not there.[96] Corresponding to this, he sees Christianity as primarily a matter of beliefs, that is, as an ideology that disregards the material and the political. Baptism, the initiation into Christianity, leaves no mark on the flesh because it symbolizes only an inner, spiritual, and mental change.[97] "We are thus dealing with a profound spiritualization of Judaism, and once this is accomplished it is almost inevitable that this version of Judaism can no longer remain tied to the religious-political destiny of the Jewish people."[98] To the extent that Christianity has retreated from history and taken refuge in the spirit, the Jewish rejection of such a posture poses a deep challenge for a church that claims to worship and follow the God of Abraham.

A second reason for the Jewish no to Christianity is that whereas Christians claim redemption has come in Christ, the actual state of the world, and especially that of Israel, appears essentially unchanged. Redemption for the Jews is expected to be an event that can be neither missed nor misunderstood, and so it remains a future hope. "The redeemed future must be an event so messianically self-evident that it would not entail the type of dispute that led to the schism of the Christian community."[99] Thus, "in Jewish belief . . . Jesus was not the Messiah precisely because he did not bring about the full restoration of the Jewish people to the Land of Israel and God's universal reign of peace."[100] Christian claims that Christ redeemed the world belie the persistently unredeemed character the world still exhibits. Hermann Cohen argues along these lines that until the coming of the Messiah the Jewish people must retain their separateness, their witness to the singularity of God and God's ways. He charged Christianity, in contrast, with a "premature surrender to the world-as-it-is."[101] For Christians to claim that the world is redeemed already is to risk consecrating the present order, capitulating to the world's unredeemed existence. It is to risk losing the necessary separateness that witnesses to and awaits God's coming redemption.

Christian theology and practice have rarely given Jews reason to reconsider these critiques. The earliest Christian theologians began to spiritualize election and the covenant, relating them to the eternal destiny of individuals rather than to the present life of God's people. Further, by its partnership with Constantine, the church relocated within the empire its material witness to redemption. Until Christians rethink these theological and political decisions, the no of Israel will retain its sting.

3

The Politics of Supersessionism

𝑰f "supersessionism" names the conviction that Christians have *replaced* Israel as God's elect and thus may claim as their own all the blessings of that election, then "Christendom" names the politics made possible by such a theology. The goal of this chapter is not to trace a direct line of causality between the church's rejection of Israel, its theology of election, and its compromise with Constantine, for these three elements are intertwined intellectually and historically in ways that would render any unidirectional account misleading. Rather, I hope to show that the church's relation to Israel and to the Gentile powers affected and was affected by the developing view of election as a private and spiritual matter and by the theological argument with the Jews concerning the visibility and presence of Christ's redemption. Two questions focus my discussion. The first is a question Christians began asking once the church became a predominantly Gentile body: How is it that God's promises to Israel now apply to the Gentiles? The second question was posed to the church by Jews who saw no visible signs of the messianic age: Where is this redemption you say has occurred in Jesus Christ?

De-Judaizing Election

The first question, How is it that God's promises to Israel now apply to the Gentiles? could be asked another way: How have Gentiles come to receive the gifts once thought to be the sole prerogative of the Jews? Included within this was the question of Israel's status before God: If the promises are now being extended to the Gentiles, while at the same time the Jews are in large measure rejecting their own Messiah, where does this leave the Jews? Christian theologians sought to answer these questions in tractates often entitled *Adversus Judaeos*—"Against the Jews."[1] Although these writings were on the one hand directed toward Jews as apologetic arguments, seeking to convince them of the truth of Christian beliefs, they were on the other hand directed to the church as attempts to answer the internal theological question of the status of Jews and Gentiles before God. Different voices answered the questions differently, but over the first few centuries a distinct pattern did emerge, a central feature of which was the de-Judaizing of the doctrine of election.

It would be disingenuous to imply that this pattern appeared only after the New Testament writings, for it can be traced to certain passages within the canon itself.[2] Of course, we must be careful not to project later religious and communal divisions back into the New Testament, since the canonical writings were produced when the "Jewish-Christian" debate was still an intra-Jewish rivalry. At issue was which of the many Judaisms of the first century would become the dominant tradition. The Jewish writers of the New Testament were not founding a new religion but were arguing for a certain construal of *Jewish* faithfulness in response to their conviction that Jesus was the Messiah of Israel. Yet as part of this argument some of the writers went so far as to imply that God's election had been transferred to a new people in light of the widespread Jewish rejection of the Gospel. Although these are not the only voices in the New Testament, and arguably not even the strongest voices, their polemical witness must be acknowledged and dealt with.

Matthew, for instance, redacts Jesus' parable of the wicked tenants as found in Mark in such a way as to make it read like a parable of supersession.[3] The parable tells of how the wicked tenants refused to pay the owner of the vineyard his due, abusing his messengers and finally killing his son in an attempt to claim his inheritance. In Mark it is clear that this parable is told against "the chief priests, the scribes, and the elders" (Mark 11:27), but in Matthew its target seems to be extended to the Jewish people as a whole. He adds a disturbing gloss to Mark's account: "Therefore I tell you, the kingdom of God will be taken away from you and given to a people that produces the fruits of the kingdom." The context of Matthew's Gospel as a whole pushes toward an allegorical reading in which the vineyard (the kingdom of God) is the fruit of God's election, the displaced people are the Jews, and the new "people" are the church.

Turning to John's Gospel, we find not only a replacement theology but even the disconcerting insinuation that "the Jews" are of the devil rather than of God.[4] Speaking to "the Jews who had believed in him," John's Jesus lashes out during a heated debate, "You are from your father the devil, and you choose to do your father's desires. . . . Whoever is from God hears the words of God. The reason you do not hear them is that you are not from God" (John 8:44, 47). As Richard Hays observes, "John makes a fateful theological step: *from the empirical fact of the unbelief of the Jews, he infers an ontological dualism.* The Jews who do not believe must be children of the devil. The reason that they do not believe is that they *cannot.* Otherwise, surely they would be convinced of the truth."[5] Anti-Jewish passages such as these in John and Matthew certainly laid the groundwork for the more developed theologies of supersessionism that arose in the first few centuries of Christian theological reflection.[6]

A crucial assumption behind the emergence of a full-blown supersessionist theology was that if God's election and promises belonged to Christians who believed and followed Christ, they could not also belong to an Israel that did not. This conviction was shaped by three features commonly associated with gnostic thought—dualism, spiritualism, and individualism. *The Epistle of Barnabas,* for instance, written probably during the first half of the second century, rebukes those who would say that both Israel and church participate in God's covenant. "This also I further beg of you . . . to take heed now to yourselves, and not to be like some, adding largely to your sins, and saying 'The covenant is both theirs and ours.' But they thus finally lost it, after Moses had already received it. For the Scripture saith, 'And Moses was fasting in the mount forty days and forty nights, and received the covenant from the Lord, tables of stone written with the finger of the hand of the Lord;' but turning away to idols, they lost it. . . . Their covenant was broken, in order that the covenant of the beloved Jesus might be sealed upon our heart."[7]

The dualistic assumption that God's covenant could not include both Jews and Christians became axiomatic, although other early writings formulate the transfer of the covenant differently. Rather than arguing that Israel's covenant was broken and an entirely new covenant made in Christ, some suggested that the Christian covenant was a continuation and consummation of the first covenant, though in a new form and with a new people. Isaac of Antioch, for instance, uses the image of a treasure being held in trust awaiting its true owner. "Abraham was stamped like a vessel because of the treasure that was in him. And the seal continued in your generations because of the treasure that was in you until now. Now . . . the treasure has come forth. . . . In you it was in custody and was safeguarded, and it was preserved under the stamp. To me it was given for use. . . . O nation [Jews], you were the guardians of the riches that were preserved for the nations [gentile Church]. . . . Its rightful owners have taken the trust."[8] The Jewish body, marked by the stamp of circumcision, had been the vessel of the treasured election and promises of God. Once the church arrived on the scene, Israel's role as caretaker of the treasure was finished. The Jewish body became an empty vessel, bearing the seal but not the substance. Like a surrogate mother, its job was done and its progeny claimed by another.

This way of narrating the covenant transfer can be termed "economic supersessionism," highlighting the conviction that Israel's role in God's economy was limited from the start to being a preparation for the coming of Christ and the church.[9] In this form of supersessionism, "the ultimate obsolescence of carnal Israel is an essential feature of God's one overarching economy of redemption for the world."[10] This obsolescence of Jewish flesh points us to a theological problem the early church ran into in its attempt to claim the covenant from Israel. As we saw in Chapter 2, election had been understood by the Jews as a carnal matter, residing in the flesh. As such, it could no more be transferred to someone else than could one's own body. Thus, election had to be reconceptualized in Christian theology in such a way that it was separable from Jewish flesh and thus could be applied to the Gentiles.

So election was reconfigured as a spiritual matter concerned with knowledge and belief—the elect or predestined being those who believed what the church taught.[11] In *The Epistle of Barnabas,* for instance, the physical mark of circumcision, which had been a sign of Israel's election, is replaced by a circumcision of the ears: "Therefore He hath circumcised our ears, that we might hear His word and believe, for the circumcision in which they trusted is abolished."[12] The elect are those who hear and believe rather than those who participate in the flesh of Israel. So Augustine warns the Jews of his day that God will cast them off like their ancestors if they refuse to believe.[13] Israel's continuation in the covenant was no longer secured by God's gracious election but was made conditional upon their proper response of faith.

Carnality came to be seen not as the locus of Israel's election but conversely as the locus of its rejection. Indeed, it was often charged that the Jews lost the covenant precisely because of their carnality, which was interpreted as "worldliness." Rosemary Ruether's analysis of this issue is illuminating.

> The theme of Jewish sensuality can be fused with the general ontological dualism of Christian theology which describes the Jews as the people of the outward "letter," against the Christian people of the "spirit." The Fathers feel full license to describe Jewish "outwardness" not merely in terms of literalism over against the Christian allegorical interpretation of Scripture, but as though the Jews were actually addicted to the vices of the flesh, in contrast to Christian asceticism. Ephrem the Syrian speaks of the synagogue typically as a "harlot." . . . The synagogue is said to have been cast off by God "because she was wanton between the legs." . . . John Damascene says that God gave the Jews the Sabbath because of their "grossness and sensuality" and "absolute propensity for material things."[14]

Israel was written out of God's story by virtue of the very flesh that once made it central.

In short, early Christian theology spiritualized and individualized election, detaching it from corporate, bodily existence and reformulating it on the basis of spirit and belief. That is to say, election fell prey to a gnostic redescription. No longer a communal claim about the formation of a people in this world, election became information about individual salvation in the next world. Instead of being forever linked to the people of Israel, Christian election was correlated with a dualistic rejection of Israel qua Israel. Election was reduced to a belief about the destiny of the individual soul rather than a calling to participate in a particular communal vocation. This meant that the Christian doctrine of election, unlike the Jewish teaching, was not considered materially determinative for the community's earthly life and practice.

The Standard Canonical Narrative

The determination to displace Israel in God's plan left the early Christians with a decision either to reject Israel's Scripture as authoritative for the church or to find a way to relativize its witness in relation to the New Testament texts. With the repudiation of Marcion in the second century, the choice was made to retain Israel's Scripture as authoritative. What was needed then was what Kendall Soulen has termed a "canonical narrative," that is, "a framework for reading the Christian bible as a theological and narrative unity."[15] A certain "standard canonical narrative" then arose and became the paradigm for the church's reading of Scripture. It reflected a decision on the part of the church to codify in an interpretive grid its theological posture of supersessionism toward Israel.

This pattern, set forth in its earliest form in Justin Martyr and Irenaeus, construes God's activity toward creation along the dual lines of consummation and redemption, resulting in a four-part story: "creation-for-consummation, fall, redemption in Christ, and final consummation."[16] The biblical story, construed according to this narrative framework, reads something like this: Genesis 1–2 tells of God's creative work as well as God's intention to consummate creation, that is, to draw it forward to its good end. Genesis 3 tells of the incursion of evil and the fall of humankind. In answer to this rupture in God's creative purposes, the New Testament witnesses to Christ as the one who is sent to redeem the world. Finally, having overcome the forces of darkness, Christ will return in the end time to complete both the redemptive and the consummating activity of God. What is most obvious about this story is that it leaves out the heart of Israel's Scripture, jumping from Genesis 3 to the Gospels. Everything in between is understood to be preparation for Christ and thus is not in itself a decisive part of the story.

This outline basically coincides with Irenaeus's *regula fidei,* and it has shaped most of the early creeds of the church. Israel is the silent partner, falling (out) between the "Maker of heaven and earth" and "Jesus Christ his only Son our Lord." In this schematic story, election must transcend Israel if it is to be decisive for salvation (since Israel is not). Thus, election can be read only as a spiritual reality that floats above history (and thus above the Jews) and provides (for the elect) a metaphysical escape route bridging the fall of humanity and the consummation of creation.

The stories of God's covenant with Israel are not rejected in principle but rather are relegated to the background. They become supporting material for the more determinative foreground narrative. Soulen calls this the "Israel forgetfulness" of the standard account.[17] "The model renders the center of the Hebrew Scriptures— the eternal covenant between the God of Israel and the Israel of God—ultimately indecisive for understanding how God's works as consummator and as redeemer engage creation in lasting and universal ways."[18] The standard model thus leads to a "double impoverishment" of Christian theology and the church's life. "On the one hand, the standard model has led to a loss of biblical orientation for Christian theology, especially with regard to the Scriptures of Israel. On the other, it has led to a loss of creative theological engagement with the hard edges of human history."[19] Soulen notes that Jesus has increasingly come to be understood in contexts other than that presented in Israel's Scripture, leading, for instance, to the modern tendency to situate Jesus in relation to universal human categories. Further, once separated from the historical sweep of Israel, the Gospel has tended to become privatized and spiritualized. Soulen refers to this as the "latent gnosticism" that infected the early church even as it battled the gnostics. It was a gnosticism not toward matter but toward history. "God's work of redemption entails liberation not indeed from creation but nevertheless from the historical dispensation that is characterized by Israel's carnal election and by the distinction between Israel and the nations."[20] The church, then, having shed its Jewish historical context, allowed itself to be grafted into the history of nation and empire.

Christendom as the Politics of Supersessionism

The patristic claim that the church superseded Israel went hand in hand with a fateful transaction. The material, bodily currency of election was cashed in for shares in a spiritual promise. The church did not realize at the time what was lost in this exchange—for without the materiality of Israel's election the church was left with a sociopolitical vacuum. Constantinianism can thus be read as a logical correlate of the church's de-Judaizing of election.[21] Because Christianity did not carry forward Israel's social and political embodiment of the covenant, because it no longer believed that election was a material matter, it possessed few resources to resist assimilation to the social forms in which it found itself.

The compromise with Rome in the fourth century can be understood, then, as a combination of the triumph of supersessionism and the church's attempt to respond to Israel's challenge: "Where is this redemption you say has occurred in Jesus Christ?" Rome continued to rule over Jerusalem, the people of Israel remained scattered, and violence still prevailed over peace. This did not look to most Jews like redemption. Indeed, even Christians had to acknowledge that the world did not *look* redeemed. Schematizing a complex story, one finds that the early church set forth three different answers to this question: (1) that redemption was visible but not present; (2) that it was present but not visible; or (3) that it was visible and present and located in Rome.

In the first response, the Christian chiliasts of the first and second centuries held on to the visible and material character of Israel's redemptive hopes, but they diminished its presence.[22] That is, they made the tangible sociopolitical aspects of redemption part of the church's future eschatological hope. Justin Martyr, Irenaeus, and Tertullian all held to this position, resisting a spiritualized eschatology and standing firmly by the conviction that Christ would return for a thousand-year reign in Jerusalem. "I and others who are 'right thinking' Christians on all points are convinced," affirms Justin, "that there will be a resurrection of the dead and a thousand year [period] in which Jerusalem will be [re]built, adorned and enlarged, as the prophets Ezekiel and Isaiah and others declare."[23] Tertullian affirms similarly, "We also hold that a kingdom has been promised to us on earth, but before [*we attain*] heaven: but in another state than this, as being after the [*first*] resurrection. This will last for a thousand years, in a city of God's making, Jerusalem sent down from heaven which the Apostle also designates as 'our mother from above.'"[24] Irenaeus points out the justice of such a visible and physical restoration on earth, "For it is only right that they [the righteous] should receive the reward of their endurance in that created order in which they suffered hardship."[25]

Although this chiliastic view retained the visibility and materiality of Israel's messianic hopes, its shortcoming was that it did not sufficiently account for the Christian claim that redemption had already been inaugurated in Christ. If the visible reality of redemption remained a purely future hope, how had Christ's coming made any real difference? This problem led to the second major response to the Jewish challenge—the spiritualizing of redemption. Taking hold in the third century under the influence of Origen, the spiritual interpretation of Israel's messianic hope "laid to rest the dreams of an earthly kingdom."[26] Origen challenged the Christian chiliasts with being too Jewish—that is, they "understood the Scriptures in a Jewish sense."[27] In contrast, Origen read the scriptures for their "elevated sense" and saw that references to Jerusalem and the land were really references to a "land above," a "sublime region."[28] Thus, concerning Christ's fulfillment of the prophesies, he writes, "None of these things that have *taken place can be seen with the senses.*"[29]

Origen's spiritualization of the messianic age was not just the result of his dualistic, Neoplatonic hermeneutic. He had before him the question posed by Jewish interlocutors—"Where is this redemption you claim happened in Christ?" Robert Wilken deftly uncovers the significance of this: "On the surface, Origen's case against the chiliasts is that they confuse physical desire, the dream of an earthly kingdom, with spiritual yearnings. But, if one probes a bit, it is clear that what disturbs him is that if the chiliasts are correct, the promises of the prophets cannot have been fulfilled in the coming of Christ and hence the messianic age has not yet begun."[30] Origen recognizes that the path of Justin Martyr, Irenaeus, and Tertullian maintains the materiality of Jewish messianic hopes only by projecting them onto an eschatological future. This, he sees, threatens the claim that Jesus is the Messiah who has brought redemption. So instead, Origen spiritualizes the promises and prophesies and thus can claim that Jesus *has* brought redemption, albeit a redemption that cannot "be seen with the senses."

The redemption of Christ seems condemned to being either visible but not present or present but not visible. Yet neither option coheres fully with the biblical narrative in which Israel's visible, historical redemption was said to be inaugurated in Christ. A third response to this challenge became possible in the fourth century with the conversion of Constantine. Suddenly the door was opened to conceive of a messianic redemption that was both visible and present. Eusebius, one of the first apologists for Christendom, rose to the challenge to give just such an account of the converted empire. In his *Oration in Honor of Constantine on the Thirtieth Anniversary of His Reign*, Eusebius reflects on Constantine's plan to extend his dominion by appointing family members to rule throughout the empire. "By this appointment of Caesars he is fulfilling the oracles of the holy prophets, who long ago declared 'the saints of the most high will receive the kingdom' [Dan. 7:18]."[31] Eusebius reads the extension of the rule of Constantine as a reflection of both Daniel's and Isaiah's messianic visions, and thus he links Christ's redemptive reign to the authority of Rome. As Wilken points out, this is "an interpretation that was unimaginable in Origen's day. Origen thought it improper even for Christians to serve as magistrates in the cities of the Roman empire."[32] Just as Origen sought to resolve the problems of the chiliasts by spiritualizing redemption, so Eusebius sought to resolve the deficiencies in Origen's spiritualization by relocating redemption in history—in the form of the newly converted Roman Empire.

Eusebius sought to answer the Jewish challenge by affirming that redemption was both visible and present in the empire. But in so doing he effected a "premature surrender to the world-as-it-is."[33] By baptizing the rule of Rome as the visible evidence of the messianic age, Eusebius lost the Jewish character of redemption. Indeed, Ruether notes that this way of understanding redemption proved to be an almost perfect inversion of Israel's hopes:

> In the period after the establishment of the Church as the religion of the Roman Empire, this argument, that the gentile Church is a messianic fulfilment, takes on a new political tone. The universalism of the nations, gathered in the Church, is equated with the universal sway of the Christian Roman Pax. The ecumenical empire comes to be identified with the millennial reign of the Messiah over the earth. . . . All nations gather into the Kingdom of Christ. The Jews alone are in exile 'among their enemies.' But since their enemies, the nations, now equal the elect gentile Church, the reversal of Jewish messianic hope is total. All nations are redeemed at the coming of the Messiah except the Jews![34]

No longer was redemption characterized by the gathering of Israel in the land and the peaceful and plentiful sharing of covenant blessings with the Gentiles. To the contrary, the redemption of Caesar came with a sword, not a plowshare; it heightened the division between Jew and Gentile; and it led to centuries of persecution for God's chosen people. Indeed, Roman "peace," as Augustine rightly saw, was but a way of naming the imposition of the will of the victor on the vanquished.[35] Nonetheless, the Eusebian answer to the question of the visibility of redemption exerted a decisive influence throughout the age of Christendom.[36]

Christendom Transformed: National Supersessionism

The end of the middle ages saw the birth of modern political liberalism that was bolstered by a new shift in theological and political claims about election, covenant, and redemption. These claims served to underwrite Western nationalism while marginalizing both church and Israel.[37] The drama of modernity remains interestingly indebted to the supersessionism enshrined in earlier Christian teaching and practice. The battle for election continues, though now there are new players in the game. As long as the church and the empire shared dual authority over a unified Christendom, they could also share the claim to being the chosen and redeemed people of God. But as the body and soul of Christendom came apart in modernity, the church and the state each laid claim to divine election. As in Solomon's decree, the child was divided equally—the church retained the soul while the new nation-states claimed the body. The church preached an election for the life to come; the states claimed election as a this-worldly prerogative. The states saw themselves superseding Israel nationally, whereas Christianity saw itself superseding Judaism religiously.

The rise of "national supersessionism" can be clearly traced through the writings of Thomas Hobbes and Baruch Spinoza—a Christian and a Jew, respectively, who turned the covenant into a general grounding for modern politics. In so doing, they displaced both Jews and Christians as such from God's economy. Judaism, with its unapologetic political claims of election and covenant, was transformed into a precursor for the nation-state, which took over the language of covenant and election. Christianity, understood spiritually or eschatologically, was replaced by the rational religion of the Enlightenment. David Novak's description of Spinoza could apply with few changes to Hobbes as well: "The symbiosis of this rational religion—maintained privately by the philosophically perceptive—and the liberal state—maintained by every citizen—can be seen as Spinoza's combining what he saw as the political strengths of Judaism with the spiritual strengths of Christianity."[38]

Following the mainstream of Christian interpretation, both Hobbes and Spinoza declared Israel's covenant terminated. Being only a temporary and conditional agreement with God, the covenant provided no eternal assurance of Israel's election. On Hobbes's reading, the covenant with Israel came to an end when Saul became king. Israel's desire to be like the nations, to have an earthly king to rule them, was an act of rebellion against God, who was their true king.[39] On Spinoza's reading, Israel lost the covenant not by trying to be like the nations but because they were always already like the nations. Thus, like all nations they were destined to rise and fall. The loss of the covenant came at the time of exile, for "God chose not the Hebrews for ever, but only on the condition under which he has formerly chosen the Canaanites," that is, on the basis of their virtue.[40] Israel's disobedience provided the just grounds for God's rejection. Yet if Hobbes and Spinoza follow the Christian tradition in declaring an end to Israel's covenant with God, neither of them identifies this rupture with the coming of Jesus. The covenant was made void not because of the rise of the church but because of national disobedience. Likewise, the covenant is taken over not by the church but by another sovereign nation.

Spinoza's belief that the covenant could not continue in exile reveals the extent to which he rejected traditional Jewish accounts of election and thus reduced Israel to a particular instance of a general understanding of nationhood. The typical Christian question— "Why have the Jews survived so long after the coming of Christ?"—is transformed in Spinoza into, "Why have the Jews survived so long after the exile?" As with the Christian question, Spinoza's question contains an implied critique—that Israel should not have survived after its reason for being was ended. Spinoza's conception of the covenant simply could not account for its continuation in diaspora. Upon being displaced into another land, the Israelites should have become subject to the rule of the local sovereign. Any resistance to the laws of the nation in which they found themselves would be counter to the covenant of that land and thus counter to God, for each sovereign is given the divine right to determine what constitutes obedience.[41] For the Jews to hold onto their communal Jewish identity would be seditious and thus in opposition to God's earthly rule. Spinoza harshly castigated Israel for its exceptionalist claims and its separatism, even to the point of blaming the Jews for the violence and hatred of the Gentiles:

> At the present time, therefore, there is absolutely nothing which the Jews can arrogate to themselves beyond other people.
> As to their continuance so long after dispersion and the loss of empire, there is nothing marvelous in it, for they so separated themselves from every other nation as to draw down upon themselves universal hate, not only by their outward rites, rites conflicting with those of other nations, but also by the sign of circumcision which they most scrupulously observe.
> That they have been preserved in great measure by Gentile hatred experience demonstrates.[42]

Israel's resistance to its displacement and destruction only increased its disobedience and suffering.

If Israel fares poorly in this modern depiction of its history, the church does not fare much better. It is displaced both from Israel's covenant and from modern politics. Spinoza parallels Origen in spiritualizing Christianity, whereas Hobbes echoes the chiliasts by deferring Christ's political relevance until the eschaton. Each is thereby able to relativize Christianity as a social force and turn it into a model of private piety.[43] Spinoza's Christ shuns politics, since he came only to teach the universal moral law in a way that would not offend or threaten the temporal order. He was not concerned with material reality but with transcendent ideas. "[Christ] taught only universal moral precepts, and for this cause promises a spiritual instead of a temporal reward. . . . His sole care was to teach moral doctrines, and distinguish them from the laws of the state."[44] Jesus' teaching had no reference to the public welfare and therefore could be no threat to the sovereign. Likewise, for Hobbes, Christ is not relevant to the present political or historical situation, though he refuses to spiritualize Christ's message. Rather, he argues that "the kingdom of Christ is not to begin till the general resurrection."[45] As do the early chiliasts, Hobbes pushes off Christ's material and political significance to the second coming. In the meantime Jesus has authorized the interim politics of the state. "The kingdom of Christ is not of this world: therefore neither can his ministers, unless they be kings, require obedience in his name."[46] Hobbes returns to a reading of Christianity that makes Christ's redemption visible but not present. As such, it becomes unclear what it means to say that redemption has occurred.

For Spinoza and Hobbes, the separation of church and state, the kingdom of God and the kingdom of this world, makes religious belief and practice serve the good of the sovereign. As Hobbes puts it, "There is nothing done or taught by Christ, that tendeth to the diminution of the civil right of the Jews or of Caesar. . . . The kingdom he claimed was to be in another world: he taught all men to obey in the meantime them that sat in Moses' seat: he allowed them to give to Caesar his tribute, and refused to take upon himself to be a judge."[47] Spinoza goes so far as to claim that there is no other voice for God than that of the sovereign: "No one can rightly practise piety or obedience to God, unless he obey the sovereign power's commands in all things."[48] Although the inward worship of God (in mind and heart) cannot be controlled by the sovereign and must be left free "within the sphere of everyone's private rights,"[49] God's work in the world is placed firmly in the hands of the state. Religion is privatized and thus tightly policed according to its usefulness to society. In short, one can believe what one wants, but one can act only in ways that serve the state's interests.[50]

What is surely right about Hobbes's and Spinoza's analyses is their determination to view election as a material and political claim.[51] Hobbes rightly recognizes that "*the kingdom of God is properly his civil sovereignty over a peculiar people by pact.* . . . The kingdom therefore of God is a real, not a metaphorical kingdom; and so taken, not only in the Old Testament but in the New."[52] The problem is that Hobbes and Spinoza read election not as a political description of the people of God but as a divine sanction for the nation-state. They thereby enshrine a new form of national supersessionism. As Joshua Mitchell observes, "Hobbes attributes to the Leviathan the same rights as those granted by God to Moses: the right of interpretation and the right to command obedience."[53] It is no longer Jesus who is the new Moses (as in Matthew's Gospel); it is Leviathan, the sovereign ruler of the nation.

This transfer of the covenant from the people of God to the state is underwritten in both Hobbes and Spinoza by a radical inversion of the doctrine of election. God's election is supplanted by human election. Hobbes reads the people of Israel as having democratically voted to transfer their rights to God (a kind of "election" moderns are much more comfortable with).[54] Israel elects God to be its king rather than God's electing Israel to be God's people. The case is much the same in Spinoza. As noted in Chapter 1, Spinoza's metaphysics determines that "God" (or "Nature"), which names the one infinite substance of reality and the necessary outworking of a closed causality, is unable to "elect" or "covenant" in any meaningful sense. Election and covenant, considered as divine activities, would require attributing to God initiative, possibility, and purpose, all three of which would be problematic within Spinoza's monistic metaphysics.[55] Spinoza makes clear that God's "activity" or "help" is identical with the fixed laws of nature. God is in no way free to intervene in human affairs in ways that would bypass, contravene, or supplement the natural order. This is not to say that God is limited by a deterministic framework but rather that God *is* this framework.[56] As an activity of God, then, election can be understood only metaphorically.[57] Spinoza writes, "We can now easily understand what is meant by the election of God. For since no one can do anything save by the predetermined order of nature, that is by God's eternal ordinance and decree, it follows that no one can choose a plan of life for himself, or accomplish any work save by God's vocation choosing him for the work or the plan of life in question, rather than any other."[58] God's "choosing" simply names the necessary conditions of one's life that predetermine one's station. To live in harmony with these determinations is the human "choice" to follow God's plan. Like Hobbes, Spinoza inverts the traditional theological understanding of election, undermining God's choice and replacing it with human choice.[59]

Because election is grounded in a human choice, both Hobbes and Spinoza reinterpret the covenant as a social contract. Individuals, being limited and directed in nature only by their own power and passion, have a natural "right" to do whatever they want and are able to do. This creates a situation of instability, where one's own desires may be foiled by others and where one's security is always at risk from the more powerful. Thus, as Spinoza puts it, "under the fear of a greater evil, or the hope of a greater good," human beings compact together to be guided by reason rather than power or desire, to "do to all as they would be done by," and to "defend their neighbour's rights as their own."[60] Similarly, Hobbes contends that a social contract includes "the mutual transferring of right," for the purpose of securing some greater good for oneself.

In light of this contractual understanding of covenant, God's call of Abraham and the promises to his descendants are reduced to a mutual agreement. Commenting on Genesis 12, Hobbes writes, "This is it which is called the *old covenant* or *testament*; and containeth a contract between God and Abraham; by which Abraham obligeth himself, and his posterity, in a peculiar manner to be subject to God's positive law."[61] As a contract, the covenant no longer serves to constitute human identity or to direct a person to the goods of life. Rather, identity and the good must be determined prior to one's participation in a covenant, since one's participation is based on the judgment that this will serve one's self-interest. In other words, the individual's participation in the covenant is based on an analysis of how the covenant will meet needs and desires that are themselves understood as separate from and prior to the covenant. Covenant, then, is functional rather than foundational; it is pragmatic rather than prescriptive.[62] As such, a covenant, even with God, cannot make an absolute claim on a person. It is an agreement entered into from a position of individual liberty—a liberty that always remains a more fundamental reality than the covenant itself.

It thus follows for Hobbes that a covenant can never constrain the use of violence, since violence may well serve the more basic human right of self-preservation—the very right that any covenant is supposed to protect. One cannot contract to be nonviolent, since "a covenant not to defend myself from force, by force, is always void. For . . . no man can transfer, or lay down his right to save himself from death, wounds, and imprisonment, the avoiding whereof is the only end of laying down any right."[63] This stands in stark contrast to a view of election in which God's choice of humanity is primary and in which there is no prior or more determinative claim than the claim God has on God's people. An act such as martyrdom could hardly be intelligible in Hobbes's world.

Once a covenant is understood as a humanly initiated social contract, the biblical stories of Exodus and Sinai must be radically reinterpreted. Upon their escape from Egypt, by Spinoza's telling, the Israelites were set free from all national allegiances and placed in a position of political autonomy. From this original situation, the people of Israel were at liberty to form whatever laws they liked and to occupy the land of their choice. Being a slave people, however, they were in no position to make wise laws, so they gave their freedom to Moses, who led them into a social contract with God.[64] "This promise, or transference of right to God, was effected in the same manner as we have conceived it to have been in ordinary societies, when men agree to divest themselves of their natural rights."[65] The Israelites agreed to obey God, and in return God promised them preservation and prosperity. The covenant becomes an act of self-determination on the part of a liberated people. Lost is any sense that the Exodus was God's act that included a determinative claim on Israel as God's people. Rather, the Exodus story symbolizes the history of every nation's rising from individual liberty to social cooperation.

Ironically, Hobbes's and Spinoza's democratization of the covenant paved the way for imperialist claims. Once the covenant was placed up for grabs among the nations, the doctrine of election became serviceable as a system of beliefs, concepts, attitudes, and rituals that gave theological justification to an independent system of economic, political, and social structure. Election came to function as ideology just to the extent that it was no longer organically connected to a particular people and a particular vocation. Election became a way of claiming divine sanction for, and thus legitimating, the oppression and domination of others. This is especially true during the "high imperial era" of Western nationalism (1880–1920).[66] "Chosenness," once detached from Israel or church, was easily exploited for the furtherance of political interests. The rhetoric of election, deprived of distinctive material content, became supple enough to justify assertions by Great Britain, France, Germany, South Africa, and the United States, among others, to be God's specially chosen instruments in history. Claims such as those of J. G. Greenhough at the 1896 meeting of the Baptist Missionary Society in Great Britain exemplify the way election served as an imperialistic ideology: "We are elect by all signs and proofs to be the great missionary nation. . . . Was [British power and prosperity] not especially with this intent—that we should be more than all others God's messengers of light and truth to the nations that sit in darkness? In all this God's voice has been calling us. God's consecrating hands have been laid on our heads. Thus saith the Lord: 'In the shadow of My hand have I hid thee, and made thee a polished shaft, and in the day of salvation have I helped thee, that thou mayest say to the prisoners: 'Go forth.'"[67] The international mission of Great Britain was ideologically grounded in its election as God's new Israel.

The ideological invocation of election drew into its sphere a distinctly racial element during the nineteenth century. As the authority of Scripture was being challenged by the rise of critical methods of reading, race provided an alternative, scientific grounding for national supersessionism that could replace or at least supplement the biblical warrant given by Hobbes and Spinoza. Thus, as claims to national election multiplied, the basis for this election came to be found less and less in an appeal to the biblical narratives or the history of Israel. The religious historian Conrad Cherry characterizes this shift as "the unhitching of the chosen people theme from its biblical moorings and its subsequent tethering to Darwinism and biological racism."[68] In short, the modern construction of "race" as a scientific category underwrote a description of the Jews as a deficient people now superseded by other races.

This portrayal can be witnessed in several nineteenth-century European developments. For instance, the Anglo-Israelite movement in Britain set forth the belief that "originally the Jews had been a blond people very similar to the modern Anglo-Saxons. After the crucifixion of Christ, according to one exegete, the physiognomy of the Jews had greatly altered for the worse. . . . But the Jews who were members of the ten tribes retained their blondness and their beauty. The Anglo-Saxons were the true Jews, God's chosen people."[69] Concurrently, in Germany the transition toward a racially grounded election led not only to the expulsion of the superseded religion but to the attempted destruction of the superseded people. Hartmut Lehmann describes the situation after the Franco-Prussian war: "In the years that followed, the notion of a new covenant between God and the German people was modified—from a theological perspective one may also say that is was corrupted—in two ways: it was filled with considerations of power politics, and it was closely linked to considerations rooted in Darwinism. After the 1880's, therefore, even among Protestants the belief in a new covenant gradually gave way to ideas of German uniqueness and German superiority based on power and race."[70] By the early twentieth century, many Western nations exhibited this unstable alliance of biblical election, racial superiority, and empire building. As we will see, the United States perhaps above all made the claim of divine election central to its identity as a nation and a people.

The Myth of American Chosenness

National supersessionism arguably reaches its zenith in the claims of the United States to be the new Israel. Though such claims were articulated in more explicitly theological terms in the early years of Puritan influence, they have not disappeared from American political discourse. Take, for instance, Bill Clinton's appropriation of the term "New Covenant" in his 1992 speech accepting the Democratic nomination to the presidency: "The New Covenant simply asks us all to be Americans again—old-fashioned Americans for a new time. . . . When we pull together America will pull ahead." In his 1995 State of the Union address, he resurrected the "New Covenant," encouraging Americans to "fulfill the eternal promise of this country, the enduring dream from that first and most sacred covenant" (which, needless to say, is not a reference to God's election of Israel but to the American dream of "life, liberty, and the pursuit of happiness"). In the end, Clinton tells us, the Pledge of Allegiance "is what the New Covenant is all about."[71] Like Ronald Reagan's "city on a hill," Clinton's "New Covenant" combines religious calling and the American way of life to encourage social unity and national supremacy. The rhetoric of exceptionalism and chosenness, even in the increasingly secular polity of the United States, continues to imply and invoke a divine sanction on the nation's goals.

Nonetheless, this language of election seems to float along the surface of public discourse, finding its way into political speeches but certainly not into the details of policy proposals. This lack of substantive content is not surprising within a polity that relegates religion to the private sphere. What work, then, is this detheologized doctrine of election doing in the American political conversation? To recall Alasdair MacIntyre's analysis, such language can best be described as a fragment that has been removed from the overarching social and narrative context that once provided standards for its intelligible use.[72] The "chosen nation" rhetoric now rattles about in American political speech, wrenched from its narrative context in the story of Israel and awkwardly spliced into the story of America—like a Tarheel logo on Duke stationery or a Pepsi machine at Emory. As such, the language of election, "chosenness," functions as an ideology, a "socially necessary illusion,"[73] providing legitimation for the American pursuit of power and domination. And though, as we have seen, other Western nations have also laid claim to being the new chosen people, the United States has declared itself, in Conor Cruise O'Brien's words, a "chosen people with tenure."[74]

One can see the roots of this belief as early as the preaching of John Winthrop in 1630. As the first governor of Massachusetts Bay colony, he articulated a Puritan vision for America that paralleled God's relation to Israel. In his celebrated sermon on board the *Arabella* as it crossed to the new land, he affirmed, "Thus stands the cause betweene God and us. Wee are entered into Covenant with him for this worke, wee have taken out a Commission, the Lord hath given us leave to draw our owne Articles, wee have professed to enterprise these Accions upon these and these ends, wee have hereupon besought him of favour and blessing: Now if the Lord shall please to heare us, and bring us in peace to the place wee desire, then hath hee ratified this Covenant and sealed our Commission [and] will expect a strickt performance of the Articles contained in it."[75] What is significant about this act of covenant making, beyond the commendable desire to build a faithful politics, is the direction of the covenant's initiation. This covenant is not grounded in God's calling and forming of a people but rather in the people's asking God to ratify the articles drawn up by the community—"the Lord hath given us leave to draw our owne Articles." The reversal of election begun with Spinoza continues here. And though Winthrop's deep Puritan piety made certain that the articles would not conflict with the moral vision of Scripture, the fundamental direction of covenant-making had shifted. God's priority was undermined, and God's people, Israel, were replaced. Later generations, not so steeped in Scripture and more enamored of national power, would come to take it as their right, too, to draw up their own articles.

Thus it was that this seed of American exceptionalism yielded a vicious harvest in the nineteenth century, when the expansion of the United States toward the West came to be seen as America's "Manifest Destiny." As Conrad Cherry notes, "The traditional doctrine of election held that the ultimate reason for God's choosing Israel was hidden in the mystery of the divine will. According to the exponents of Manifest Destiny, God's New Israel was elected for clear or *manifest* reasons—because of her superior form of government, her geographical location, her beneficence."[76] This reversal of election, making it a reward for America's goodness rather than a witness to God's grace, turned the claim to chosenness into a justification of American power rather than a vocation to be a holy people. In the middle of the nineteenth century, this American (and Anglo-Saxon) vision was clearly articulated by one of the country's most renowned authors, Herman Melville:

> We Americans are the peculiar, chosen people—the Israel of our time; we bear the ark of the liberties of the world. . . . God has predestined, mankind expects, great things from our race; and great things we feel in our souls. . . . Long enough have we been sceptics with regard to ourselves, and doubted whether, indeed, the political Messiah had come. But he has come in *us*, if we would but give utterance to his promptings. And let us always remember that with ourselves, almost for the first time in the history of earth, national selfishness is unbounded philanthropy; for we cannot do a good to America, but we give alms to the world.[77]

The American attempt to claim chosen status before God meant leaving Israel behind and replacing them, both politically and racially, as the covenant people. God's election of Israel gave way to America's election of itself.

At the turn of the twentieth century, Senator Albert Beveridge carried this national calling to its logical next step. Urging extension of America's westward mission to the Philippines and beyond, he professed, "Of all our race [God] has marked the American people as His chosen nation to finally lead in the redemption of the world"[78] Beveridge tellingly describes what this "redemption" looks like: It is "the eternal movement of the American people toward the mastery of the world."[79] Some have suggested that such arrogant and nationalistic interpretations of chosenness are but a corruption of what was once a more humble and noble sense of America's singular mission. Robert Bellah, for instance, urges a recovery of the biblical covenant tradition not as a mere justification for the pursuit of American interests but as a set of obligations and responsibilities, the neglect of which brings righteous judgment. This strand of American political thought was, he regrets, largely pushed to the margins with the rise of utilitarian and individualist ways of life:

> In the 17th and 18th centuries . . . freedom was part of a whole articulated framework of moral and religious values—it meant freedom to do the good and was almost equivalent to virtue. Under the rising criticism of utilitarianism, first in the late 18th century and then with ever greater insistence in the 19th and 20th centuries, freedom came to mean freedom to pursue self-interest, latterly defined as "freedom to do your own thing." . . . As the older moral pattern declines in persuasiveness, the only remaining category for the analysis and evaluation of human motives is interest, which by now has replaced both virtue and conscience in our moral vocabulary.[80]

Bellah believes that the American covenant tradition, rooted in Puritan faith and responsibility, must be reclaimed to combat the unqualified pursuit of self- and national interest. The churches are needed in this restoration project to "provide us with a national sense of ethical purpose" and "to serve as a school for the creation of a self-disciplined, independent, public-spirited, in a word, virtuous citizen."[81] Yet in so conceiving of the Christian mission he reduces the church to a supporting role in the national drama, nurturing the civic religion and creating well-formed citizens.

Bellah remains caught in the American myth of chosenness just insofar as he seeks to recover a purer, truer moment in the nation's covenant tradition. He refuses to believe that the American project, despite its claim of God's favor, might have been flawed from the start. He does succeed in resisting the self-aggrandizing possibilities in the claim to "chosenness," and he lets no one off the hook: "A conception of chosenness that slips away from the controlling obligations of the covenant is a signpost to hell."[82] Nonetheless, he never asks the deeper question, whether a conception of chosenness that slips away from the life and witness of Israel is likewise a "signpost to hell." That is, Bellah continues to assume that "covenant" and "chosenness" are terms appropriately applied to America. He does not investigate the extent to which the designation of America as "chosen nation" masks a perilous form of national supersessionism.

Perhaps this nation, in seeking to own a designation meant only for Israel, has taken its place alongside the nations of Psalm 2:

> Why do the nations conspire,
> and the peoples plot in vain?
> The kings of the earth set themselves,
> and the rulers take counsel together,
> against the Lord and his anointed, saying,
> "Let us burst their bonds asunder,

and cast their cords from us."
He who sits in the heavens laughs;
the Lord has them in derision.
Then he will speak to them in his wrath,
and terrify them in his fury, saying,
"I have set my king on Zion, my holy hill." (Ps 2:1–6)[83]

Claiming to be God's chosen people, America sought to break free from any necessary bond to God's anointed Israel, to resist the possibility that God's rule had been set in Zion. However, being extracted from Israel's story and renarrated into America's story, election lost its grounding in God's economy and was laid open to nationalistic manipulation. Outside of Israel and the ongoing narrative of this people, the designation became indeterminate, infinitely fluid, a ready-made prop for the pursuit of national interests.

Later in his life Melville, in sharp contrast to his earlier nationalistic panegyric, began to hear the darker rumblings beneath the surface of the American experiment. He discerned that the true end of the human being "Left to himself, his natural bent,/ His own devices and intent" was a people who would rise up against God, challenging God with the utilitarian refrain:

How profits it? And who are Thou
That we should serve Thee? Of Thy ways
No knowledge we desire; *new* ways
We have found out, and better. Go—
Depart from us.[84]

The claim to divine election turned out to be a way of validating and securing the American commitment to voluntarism and violence. The irony is that election is the very doctrine that should call such an ethos into question. But as long as the church's doctrine of election remains a disembodied belief, it remains open to manipulation as it is combined and recombined with divergent political practices. Only as the church (along with the synagogue) begins to recover the distinct communal life internal to the narrative of the election of God's people, and thus to reconceive its life as a political witness to the covenant, will the nation's self-serving appropriation of God's favor be effectively demythologized.

John Howard Yoder has challenged Christians to "deconstantinize" and "disestablish" the church.[85] As it turns out, the state has been more than willing to disestablish the church (now in practice as well as theory), but it is not clear that the churches know what to do with this new situation. And so the call to "deconstantinize" must be paired with a call to "re-Judaize." By returning to its roots in the people of Israel, the church can recover a doctrine of election that is not mere information (which can so easily become ideology) but rather formation or, better yet, conformation to the ways of the triune God.

4

Rereading the Tradition

*W*hatever differences Calvinist and Barthian Christians have with Judaism over the ultimate meaning of election—and they are crucial—these Protestants are not offended by the Jewish doctrine of the unconditional election of Israel, which is not the case with most of their more liberal co-religionists."[1] In pointing to the legacies of John Calvin and Karl Barth, David Novak calls attention to two Christian theologians who refused to accept the church's traditional repudiation of Israel. Although in the latter half of the twentieth century their voices have been joined by a chorus of others, their witness remains a crucial starting point for any serious rethinking of the Christian doctrine of election and the Christian theology of Israel. Both figures remain, in the last analysis, insufficiently attentive to the Jewish character of election, yet they each reread the tradition of supersessionism through the lens of God's unconditional election of Israel.

John Calvin

John Calvin rightly reminded the Reformation church that its own salvation was always only an inclusion in the fellowship of Israel: "Christ the Lord promises to his followers today no other 'Kingdom of Heaven' than that in which they may 'sit at table with Abraham, Isaac, and Jacob' [Mt. 8:11]."[2] As this passage suggests, Calvin recovered a surprisingly positive portrayal of Israel in his theology, and thus he at least gestured toward a recovery of Israel's witness for the church. Contrary to the *Adversus Judaeos* tradition in patristic theology, Calvin refused to believe that God's election of Israel had failed. The Jews were not cut off, despite their disobedience, since their election was not founded upon obedience but upon the grace of God. Calvin, perhaps more than any Christian theologian before him, realized that a strong doctrine of election carried with it a high appraisal of Israel's role in God's economy. Or perhaps it was the other way around: Calvin came to understand the importance of God's ongoing commitment to Israel and thus recovered the centrality of election. Either way, the two doctrines were intertwined for Calvin—both the people of Israel and the doctrine of election pointed to the gracious freedom and sovereignty of God.

Calvin therefore rejected the flat economic supersessionism that had come to dominate Christian theology. God's covenant with Israel was not brought to an end by the new thing God did in Jesus Christ. For as Calvin reminds us, "The covenant made with all the patriarchs is so much like ours in substance and reality that the two are actually one and the same" (II.x.2). Though Irenaeus made this point as well , for Calvin it meant that the living people of Israel must still, somehow, be a part of God's continuing covenant with the elect of humanity.[3] Because the covenant is the same, one cannot speak of the new covenant's "replacing" the old or the church's "replacing" Israel. Indeed, both the election and the promises are still in force for the Jews, despite their rejection of Jesus Christ. "Do you see how," Calvin writes, "after Christ's resurrection also, [Paul] thinks that the promise of the covenant is to be fulfilled, not only allegorically but literally, for Abraham's physical offspring?" (IV.xvi.15). Here Calvin does not allow us to substitute a spiritualized "true Israel" for the actual physical descendants of Abraham. Such allegorizing away of God's promises was unacceptable for Calvin. Because God's promises are sustained by God alone, they continue not just for the faithful Jews who come to believe in Christ but for all the physical offspring of Abraham. This is an obvious point for Calvin since he understands that election is never contingent on human response, including the response of belief, but is and was the free gift of God's grace—a grace not just for this life but for eternity. Thus, Calvin follows Paul in asserting that "the covenant which God had made once for all with the descendants of Abraham could in no way be made void. Consequently, in the eleventh chapter [of Romans] he argues that Abraham's physical progeny must not be deprived of their dignity" (IV.xvi.14). Such references to the fleshiness of election, the physicality of the chosen people, urges a strong reconsideration of the church's spiritualizing tendencies.

Nonetheless, Calvin proves unable to maintain this position as he presses on with his doctrine of election. Since he believes that the *individual* is the true and final object of election, Calvin is forced to retreat, in sometimes inconsistent ways, from his powerful affirmations of Israel's chosenness and God's faithfulness. Calvin shifts his gaze from the biblical witness of God's election to his own observation that some individuals believe and some do not (III.xxi.1; III.xxiv.15), and in this shift Calvin creates for himself a problem—how can he still speak of Israel's communal election when he has come to see election as primarily an individual matter? Stretching for an explanation to hold together these competing claims, Calvin introduces "a second, more limited degree of election," based on God's "special grace" (III.xxi.6). He writes, "It is easy to explain why the general election of a people is not always firm and effectual: to those with whom God makes a covenant, he does not at once give the spirit of regeneration that would enable them to persevere in the covenant to the very end. . . . That is why Paul so carefully distinguishes the children of Abraham according to the flesh from the spiritual children who have been called after the example of Isaac [Gal. 4:28]" (III.xxi.7). So Calvin invokes a second, individual election to explain why not all the Jews are part of God's "true Israel." God's "general election of a people is not always firm and effectual," Calvin claims, apparently without concern that this creates an antinomy in his theology. If God's election is a sign of God's pure grace and sufficient power, than what sense can be made of the need for a second election? And if God's election of a people "is not always firm," then why should anyone trust that God's election of individuals will be?

In short, two voices compete in Calvin—the one that would hold fast to God's promises even for a disobedient Israel, and the one that would relativize God's election of Israel in favor of an individual election. Despite his better insights, in the end Calvin remains captured by an insufficiently Jewish understanding of election. The spirit of the church is affirmed, but the flesh of Israel is cut off. And just as we saw in the patristic period, a naked soul cannot long survive—a body must be found somewhere. Thus, when Calvin, at the end of the *Institutes,* comes to discuss the relation between the church and the magistrate he tells us that "whoever knows how to distinguish between body and soul, between this present fleeting life and the future eternal life, will without difficulty know that Christ's spiritual Kingdom and the civil jurisdiction are things completely distinct. Since, then, it is a *Jewish vanity* to seek and enclose Christ's Kingdom within the elements of this world, let us rather ponder that what Scripture clearly teaches is a spiritual fruit, which we gather from Christ's grace; and let us remember to keep within its own limits all that freedom which is promised and offered to us in him" (IV.xx.1, emphasis added). Because Calvin has already relativized the ongoing communal election of the Jews, and because his reflections are driven by the metaphor of a body-soul dualism, he rejects as "Jewish vanity" Israel's witness to the public, political embodiment of God's reign. He thus reinforces the basic structure of Christendom and remains trapped in a politics of supersessionism—the "vanity" of a Jewish embodiment of God's reign is replaced by a civil jurisdiction that circumscribes Christ's kingdom as a body does a soul.

Alongside this lapse into supersessionism, we find in Calvin the continuation of another problematic aspect of the church's traditional accounts of election. Because from at least Augustine forward election was believed to involve an eternal (pretemporal) decision about the soul's eternal (posttemporal) destiny, the subject of the electing act was conceived of as the eternal God, God the Father or God as an abstract unity, removed from time and history. As theology became more systematically arranged in the Middle Ages, this assumption led to the placement of the topic of election (or predestination) within the doctrine of the perfections of God, prior to discussion of Trinity or creation. Thus, in his *Summa Theologica* Aquinas discusses predestination as a work of God in God's unity—prior to and therefore without reference to his discussion of God's trinitarian procession.[4]

Alternately, in the final edition of the *Institutes,* Calvin considers predestination and election at the end of his soteriology. Because of his closer attention to scripture on this matter, Calvin does note the interworking of Father and Son: "If we have been chosen in [Christ], we shall not find assurance of our election in ourselves; and not even in God the Father, if we conceive him as severed from his Son. Christ, then, is the mirror wherein we must, and without self-deception may, contemplate our own election. For since it is into his body the Father has destined those to be engrafted whom he has willed from eternity to be his own . . . we have a sufficiently clear and firm testimony that we have been inscribed in the book of life if we are in communion with Christ" (III.xxiv.5). Yet if Calvin's reference to Christ as the "mirror" of election does hint at an openness to viewing election as a trinitarian activity, this insight does not materially impact the shape of his doctrine. Predestination remains firmly ensconced in the eternal decree of the Father from before all time.

In Reformed theology after Calvin, predestination rebounded to its former locus within the doctrine of God, and there it ossified into an eternal principle hardly distinguishable from Stoic fate.[5] Although hints of this turn can be traced back to Calvin himself, it owes even more to his successor Theodore Beza. Calvin was very careful not to say more about election than seemed to be warranted biblically. "Let this, therefore, first of all be before our eyes: to seek any other knowledge of predestination than what the Word of God discloses is not less insane than if one should purpose to walk in a pathless waste, or to see in darkness" (III.xxi.2). That Calvin's restraint was not always practiced by his followers is clear when one observes how Beza codified the doctrine of election into a matter of such certainty that it could be the hinge upon which his entire theology turned.[6]

As I hope to show, insofar as the doctrine of election has failed to be sufficiently Jewish it has also failed to be sufficiently trinitarian. Thus, the Christian recovery of the former opens possibilities for the recovery of the latter. For the electing God conceived as an abstract divinity who asserts absolute (at times, capricious) power is just as far from the Father, Son, and Holy Spirit as from the God of Abraham, Isaac, and Jacob. The God of Israel's election, who engages history, calls and forms a people, and moves this story of election toward its final redemption, is the same God Christians have come to know as Trinity. This God has little in common with the abstract God of the eternal decrees.

Karl Barth

Karl Barth shook the foundations of the classical doctrine of election, and he did it primarily by removing election from the hidden counsel of a distant God and refocusing it in the person of Jesus Christ. That is, Barth began to move the doctrine of election in a more trinitarian direction and thus toward history and materiality. At the same time he, like Calvin, saw that no faithful Christian doctrine of election could proclaim that the Jews were now excluded from the covenant. God's election is God's doing, and thus even Jewish unfaithfulness could not abrogate the faithfulness of God. Indeed, Israel's eternal election is the eternal basis for the church's communion with God. As Barth puts it in the *Church Dogmatics*, "the Gentile Christian community of every age and land is a guest in the household of Israel. It assumes the election and calling of Israel."[7] Israel can never be replaced as the locus of God's covenanting activity and God's election of grace. Barth therefore undertakes to refigure both the subject and the object of election.

It is worthwhile to note the setting in which Barth composed his discussion of election in the *Church Dogmatics*. The nationalistic affirmation of Germany's divinely chosen status had gained strength among Evangelical Protestants between 1848 and 1914.[8] Although the defeat of 1918 created difficulties for those who had claimed God's blessing for the German war effort, the assurance of God's special calling for this people did not dim. Indeed, "on 29 November 1918 . . . the leading Protestant weekly explained that 'no people had ever understood the biblical message as well as the German people, and no people had given expression to the biblical message as well as they had.'" It went on to advocate that Germany's "godly mission should be preserved."[9]

Barth attacked these exceptionalist claims head on, both in his political activity and in his theology. It was no mere coincidence that as the sounds of war began to be heard in the autumn of 1939, Barth began writing and lecturing on the topic of election for his *Church Dogmatics*. He noted the importance of this "wartime background," commenting, "It is a good thing that the properties of God and predestination and all the rest could be put on paper and printed in the middle of this."[10] Within this context, Barth's reformulation of the object of election can be read as a response to the modern rise of national supersessionism, especially in Germany. But as I noted above, it was also a response to the failings of traditional Calvinist theology. Although Barth opposed any national, familial, social, or racial grounding for election, he also resisted Calvin's individualized election. In the end Barth held these aims together only very tentatively and with questionable success, for by avoiding the communal claims of the one he tended to fall back into the individualistic claims of the other.

This tension between the communal and the individual comes to the fore when Barth argues, "There are no predestined families and no predestined nations—even the Israelite nation is simply the first (transitory) form of the community—nor is there a predestined humanity. There are only predestined men—predestined in Jesus Christ and by way of the community" (II/2, 313). Barth left no room for a nation or a people to choose themselves or to claim election or exception based on their communal identity. He did this at least in part by locating election, in its most determinative form, at the level of the individual.[11] Yet he resisted making election a purely individual matter, as the tradition had largely done. "The Subject of [election]," Barth writes, "is indeed God in Jesus Christ, and its particular object is indeed men. But it is not men as private persons in the singular or plural. It is these men as a fellowship elected by God in Jesus Christ and determined from all eternity for a peculiar service." He goes on, "Only from the standpoint of this fellowship and with it in view is it possible to speak properly of the election of the individual believer (which tradition has been far too eager to treat as *the* problem of the doctrine of predestination)" (II/2, 196). Thus, for Barth there can be no talk about individual election without first talking about the election of the community, which includes both Israel and the church.

The lingering question, then, is how Barth will hold together (in his typically dialectical fashion) his appeal to the individual to critique a distorted collectivism and his appeal to the community to critique a one-sided individualism. He tries to do this by locating God's true and eternal election neither in the individual nor in the community but in the person of Jesus Christ, who is both the subject and the object of the divine election, both the electing God and the elected human being. In him, all others have their election. In and with Christ the people of Israel and the church have their election. And in and through the life and witness of this one elect community, individual human beings find themselves called and claimed as the elect of God. Christ, community, and individual together form the threefold object of election. Yet Christ remains the principle object, for in him humankind is chosen before creation, and in him God chooses to be for humanity. Christ is the object of *both* God's election and rejection, but the divine rejection is always ordered to the divine election. Christ therefore is God's yes, to which God's no can only bow in service. There can be no talk of two parallel eternal decrees—one to election and the other to rejection. This is a fundamental mistake, Barth was convinced, as it turned God's election from good news into bad news, or at least ambiguous news.

In Christ, the community of Israel and church is elected as a witness to God's election and rejection in Christ. By making Israel a continuing and necessary part of the one chosen community, Barth stands over against the tradition of supersessionism and affirms the unconditional and eternal election of the Jews. God will not forsake God's people. As Barth asserts, "Without any doubt the Jews are to this very day the chosen people of God in the same sense as they have been so from the beginning, according to the Old and New Testaments. They have the promise of God; and if we Christians from among the Gentiles have it too, then it is only as those chosen with them; as guests in their house, as new wood grafted onto their old tree."[12] Unlike Calvin, who equivocated on the identity of the "true Israel," Barth makes no distinction between a general and a special election. The Jews have been called, and, as Jews and without becoming Christians, they remain God's elect people to this day.

Yet despite the ways in which Barth reformulated the tradition and stood against the many forms of supersessionism he saw around him, and despite his careful attentiveness to the Jews, Barth's theology remains latently supersessionist, and thus he also fails to avoid the danger of spiritualizing and individualizing the covenant. As noted above, Barth views the election of the community as a representation of the election of Christ. Thus, just as the elect Christ bears both the election and rejection of humanity, so the community witnesses to both the yes and no of God's grace and judgment. At this point, perhaps to make as visible as possible the dialectical nature of this election, Barth divides the one elect community into that part which witnesses to God's rejection—Israel—and that which witnesses to God's election—church. Israel represents and only represents the human rejection of God and thus bears God's rejection of that rejection. Israel, Barth tells us, exhibits "the unwillingness, incapacity and unworthiness of man with respect to the love of God directed to him. . . . In its existence it can only reveal the passing of the old man who confronts God in this way" (II/2, 198).

Barth is clear, however, that this characterization is not a denial of Israel's election. Rather, together Israel and church are the one elect people in two forms (II/2, 199). But as the elect ones who *resist* their election in Christ, the Jews witness as those who are passing away, those who could live on only in affirmation of their election in Christ and thus in their joining with the church. The problem is that by setting up the dialectic in this way, Barth is unable to affirm any ongoing positive witness of Israel, even in the midst of its sin. As Michael Wyschogrod put the question, "Why do Christians, and why did Barth, find it so easy to overlook the positive side of Israel's response and focus exclusively on the disobedience?"[13] Barth saw in Israel only an example of what *not* to be as God's people, and therefore, his ear was deaf to the ongoing constructive and faithful witness of the Jewish people.

Given this move, we should not be surprised to see Barth at times resorting to the classic division between Jews as a carnal people and Christians as a spiritual people. He critiques Israel because "it takes a rigid stand on a carnal loyalty to itself and on a carnal hope corresponding to this loyalty" (II/2, 263). Again Barth adds, "[The Jew] can repeat again and again the old sins of Israel and suffer again and again their old punishment. But he cannot remove the promise of God which confronts his whole typically carnal being as such" (II/2, 264). In these passages Barth sees the "typically carnal being" of the Jews as one with their rejection of God's election. This renunciation of Jewish flesh paves the way for Barth to subordinate the communal aspect of election to the individual.

Above it was noted that Barth used the individual to gain leverage against a distorted collectivism and he used the community to gain leverage against an excessive individualism. Yet how the two are ordered in Barth's christological election is not always clear. He gives a hint, however, when he writes, "The *particula veri* of 'individualism' is not curtailed but genuinely assured and honoured when we understand the election of the 'individual' as the *telos* of the election of the community" (II/2, 311). The elect community serves in the end only as a mediator, a messenger, between Christ and the individual. The community exists and is elected to proclaim to the individual the good news of her or his election. "The community is [election's] necessary medium. But its object . . . is individual men" (II/2, 313). The community is functional, not foundational. Indeed, it is striking that for Barth neither Christ's election nor the individual's can be forfeited, but the election of the community *can* be (II/2, 316–317). This is because the formation of the community is not God's final goal of election but only the medium by which God calls individual human beings into fellowship with Christ. So Barth can say, "If the community tries to be more than [Christ's] environment, to do something more than mediate, it has forgotten and forfeited its election" (II/2, 196).

Although Barth does manage to undercut any claims to elect status on the part of race or nation in Germany, he does this at a price. Rather than opposing the "German Christians" with a politics of election embodied in church and Israel, Barth spiritualizes election in the very Calvinist mode he had attempted to critique. Election remains an individual, noetic matter, and this in turn pushes Barth's ecclesiology in an abstract direction. As Nicholas Healy rightly sees, "The irony is that the more Barth reduces Christianity to a matter of knowledge, the more he unwittingly encourages its appropriation and domestication within a non-Christian framework. One result of the loss of sociocultural particularity could be that Christianity becomes a more or less dispensable part of an individual's private world-view. This 'neo-Protestant' outcome is clearly the last thing that Barth would want."[14] In the end one wonders how adequately Barth's ecclesiology and doctrine of election have armed the church against the very *Kulturprotestantismus* (cultural Protestantism) he attacked.

When Barth undertook his massive reformulation of the doctrine of election, he asked what difference it would make to acknowledge that in Jesus Christ one encounters both the electing God and the elected human. In election, he argued, one has to do not with an alien and unknown God making capricious decrees of absolute power, but with the God whose loving grace is embodied in the life and witness of Jesus Christ. Nonetheless, Barth failed to press on with a *fully* trinitarian transformation of the doctrine, which would have required attention to the ways in which, as Robert Jenson puts it, "the Holy Spirit is the choosing God."[15] The tendency in the classical formulations to raise election above history, to make it a divine decision that applies only in eternity, slipped in through Barth's back door, making God's decision for humanity a transhistorical and still pretemporal transaction between Father and Son. More attention to the Spirit may well have led Barth to give a more thoroughly ecclesial reading of election.

Post-Holocaust Theology

In the aftermath of the Holocaust, and in part under Barth's influence, a new group of theologians has attempted to rethink Christian teaching in relation to Judaism. These theologians have argued that the church's widespread repudiation of supersessionism must lead to a reconsideration of Christian theology from the ground up. Although this basic insight is certainly correct, I remain concerned about the troubling tendency among these thinkers to reject or minimize central Christian claims about the identity of God. Christian particularity is too often sacrificed in order to find common ground with Judaism, and all too often this has meant a denial of Jewish particularity as well.

For instance, at the end of her groundbreaking book, *Faith and Fratricide*, Rosemary Ruether poses what has become a defining question for any attempt to reform Christian theology in the shadow of Auschwitz:

Our theological critique of Christian anti-Judaism . . . must turn to what was always the other side of anti-Judaism, namely Christology. At the heart of every Christian dualizing of the dialectics of human existence into Christian and anti-Judaic antitheses is Christology, or, to be more specific, the historicizing of the eschatological event. . . . Is it possible to purge Christianity of anti-Judaism without at the same time pulling up Christian faith? Is it possible to say "Jesus is Messiah" without, implicitly or explicitly, saying at the same time "and the Jews be damned"?[16]

These questions must be posed to any Christian theology that attempts to redress the sins of supersessionism. Can one cut away the cancer of anti-Jewish polemic without destroying the patient? Or is it the case that Christianity is structurally dependent on anti-Judaism such that the building would crumble if this pillar were removed?

The assumption of the self-described "post-Holocaust" theologians, including Ruether, Paul van Buren, and Clark Williamson, is that Ruether's first question can be answered affirmatively—yes, one can maintain Christian faith without anti-Judaism. But it is not so clear to them that her second one can. That is, these theologians who have thought extensively about how to reconstruct Christian theology without its anti-Jewish elements have been markedly lacking in their willingness to affirm either the christological claims inherent in the New Testament designation "Christ" ("Messiah") or the Nicene and Chalcedonian christological (and thus trinitarian) claims (e.g., "the only-begotten Son of God," "true God from true God," "perfect both in deity and also in human-ness").[17] In short, for them Christianity can be salvaged, but what will remain of Christology is far from clear.

Ruether herself solves these problems by retreating to an "experiential-expressivist" position in which she, to use Lindbeck's language, "interprets doctrines as noninformative and nondiscursive symbols of inner feelings, attitudes, or existential orientations."[18] More specifically, she interprets Jesus as the paradigmatic expression of the experience of eschatological hope.[19] The resurrection symbolizes the fact that the followers of Christ reaffirm their hope in God's Kingdom by remembering Jesus. Such remembrance allows for ever new "breakthrough experiences" to occur among his followers.[20] Ruether affirms that other paradigms, such as the Exodus, will provide the same symbolic and evocative function for other religions. Only when Christians come to realize that Easter means the same thing as Exodus will they finally be able to end their anti-Jewish polemic.[21] This construal, however, does no favors to the Jews, for it relativizes Jewish claims of chosenness just as much as it does Christian claims about Christ.

Though van Buren and Williamson largely avoid this level of reductionism, when it comes to the resurrection they follow Ruether's path—reading resurrection as the experience of faith reborn in the disciples.[22] Such an interpretation follows from their overall approach to Christology, which makes clear that Jesus is simply a human instrument through whom the God of Israel works to bring knowledge of salvation to the Gentiles. As van Buren writes, "[Jesus] was and is a man, a Jew, not a second God, heaven forbid, not a deified man, but just a man. Only the LORD is God. But in the words of Jesus . . . many Gentiles have heard God's Word for the first time. . . . For us Gentiles in the Way, then, Jesus is not the LORD, but our Lord, the one Jew who has given us access to the God of the Jews."[23] The meager christological content in both van Buren and Williamson yields an impoverished doctrine of the Trinity. Drawing heavily on 1 Corinthians 15:28, "When all things are subjected to [Christ], then the Son himself will also be subjected to the one who put all things in subjection under him, so that God may be all in all," van Buren and Williamson both present a Monarchian view of God.[24] Anything that is attributed to Christ must finally be passed on to the Father, who is the one and only God. The resulting Christology is adoptionist at best, for it is not exactly clear how Jesus differs from the prophets. Both van Buren and Williamson make much of the fact that Christ must step aside for the final consummation to occur, for in the end it is the God of Israel alone, the one whom Jesus calls "Father," who is glorified. Christ becomes something of a window through whom one may see and worship God; or alternatively, he becomes a message in a bottle, bringing good news from God on the far shore.[25]

For Williamson, then, Jesus Christ and Holy Spirit are "symbols" of the "salvific self-disclosure of God."[26] For van Buren, they are instruments: "By His Spirit and through Jesus Christ, the Jew of Nazareth, the God of Israel has made Himself to be our Father as well."[27] Hence, it is not surprising that van Buren refuses to make the Holy Spirit anything like a "person" of the Trinity, noting that "as God is with His people in the Way as what they call the *Shekhinah,* so God is with His church in the Way as what we call the Spirit."[28] Here van Buren comes close to Ruether's move by locating a common substance of faith that resides below the differing linguistic formulations of Jews and Christians.[29] In their attempts to formulate a doctrine of God that is not anti-Jewish, van Buren and Williamson have erred on the opposite side. Their formulations may avoid anti-Judaism but at the expense of emptying Christianity of its distinctive witness to the identity of God. They have not, in the end, shown that they are able "to purge Christianity of anti-Judaism without at the same time pulling up Christian faith."

Ironically, it is from Jews engaged in Jewish-Christian dialogue that concern has been expressed about this kind of Christian position. Wyschogrod, for instance, has noted that van Buren's position seems to be a "Jesusology" rather than a Christology,[30] and thus it is unable to account for the church's description of Christ as "true God from true God." Novak has also expressed concern about the trend toward a dedivinized Jewish Jesus:

One result of this process of liberalization in Judaism, as developed by some American Reform thinkers, was to see the de-Christologized Jesus [of Protestant liberalism] as an important *teacher* of this delegalized Jewish *teaching.* He could now be the basis for Christians who had risen above traditional Christian dogma to relate to Jews who had risen above traditional Jewish dogma. . . . "Liberal Jews" and "unprejudiced Christians" can find common ground together when Jesus is seen as superlatively human (contrary to traditional Judaism) and less than divine (contrary to traditional Christianity). . . . If this de-Christologized Jesus is accepted, it marks a break with both Judaism and Christianity to such an extent that dialogue between them becomes a new monologue containing them instead.[31]

Given that neither Novak nor Wyschogrod welcomes a dedivinized Jesus as particularly helpful for Judaism or Jewish-Christian dialogue, one wonders what is really gained by the Christian move to jettison traditional christological and trinitarian claims. Surely dialogue is both more interesting and more fruitful when it resists, from both sides, becoming a monologue in which the original parties are no longer recognizable in their differences. The goal of "post-Holocaust" theologies to set forth a presentation of Christian doctrine that does not denigrate Israel is one that all Christian theology must now make its own. What is needed, however, is a way to do this that does not empty the faith of the particularities that identify the God Christians worship.

Kendall Soulen's Economy of Blessing

Kendall Soulen is well aware of the dangers of dividing Christian dialogue with Jews from Christian claims about God as Trinity. He writes, "In the post-Constantinian situation, the church has a fresh opportunity to answer the question, 'Who is the God revealed in the gospel?' in faithful and timely ways. Both the trinitarian revival and the church's reconsideration of its relation to the Jewish people have essential contributions to make to this task, contributions that are imperiled to the degree that they are taken apart from each other."[32] Soulen is thus attempting in his own work to rethink the Christian ways of identifying God in light of a nonsupersessionistic canonical reading. He challenges the "Israel forgetfulness" of the "standard canonical narrative" and attempts a renarration of God's economy that highlights God's continuing faithfulness to Israel. He then asks how this reformulation of the church's *regula fidei* affects our understanding of God as Father, Son, and Holy Spirit. He is intent on showing that one can affirm both God's trinitarian identity and God's identity as Hashem, the faithful God of Israel. Yet in his work *The God of Israel and Christian Theology* he makes certain moves that come perilously close to the mistakes of van Buren and Williamson.

Soulen realizes that altering the church's posture toward Israel is not just an "interfaith" issue. It calls for a fundamental rethinking of Christian theology. To go back and reject the church's supersessionistic teaching is to reject the doctrines that were built upon that presupposition as well as to rethink doctrines that were impoverished by their neglect of Israel's witness. Soulen starts at the roots by seeking to reform the church's *regula fidei,* and he does this without the liberal reductionism of Ruether, van Buren, and Williamson. That Soulen does not need to demythologize the resurrection is a significant indication that he is not doing "post-Holocaust" theology as a means of producing new variations of an old Protestant liberalism (the impression one gets with Ruether, van Buren, and Williamson).[33] Soulen does not seek common ground with Israel through "universal human experience" (Ruether), through "different paths to the same goal" (van Buren), or through a Bultmannian-Tillichian search for "ultimate meaning" and "self-understanding" (Williamson). Soulen is not interested in finding a least common denominator or in underwriting a reductionism of Judaism or Christianity. He therefore grapples with the biblical story much more profoundly than his predecessors, and rather than trying to conform the story to modern sensibilities, he constructs a framework for telling the story that is manifestly *more* faithful to the entirety of the biblical witness than was the standard canonical narrative. Soulen has taken a distinct and necessary step forward by giving us a taste of what a theology that is both post-Holocaust and postliberal might look like.

He makes Israel determinative in God's economy by refocusing the central canonical story on consummation rather than redemption: "Christians should acknowledge that God's history with Israel and the nations is the permanent and enduring medium of God's work as the Consummator of human creation, and therefore it is also the permanent and enduring context of the gospel about Jesus" (110). Soulen proposes a twofold reading of Israel's Scriptures—both as a witness to the blessings contained in God's economy of consummation and as a witness to the threat of sin that denies this economy, brings God's curse, and creates the occasion for redemption. God's creation-for-consummation intends an economy of mutual blessing and dependence between those who are irreducibly other (111). This emphasis on the economy of consummation leads us to read the story of Israel that begins in Genesis not as a prefigurement of the solution to sin (and thus purely as a prelude to Christ) but as the initiation of God's plan to consummate creation. Here Soulen picks up on Barth's affirmation that covenant is grounded in creation. But sin intrudes into God's intended order of blessing. It is "the incomprehensible fact that the human family cuts itself off from God's economies of mutual blessing and instead seeks to procure blessing on its own terms at the other's expense. Male seeks blessing at the expense of female, Gentile at the expense of Jew, Jew at the expense of Gentile. In these ways and others, the human family turns its back on God's blessing and does violence to the human other. The economy of difference and mutual dependence becomes an economy of curse rather than blessing and is therefore overshadowed by the curse of God" (141). The curse that triumphs where there should be blessing calls into question God's prior determination to consummate creation in blessing. The prophets now envision the possibility that Israel will be blessed but the nations cut off in curse (e.g., Hag. 2:21–23) or even the possibility that Israel's own end will be curse instead of blessing (Amos 5:18–20).

In the face of this threat, God responds to sin and evil by engaging creation as its Redeemer, recovering blessing where it appears to be cut off entirely. Although the Exodus and the Jubilee year witness to God's desire to redeem (148–151), on

Soulen's reading Israel's Scriptures leave an open-endedness about whether curse or blessing will finally triumph. The significance of Christ and the Apostolic Witness (Soulen's term for the New Testament) arises specifically out of this indeterminacy at the end of Israel's biblical story. The Apostolic Witness is the good news that God's reign will be consummated through the overcoming of curse by blessing. "The gospel is good news about the God of Israel's coming reign, which proclaims in Jesus' life, death, and resurrection the victorious guarantee of God's fidelity to the work of consummation, that is, to fullness of mutual blessing as the outcome of God's economy with Israel, the nations, and all creation" (157). Jesus is himself "the victorious guarantee of God's end-time fidelity to the work of consummation" (165). He is "victorious" because in the resurrection God vindicates Jesus' life of blessing. He is a "guarantee" (and not the fulfillment) because the fullness of God's eschatological reign is still awaited (165). Jesus' resurrection is the first fruits of God's consummating work, which will in the end extend to all Israel (160–166). Jesus confirms God's consummating intentions through his hope, trust, faith, and expectation of God's coming reign. He is the "proleptic enactment," the "carnal embodiment," of God's fidelity to Israel and to the eschatological *shalom* between Israel, the nations, and all creation (166).

Soulen's proposal properly reorients the Christian vision from a purely redemptive reading of the canon to a reading that places redemption within the context of God's consummating work mediated through Israel. Yet it remains unclear at points just how the Apostolic Witness, and thus Jesus himself, adds anything new to Israel's story. This is to say that here again Christology seems to be minimized just to the extent that Israel's significance is maximized. One of the central features of Soulen's account of Jesus as Redeemer seems to be that his life, death, and resurrection are the guarantee of God's faithfulness, that is, the assurance that the consummation will be one of blessing for all and not curse. The consummation has become "a future event whose character as victorious fidelity can no longer be in doubt" (166). But given Israel's witness to God's irrevocable election, was it ever in doubt? Soulen seems to underestimate Israel's trust in God's faithfulness. Neither the Jews of Israel's Scripture nor the Jews today need Jesus in order to trust that God will be faithful to God's promises. The irrevocability of the covenant is the abiding assurance of God's election, which is eternal and unconditional. As Soulen himself notes, Israel's Scripture affirms that "as Redeemer, God acts in fidelity to God's work as Consummator by refusing to let curse have the last word" (148). If this was already known before Christ, it is unclear what Christ has brought that is new. What exactly is the content of Christ's redemptive work? In him the promises are confirmed (165), but are they not already confirmed in the Exodus, the return from Exile, and the prophetic visions of messianic peace? If one trusts that the promises of God's election are "irrevocable," as the apostle Paul does (Rom. 11:29), then from the very start the tension between blessing and curse is subsumed by the more determinative assurance of God's election.

The lingering question for Soulen's Christology is this: If Jesus does not inaugurate Israel's redemption but only confirms it, then how is Jesus different from other faithful Jewish witnesses? To put it another way, it is just not clear that one needs more than an adoptionist Christology to affirm what Soulen wants to affirm. For instance, Jesus' life witnesses to his place in the overarching economy of consummation by looking back in the genealogies and forward in his proclamation (159). His genealogy links him to the whole unfolding story of Israel, and it "catches up in the briefest possible compass all the manifold dimensions of God's work as Consummator" (159). But in what sense is Jesus' genealogy his own as a mark of irreducible identity? Would not Joseph's and Mary's genealogies link them to this same history of mutual blessing and God's consummating work? Likewise, the claim that Jesus' proclamation ties him to the future of God's consummation does not decisively set him apart from John the Baptist or other Jewish prophets. Soulen admits that Jesus was not the first to preach the coming of God's reign; "yet," he argues, "in one crucial respect the message about God's coming reign takes on a distinctive character on Jesus' lips: it becomes *gospel,* an unambiguous proclamation of good news" (159). Why? Because "First, Jesus trusted God's reign to consummate the economy of mutual blessing between God and the house of Israel, and therefore between God and the nations as well. Second, Jesus trusted God's reign to consummate Israel and the nations in a manner that reclaimed, redeemed, and restored the lost" (159). But one would have to admit that such trust was not unique to Jesus. Many of the prophets and indeed Abraham himself trusted God for this. And even if none before had so trusted, Jesus would then be best understood as a remarkably faithful Jew. This is no small feat, but it is not yet clear what sets him off in such a way that Christians have come to worship him.

Furthermore, in Soulen's reading, Jesus' death witnesses to his willingness to go to the outer limits with the lost and forsaken, trusting even there in God's fidelity to the economy of blessing. Here also we have the remarkable witness of a Jewish martyr, faithfully trusting the God of Abraham and embodying that trust as a witness to others, but surely Jesus was not the first or the last faithful Jewish martyr. It is true that Jesus' pattern of cruciform faithfulness to a life of peaceful blessing is crucial to his identity and gives a distinctive shape to covenant obedience. But this, too, is compatible with an adoptionist Christology. Soulen adds that in the resurrection of Jesus, "God vindicates Jesus' trust in the triumph of blessing over curse, life over death, communion over isolation" (165). Yet even here Jesus is the first fruit of many brothers and sisters (165). His being raised by God does not define his identity in a unique way unless his resurrection inaugurates redemption rather than just confirming it.

All that Soulen says about Jesus seems amenable to an adoptionist Christology, and thus it is unclear what might make us worship Christ. One could argue that Soulen's position is amenable to a "higher" Christology, even if it does not require it. However, as Lee Keck has noted, "Christological correlations tend to obey the

law of parsimony. That is, generally speaking, christology and soteriology/anthro-
pology are not wasted on each other, because the understanding of Jesus' identity
and significance should not exceed what is required to resolve the human
dilemma."[34] Given this, Soulen's discussion of Christ's life, death, and resurrection
does not require that we attribute to Jesus any more than that he was an extremely
faithful Jew, trusting in God's promises and living the way of blessing faithfully
even unto the cross. God adopts this one and vindicates this faithful life as a sign
and guarantee to others that such faithfulness will be matched by God's own faithfulness to the promises of consummation. Such a depiction of Jesus' identity
would seem to be all that is required, and thus, if Keck is right, all that is appropriate. What is still needed is an account of Israel's place in the Christian story that
does justice both to the ongoing significance of the Jews and to the christological
claims that make Jesus worthy not only of imitation but of worship.

Oliver O'Donovan's *Desire of the Nations*

Oliver O'Donovan has given us one of the most interesting of recent attempts to
rethink the place of Israel in the church's theological reflection. In *The Desire of
the Nations: Rediscovering the Roots of Political Theology,* O'Donovan looks to
Israel to help him articulate a theological alternative to the politics of late-modern liberalism.[35] O'Donovan reads late-modern liberalism as a falling away from,
a prodigal squandering of a prior Christian social order (275). His critique focuses on the triumph of the individual will paired with concomitant contractual
theories of society. In this situation freedom is turned into "free will," which,
without any orienting telos, serves only the pursuit of self-interest. Such a victory
of voluntarism "means that society's demands are justified only in so far as they
embody what any individual might be expected to will as his or her own good. It
rejects the Christian paradox of freedom perfected in service" (275). O'Donovan
adds, "Once society is thought of as an agreement between competing wills, the
cloud of competition never lifts from it. Each new public endeavor serves as a further action in the war" (278). Suffering, no longer understood in terms of Christ's
own passion and the vicarious suffering of the church, loses all intelligibility and
becomes an unredeemable evil. Further, "free speech," once based on and serving
the church's prophecy, prayer, and proclamation, is reduced to "the conflict of
competing wills," having "lost its orientation to deliberating on the common
good" (282).

This deterioration of the political order is marked also by a widely accepted
split between theology and politics (6–12). This split rests on two deep suspicions
in late-modern thought. On the one hand, there is a suspicion that church-state
cooperation will ruin religion, turning it into an ideology that underwrites the
interests of the rulers. On the other hand, there is a suspicion that a close tie between church and state will ruin government, turning it into a means of enforc-
ing religious conformity. These two suspicions have come together in the West to

produce a strong argument for the separation of church and state. Yet, O'Donovan notes, a truce that would carve out autonomous spheres of politics and religion is not finally a happy one—either for the church or for government.

In light of this situation, O'Donovan seeks to recover a Christian political vision through a recovery of the political significance of Israel. He notes that from the beginning "failure to attend to Israel is what left Christian political thought oscillating between idealist and realist poles" (27). That is, once Israel's political influence was lost to the early church, it found itself bouncing between the untenable positions of simple "political disinvolvement" and uncritical "political affirmation," between pietism and theocracy, between an idealism that failed to touch human political structures and a realism that failed to change them (25–27). To discern God's desire for human political arrangements, Christians must look where God has chosen to disclose God's will—among the chosen people. "Any question about social forms and structures must be referred to a normative critical standard: do they fulfil that will of God for human society to which Israel's forms authoritatively point us?" (25). In affirmations such as this, O'Donovan stands firmly against the classical economic supersessionism that would leave Israel behind. In contrast, he admits the church's ongoing debt to Israel and understands the ways in which a repudiation of supersessionism calls on the church to rethink politics. Drawing on Paul's discussion of Israel in Romans, O'Donovan concludes that the Jews have not been rejected by God and that in fact they continue to bear forward a *"public* tradition—the adoption, the glory, the covenants, the giving of the law, the worship and the promises . . . the patriarchs and . . . the Messiah" (Rom. 9:4–5) to which the church must attend (132).

The enduring significance of Israel's social witness reminds Christians that church and theology are by their very nature political. One does not, for instance, work out a theology and then *apply* it politically. Rather, "theology is political simply by responding to the dynamics of its own proper themes. Christ, salvation, the church, the Trinity: to speak about these has involved theologians in speaking of society, and has led them to formulate normative political ends" (3). Likewise, the church does not simply have a political agenda but in fact *is* a political body. Through the church the future age that Christ proclaimed "has a social and political presence. A community lives under the authority of him to whom the Ancient of Days has entrusted the Kingdom" (158). O'Donovan does not spiritualize the Kingdom, nor does he push it off to some distant eschatological future. The reign of Christ is made visible in the politics of the church as the people who live already under that reign.

Thus, this is not a dominion that looks like that of the nations (159–174). In contrast to the Gentile rulers who lord it over others, the church is called to service and suffering, and thus its authority and political witness, in one sense, lie hidden until Christ's return (see Mark 10 and Luke 22). That is, from the outside there appears to be no particular political form to the church. But this is only because what makes the church a political witness is not its official structures of power. Rather, and here O'Donovan makes a very helpful move, the church's politics is found precisely in the practices that conform the church's life to the life of Christ. Thus, the church is political insofar as it gathers and baptizes, suffers and celebrates Eucharist, rejoices and keeps the Lord's Day, speaks the words of God and lays on empowering hands. Locating the church's political witness in this distinct pattern of practices not only highlights that this is a different politics from the world but also engages the full membership of the church, not just the ordained leaders, in its political witness.

O'Donovan understands the heart of his constructive project to be the search for "true political concepts" (15). Turning to the Old Testament, he analyzes Israel's history in order to identify the central political concepts that constitute God's authority over Israel and over all creation. The affirmation "*Yhwh malāk*," "Yhwh reigns," is found to include a constellation of central concepts: salvation (also power/triumph), judgment, and possession (also tradition/community identity). Israel affirms the rule of God through its praise as a separate but necessary moment in the establishment of God's authority. This fourfold architectonic—salvation, judgment, possession, and praise—weaves throughout the rest of the work like a thread marking the path on a long journey. Alongside these chief concepts O'Donovan traces the history of "dual authority"—those times and places where God's people have found themselves tensely situated between conflicting powers (82ff.). "It would be difficult to exaggerate the significance of the Babylonian experience for Israel," O'Donovan writes. "One could say that it became the paradigm of Jewish existence thereafter" (83). This situation of exile called for careful engagement with the empire that wielded power over God's people. Daniel, especially, warns Israel "against optimism about the compatibility of the two kingdoms, bred, perhaps, by too facile a reading of the stories of Joseph or of Esther. The co-operative relation between Israel and the empire is not a right, and to make a priority of preserving it can lead to fatal compromises" (87).

With his inauguration of the kingdom, Christ put an end to the spatial tension of dual authority by gathering up all political authority in himself. But in so doing, he inaugurated an analogous period of temporal tension between two ages. "In Jesus' proclamation the duality of Babylon and Israel has become a frontier in time" (158). The spatial duality of Israel's exile becomes a temporal duality in the church's life. In the time between the times, between Christ's advent and his return, the old age is passing away but has not yet vanished. Thus, the passing forms of the world and the coming age of Christ's reign coexist precariously in one time. The church embodies the new age in its social and political life, whereas the secular[36] rulers embody the old and passing age.

Christ also transforms the dual authority of church and secular power into a sign no longer of exile and alienation but of Christ's triumph. The pagan rulers have been made to cooperate in Christ's rule and must either serve the church or stand on the side of Antichrist. There is no neutral territory after the victory of Jesus. The pagan rulers are paradoxically dethroned and reauthorized by Christ's coming. On the one hand, through his embodiment of God's Kingdom, Jesus disarmed the kingdoms of this world. On the other hand, these passing forms maintain a relativized and minimized place in God's ordering of authority during the time between the times.

To explicate the continuing role of the passing age in God's economy, O'Donovan turns to Romans 13. He notes first of all that we must read Romans 13 in the context in which Paul has placed it, that is, alongside "his claim for the continued significance of Israel as a social entity in God's plans for final redemption" (147). What Paul says about the authorities is based on his conviction that Christ has brought Israel's promised victory over the nations. Thus, "the authorities are claimed for obedience to Israel, chastened and reduced to the familiar functions that were once assigned to Israel's judges" (147). A certain limited judgment is all that is left for earthly authorities to exercise, but this is their role, and the church is both to respect and to oversee this activity of the rulers. Although the church is to bear witness to God's mercy by abstaining from judging, the secular rulers are to wield the sword of judgment as a witness to the coming judgment of Christ, at which time secular rule will pass away.[37]

O'Donovan tells the story of Christendom as the story of the dual authority that exists in the time while the two ages overlap (193ff.). He reminds us that Christendom is about *mission*—the mission to the Gentiles that reaches even to the rulers. Christendom is about what happens when mission succeeds and the lords of the Gentiles are claimed for Christ's service. The empire then becomes not only the object of mission but also the servant of mission. Alongside the church the secular rule is called to the service of Christ's kingdom. It is called to support and promote the life and work of the church. The "Christendom idea," as O'Donovan calls it, is not about the church's seizing secular power for its own ends but is rather "the idea of a confessionally Christian government, at once 'secular' (in the proper sense of that word, confined to the present age) and obedient to Christ, a promise of the age of his unhindered rule" (195).

O'Donovan, however, is not naive about the dangers of a Christian compromise with secular authority. "The question which created the turbulence of church-state relations in the West was how the sign of Christ's victory could be protected against subversion, which would leave the church in a Babylonian captivity to its own Christian rulers" (196–197). Whether this subversion could be prevented or whether it was intrinsic to Christendom is the question that divides O'Donovan from theologians such as Stanley Hauerwas and John Howard Yoder. O'Donovan clearly wants to uncover a normative Christendom, a "deep Christendom," which, despite its distortions along the way, reflects a true ordering of dual authority as ordained by God until the eschaton. Christendom was not a mistake from the beginning, even though some wrong turns were made as the cooperative enterprise was played out.

Two crucial points had to be remembered in order to maintain the proper ordering of the dual authority. First, it always had to be clear that the church, as a political body, represented the coming age, the new rule of God in Christ. As a distinct social reality, it witnessed to a new time that could not be confused with the social structures of the old age that were passing away. Whenever these two societies were merged into one, the witness to the new age was clouded. Second, the church always had to remember that its own witness was to a renunciation of coercive judgment as a response to the merciful judgment of God pronounced in Christ. The state, in contrast, maintained the authority of passing earthly judgments and thus of wielding the sword for just causes. Christians could never ask the state to promote the church through violence since this would be to misuse an alien power and thereby jeopardize the church's witness to mercy. Forced conversions and persecution of Jews and Muslims were always perversions of what Christendom was supposed to be. O'Donovan remains convinced that such misuse of power was not built into the model of shared authority but rather was a distortion that could be peeled away to reveal the true Christendom legacy.

On this reading of Christian history, the true rejection of God's reign came not with the Constantinian compromise nor with the rise of modern liberalism but more specifically with the descent into liberalism's late-modern form. Looking for an answer to the growing chorus criticizing modernity, O'Donovan cautions us not to dispense with the legacy of Christendom in its modern liberal form too hastily. Rather, he argues, what is needed is a recovery of the Christendom idea, which was in some ways embodied most faithfully in early-modern liberalism, when church and state were held together in a cooperative relationship of mutual service under the reign of Christ. O'Donovan unabashedly promotes a political vision in which the state understands and facilitates the church's mission, though not to the point of engaging in coercive activity to defend or support the church's work (217–221). O'Donovan persuasively argues against the late-modern notion of a neutral state, making clear that the rulers of the nations are either for Christ or against him.

It is perhaps ironic that the greatest weakness in a book that pays so much attention to Israel is the lingering supersessionism that keeps O'Donovan from finally attending to the Jews as he himself claims we should. Indeed, this way of putting the problem is instructive—O'Donovan attends to Israel, but the role of the Jews is unclear. I have attempted throughout this book to use these two terms interchangeably, thus noting that one cannot separate "Israel" from the actual flesh of the Jews. O'Donovan, however, seems to give an account of "Israel" that is at least theoretically separable from Jewish bodies. So it is not always clear who "Israel" is in *The Desire of the Nations*. It seems that the people of Israel fade out of the story, whereas the concept of Israel is carried forward. In the end this reproduces the politics of supersessionism by which the church's political identity comes to be named by a certain partnership with the nations rather than its shared covenant with the chosen people.

Israel, as the chosen people of God, is relativized in O'Donovan's work in two specific ways. First, the distinctive identity of this people is lost through

O'Donovan's hermeneutical method of abstracting "political concepts" from the Old Testament story. Second, Israel drops inexplicably out of view once Christ enters the picture. The kind of "structural supersessionism" at work here is subtle, and it belies O'Donovan's own best attempts to combat traditional supersessionistic readings of the Scriptures (130ff.).[38] Structural supersessionism does not include any specific repudiation of Israel as such; rather, the Jews are simply allowed to fade into the background of the Christian story. The unity of the biblical story is structured in a way that makes Israel's own history relevant but indecisive in reference both to the identity of God and to the nature of God's redemptive and consummating work. Israel is not conspicuously rejected but is rather made inconspicuous; Soulen calls this the "Israel forgetfulness" of structural supersessionism.[39]

This form of supersessionism shows through in O'Donovan's conceptual analysis of Israel as well as his depiction of Christendom. As the focus of his book shifts from the Old Testament to the New, his exegetical method shifts from a search for political concepts to a presentation of the narrative. "To speak of God's rule from this point on," he writes, "must mean more than to assert divine sovereignty, or even divine intervention, in general terms. It means recounting this narrative [of Christ] and drawing the conclusions implied in it" (133). O'Donovan stresses the importance of narrative in the New Testament and its irreducibility to concepts, and thus his analysis focuses on moments of Christ's mediation of the kingdom—Advent, Passion, Restoration, Exaltation. Here his categories parallel the narrative in a way that his concepts did not in his treatment of the Old Testament. One wonders why the New Testament demands a different hermeneutical approach, that is, why "general terms" are sufficient for the Old Testament but not for the New. O'Donovan's hermeneutic simply does not honor the particularity of the Old Testament. This is not to take away from the thorough and insightful exegesis of the Old Testament in *The Desire of the Nations,* but it is to point out that O'Donovan finally mines the Old Testament for concepts that are then carried forward in a way that leaves behind the chosen people themselves.

Although he mentions this difference in hermeneutical strategy only in passing, I would argue that this turns out to be a difference that makes a difference. For by abstracting general concepts that can then be applied either directly or analogously to other nations, O'Donovan makes Israel into a paradigm (23), a model (73), or an archetype (83) of political authority. And although such a paradigmatic role could be combined with an affirmation of Israel's continuing distinctness by virtue of its election, O'Donovan does not do this. Thus, Israel threatens to be reduced to *only* a model or an archetype or a political order that can in principle be embodied by another (nonelect) people. So we read, "The unique covenant of Yhwh and Israel can be seen as a point of disclosure from which the nature of all political authority comes into view. Out of the self-possession of this people in their relation to God springs the possibility of other peoples' possessing themselves in God" (45). The uniqueness of Israel as the chosen people is lost from view.

This explains why O'Donovan grounds Israel's politics finally not in God's covenant with Israel but in creation (19). The divine rule avoids the arbitrariness of modern political voluntarism by being grounded in the history of God's restoration of "creation order" (19–20). Insofar as divine authority is rooted in and ordered to the goods of creation, human beings can trust that it serves their deepest good. This grounding of divine authority in creation (rather than in the particularity of the covenant with Israel) parallels the structural supersessionism of which Soulen warns, just insofar as the people of Israel are no longer determinative for God's politics but only exemplary. Israel's politics is grounded in its acts of praise, but so is the politics of every society (49); Israel's social order is governed by law, but so is every society (72); Israel witnesses to the divine rule by responding in praise to the unified authority of God's power, judgment, and possession, but then, so does every society (45, 49, 72).

Further, it seems that the characteristics of divine authority that O'Donovan locates in Israel do not in fact arise organically from an analysis of Israel's distinct political existence. This is especially clear if one looks back at O'Donovan's earlier work *Resurrection and Moral Order.* Here he sets forth some of the themes that he takes up and expands in *The Desire of the Nations.* What is telling is that already in *Resurrection and Moral Order* O'Donovan locates God's authority in the threefold form of "might," "right," and "tradition" paralleling "power," "judgment," and "possession."[40] Yet in this earlier book O'Donovan does not attempt to draw these concepts out of an analysis of Israel; indeed, he hardly mentions Israel. Rather, he grounds them in the natural order—"might" and "tradition" he calls "natural authorities," and "right" he names a "'relatively natural' authority."[41] One cannot help but wonder then, upon turning to *The Desire of the Nations,* if O'Donovan's conceptual analysis of Israel is really just a matter of setting a predetermined template over the Old Testament. My criticism is not a complaint about O'Donovan's exegesis but rather a suspicion that O'Donovan has found in Israel a helpful example of a political analysis that was arrived at on other terms altogether and is grounded finally in creation itself rather than the distinctive life of the Jews.[42]

It may be, then, that Israel departs early from O'Donovan's story because in fact the Jews were never decisive for his analysis in the first place. Once Christ arrives on the scene, O'Donovan focuses his discussion on the two ages that coexist until Christ's return. Christ inaugurates the new age, and the church embodies this age socially and politically. The old age lives on but is destined to pass away. Where, one wonders, do the Jews (not just "Israel" as a political concept) fit? O'Donovan never clearly tells us. At one point he places the rulers of Israel on the side of the passing age, which has no future in the coming kingdom: "Jesus . . . stands at the moment of transition between the ages where the passing and coming authorities confront one another: the rulers of Israel representing the one, the Son of Man the other" (158). The rulers of Israel represent Babylon, whereas Jesus takes over the place of Israel. To give O'Donovan the benefit of the doubt, one might emphasize that he refers here only to "the *rulers* of Israel." Perhaps he means to imply that others in Israel do remain part of the coming age. But it is not clear in what form. That is, "Israel" as a concept continues through its fourfold pattern of authority, but are the Jews part of the new age? I assume that for O'Donovan the Jews who become Christians participate in the new age, but the Jews qua Jews are destined to pass away as part of the old.

O'Donovan's analysis of the structures of Christendom continues this "Israel forgetfulness." This is in one sense understandable, since Israel had no positive role in the ongoing story for the Christians of Christendom. Thus, to follow their lead is to make Israel irrelevant for the church's politics. But O'Donovan is not writing a history; he is doing constructive theology. He is not bound to follow the lead of Christendom on this point. The truly puzzling thing is that O'Donovan himself notices this and comments on it toward the end of his book. Reflecting on the dangers of religious coercion in a Christendom model and noting particularly the sustained persecution of the Jews, O'Donovan writes:

> Perhaps the whole problem lies with the structure of the doctrine of the Two: where is the third realm, the heir of the covenant? One would have expected to see a doctrine of the Three. At the base of the triangle, the two poles of Israel and the nations, linked by a line of hope in Yhwh's covenant-promises for the twofold gathering of Israel and the nations. At the apex the church's witness to the fulfilment of the promises, subduing the nations' lords on the one side for the sake of Israel on the other. But the patristic and medieval church thought it had so wholly taken over Israel's identity that no further engagement between church and synagogue was called for. The third realm became invisible. . . . The apostolic church's view of its double mission, to secure the identity of Israel on the one hand and the obedience of the Gentiles on the other, had been lost sight of. In its place was a one-sided mission to the Gentiles and a rather petty determination to triumph over Israel. (220)

O'Donovan ironically provides here a critique of his own work. This observation occurs in the small print of O'Donovan's text, and remarkably, upon return to the large print, it is as if O'Donovan had already forgotten what he had just written. This acknowledgment of the failings of Christendom theology in relation to Israel should have caused O'Donovan to rethink and make adjustments in the Christendom model. Unfortunately, he does not. O'Donovan's awareness of the problem makes it all the more disappointing that he does not take this seriously as a critique of his own project.

At the end of the above excursus, O'Donovan draws an analogy with the angel wrestling Jacob at the Jabbok. Christendom theologians (including Augustine) pictured the church in the role of Jacob encountering Esau (the nations and/or Israel) (220). But O'Donovan suggests the church should be seen as the angel that wrestles with Jacob (Israel). With this shift in the analogy, he goes on to redescribe the posture of early Christendom: "It was as though the angel left Jacob sleeping by the Jabbok and went off to wrestle Esau instead. The angel who does that had better beware that it does not learn from the Gentile lords to be a lordly angel, and so, in the end, a fallen angel!" (220–221). Right again. And yet what does O'Donovan leave us with but a picture of the church wrestling with the secular authorities, the two ages living in a tensive mutual service, with Israel nowhere to be seen.

O'Donovan's proposal is especially helpful in that it reveals, even as it falls prey to, the deep antinomy that lies at the heart of Christendom. Stated simply, Christendom purports to be a result of the church's mission to the Gentiles and the conversion of the rulers. But in fact, as noted earlier, the Christendom idea presupposes the necessity of an incomplete conversion and thus a partially failed mission. Indeed, the church requires that the structures of the old age remain in place to provide coercive judgment and thus to create a space in which the church can work. If the church were truly concerned to convert the Gentiles, then the goal would be to draw them fully into the new age of God's reign. But this is in fact *not* the goal of Christendom, which requires that the old age remain partially unconverted in order to wield the sword that the church repudiates. Ironically, then, Christendom requires that the church affirm the very thing it denies, that the church sustain the very structures it combats, that the church embrace the very violence it abjures. This antinomy haunts O'Donovan's proposal as it does all apologies for Christendom. Thus, the "Christendom idea," far from being a purified Christian politics, actually deconstructs under its own weight. There are few better examples of a totalizing discourse that carries within it an aporia that undermines the structure yet is also a necessary element of it. Christendom relies on a hierarchical dualism (the new age and the old, church and empire) in which the "lesser" element is both denied and affirmed and thus the claimed purity and superiority of the "higher" element is subverted.

Another tension that reveals this instability is that between Christ's "subjugation" of the rulers and God's "authorization" of them. God is pitted against God's own self insofar as full subjugation would require a deauthorizing of the nations, whereas authorization requires that subjugation not be complete. O'Donovan maintains that "in Israel's experience . . . dual authority corresponded to the fractured and enslaved condition of God's people. Now [after Christ] it corresponds to the progress of the victory that God has given them" (158). He goes on, "The duality assumes a conflictual, aggressive note, as the rule of Christ within the church presses back upon the old and withering authority of empire. It was not protection that was needed, but that the secular authority should give way" (158). Yet God cannot really want it to give way entirely, since the old age is still required to fulfill its role in the divine design of dual authority. What O'Donovan is describing here is not simply an eschatological tension, not simply the "already/not yet" of Pauline theology. Rather, it is the decisive justifying of a union with the old age, such that Christ's full victory over the nations would actually be a defeat for Christendom and for the divinely authorized cooperation.

Another way of analyzing the problem is to look at O'Donovan's question of whether Christendom is a matter of "mission or coercion" (211). This question sets up the aporia nicely, since Christendom must secretly presuppose an answer of "both" while outwardly professing that the answer is purely "mission." O'Donovan asks, "To what extent is secular authority compatible with this mission and, so to speak, re-authorised by it? If the mission of the church needs a certain social space, for men and women of every nation to be drawn into the governed community of God's Kingdom, then secular authority is authorised to provide and ensure that space" (146). O'Donovan purports to show that Christendom is the outgrowth of mission to the Gentiles and thus must maintain a mission focus rather than seeking coercive support from the rulers. But this leaves the church in a highly ambiguous situation. It must seek the conversion of the nations to Christ's rule, while at the same time authorizing and making use of the unconverted elements of the old age (specifically, coercive judgment) in order to create "a certain social space" for the church's growth. The secular rule must remain only partially converted for Christendom to continue, and thus the church's mission must end at the point where it would finally call the authorities of the old age wholly into the new. Indeed, it is clear that the church's mission is threatened, rather than supported, by this Constantinian arrangement.

Thus, even though O'Donovan claims to locate a "Christendom idea" that does not require the state to advance the church's cause through violence, this is in fact at the heart of Christendom, even on his own account. "The Christendom idea," he tells us, "describes a *mutual service* between the two authorities, predicated on the difference and the balance of their roles" (215). This difference resides in the right of secular authorities to exert coercive judgment, to bear the sword, to use violence to uphold the good, though, to be sure, this judgment is tempered by mercy and disciplined by justice. Although the church witnesses to the coming reign of Christ, the secular rulers are authorized "to provide and ensure" that "social space" needed for the church's work (146). This social space is created by the use of coercion. Thus, when O'Donovan argues that there is a Christendom idea that can be cut free from the "parasite" of religious compulsion or violent defense of the church (221), one wonders how this can be. For, to repeat, if the secular rule is defined as the arena in which coercive judgment is still used, and if the role of this authority is to ensure a social space for the church, then, however indirectly, coercion is going to be used to the end of furthering the church's mission. Indeed, O'Donovan's Christendom idea remains parasitic on the very secular violence that it appears to reject.

By following the Christendom model of dual authority, O'Donovan has proposed a partnership between the old age and the new, and thus he has given the structures of the old age too much of a place in God's good order. To say that there are still authorities from the old age that linger in the new and even that God uses them and that Christians must at times work with them is far different from saying that the old authorities are given a specific role to fill in the present time; for so doing threatens to justify the powers in their resistance to Christ's rule. O'Donovan looks for the conversion of the rulers, but he does not sufficiently address the fact that these rulers continue to serve in structures that are determined by the old age and thus by their resistance to the new.[43] To recall Cohen's critique of Christianity, O'Donovan's Christendom idea, though chastened and purified, remains susceptible to the charge that it is a "premature surrender to the world-as-it-is."[44]

In many ways O'Donovan and I share a fundamentally similar project. Our critiques of modernity focus on the same crises—the post-Christendom separation of theology from politics along with the triumph of voluntarism and violence—and we seek to counter these challenges with a return to Israel and a recovery of the covenant charter of God's reign. However, our constructive proposals remain significantly at odds. Unlike O'Donovan, I have tried to show that Israel does not *reveal* God's politics but rather Israel *is* God's politics. Such a conviction makes it harder to drift away from the actual people of Israel as O'Donovan does, since it is in this people and their story that God's reign is embodied. O'Donovan recovers "political concepts" that are revealed by Israel but are in principle separable from this particular people. This leads to the possibility that the "Christendom-idea" can represent the form of divine politics despite the ways in which Christendom presupposes the detachment of the church from its material continuity with God's chosen people. In contrast, my attention to Israel is not a search for detachable political concepts but rather for a people whose very existence constitutes the reign of God. There can be no separation of God's reign from the people whom God has chosen to embody it. When seen in this light, Israel's constitution as the elect people of God becomes the church's principal political claim. The social structures of God's people as defined in the story of election, covenant, and redemption come to the foreground. The church's political witness must be understood as an ingrafting into this people and their redemption.

5

Trinitarian Election

$\mathcal{H}$ow is it that God's promises to Israel now apply to the Gentiles?" the early church asked itself. And Israel asked, in turn, "Where is this redemption you say has occurred in Jesus Christ?" In short, how have Israel's election, covenant, and redemption come to be predicated of this largely gentile gathering called church? What does this say about the church's identity and mission? What kind of relationship does this create between church and Israel? Many voices are now proposing creative and faithful answers to these questions. Yet it is also clear that we do not yet know how to move forward without losing Israel again or relativizing central Christian affirmations about the identity of God. Although certain strands of the tradition, from Calvin to O'Donovan, have kept alive alternative readings of Israel, church, and election, the church's story (its canonical narrative) has yet to be articulated so that it sufficiently holds together the true object of election, Israel, with the true subject of election, the triune God.[1]

The "New Covenant"

The language of "new covenant" has been a hot spot for Christian-Jewish controversy, and it has long served as a biblical grounding for supersessionism. What are we to do with this biblical description in the wake of the Holocaust? Should we repudiate it altogether, excising it from our Christian imaginations? Or is there a way to reinterpret it in a nonsupersessionist way?

The belief that God made a "new covenant" with the Gentiles to *replace* the covenant with the Jews has long served as a Christian answer to the question about how God's promises to Israel now apply to the Gentiles. On this reading, "new covenant" means replacement covenant. Even in the post-Holocaust world, such a view still governs much of our Christian discourse. For instance, the New Testament scholar N. T. Wright interprets Romans 9–11 as saying that Israel's calling was to a distinct yet limited place in God's plan.[2] There is no *eternal* covenant here, only a specific, circumscribed role to be played in God's drama. Specifically, Israel was the nation that God chose as a receptacle for the sin of the world. The role of the Torah was, from the start, to multiply Israel's sin, to entice Israel "into 'national righteousness', becoming the place where Adam's pride found its full outworking."[3] The plan was for Israel to take the world's sin, for Jesus to bear Israel's sin, and for all sin to be put to death on the cross.

In the aftermath of the cross, then, the people of Israel stand on exactly the same footing as the Gentiles. They have an "equal opportunity" for salvation through faith in Christ, though they are no longer considered the chosen recipients of a special promise. Wright argues that this understanding of Israel does not nullify God's faithfulness, since "God's plan, the righteous plan which he had always indicated he would follow, and therefore in which (9:6) his word has not failed, was always to cast Israel away that the world might be saved."[4] Wright's picture of God "casting away" Israel, however, makes a parody of the pervasive Old Testament description of God as Israel's faithful spouse.

Wright does attempt to diminish the triumphalism of this view by giving the church a role similar to Israel's. "The Spirit thus accomplishes within the church what, *mutatis mutandis,* the Torah accomplishes within Israel. Just as the sin and death of the world were concentrated, by means of the Torah, on Israel . . . , so now the pain and grief of the world is to be concentrated, by means of the Spirit, on the Χριστός, the family of the Messiah, so that it [the world] may be healed (Rom. 8:18–30)."[5] But does this mean that the church may yet be cast away, as was Israel? If Israel was rejected once it had served its purpose, why should the church think its fate would be any different? The problem with becoming a replacement people is that one has no assurance one will not meet the same fate as those who went before. In the end our trust in God's faithfulness is undermined by Wright's position.

The temptation, in response to this "equal opportunity" reading of the new covenant, is to err on the other side, by dividing Jews and Gentiles into two parallel covenants—a "separate but equal" approach. Paul van Buren, for instance, argues that "the Way which we [Jews and Christians] walk is one in that its goal is one, but the ways in which we walk it differ. . . . The differences between us arise not because one of us is right and the other wrong, but because they are God's elect people whereas we are God's elect church."[6] These two elections create two fundamentally different though complementary communities.[7] Commenting on Romans 11:28, he writes, "In other words, God has kept the Jews out of our path and given them their own instructions to continue in the Way so that we Gentiles might find our *own* manner of walking in the Way. But for all that, they remain God's beloved people, ever before us as evidence of God's faithfulness."[8] Despite his better moments, van Buren continues to reproduce a liberal account of Judaism and Christianity that relativizes the claims of both by pluralizing the paths to God. His attempt to overcome supersessionism and his insistence on the church's learning from Israel are both welcome changes from what has gone on in the conversation for centuries. Nonetheless, van Buren fails to take either tradition seriously enough just at the points where they make their most distinctive claims about their relationship to God.

Van Buren and Wright turn out to be but two sides of the same coin. Each in his own way relativizes the importance of Israel for the church's ongoing life and thought. If, for instance, Israel is replaced by the church, then there is no need for Christians to listen to the contemporary witness of Judaism. Likewise, if Israel and church are traveling separate, parallel paths to God, then their callings are different enough to mitigate the significance of Israel's witness for the gentile journey. Both readings of "new covenant" serve to insulate the church's own identity and mission from any necessary engagement with the Jews. Further, both Wright and van Buren fail to acknowledge sufficiently the Christian canon's claim concerning Israel's unique, eternal covenant with God (Gen. 17:4–19; Rom. 11:26–28). Israel's place in God's economy can neither be given up (as with a replacement covenant) nor relativized (as with a parallel covenant). Put most bluntly, the biblical story reveals that the one way to God is through Israel. The exclusivity of this claim makes most moderns uncomfortable, even (sometimes especially) modern Jews. But the fact is that the logic of Christianity ought to lead us to make this claim about Israel. Jesus came to restore the Jews, to embody the promises of God to Abraham and David. Jesus came to preach good news to Israel, and by God's grace the Gentiles overheard.[9] Through the coming of the Holy Spirit, they, too, share in Israel's covenant blessing—not by displacing them or finding a separate path but by being grafted into Israel's story, for "salvation is from the Jews" (John 4:22). As we saw in Chapter 2, Israel's own traditional witness to election coheres more closely with the view of a single covenant into which the Gentiles are grafted than with a metareligious theory of many paths or many covenants.

The difficult twist in the story for Christians is that by and large the people of Israel have not recognized Christ as their redeemer. So in this time between the times there is a rupture in the one covenant. It is not, however, a rupture created by one people's replacing another; nor is it a permanent rupture between two peoples who have simply gone separate but equal ways. The church exists as part of the same story of Israel, grafted into the same covenant yet living, temporarily, in a different part of the story. Time is, in a sense, bent back on itself, and so the church represents those, as Paul has put it, "on whom the ends of the ages have come" (1 Cor. 10:11; cf. 1 Pet. 1:20). The fullness of the eschaton has not arrived, and thus the church lives between the times, or in two times at once. Israel, in contrast, lives as though the end of time has not been inaugurated in Christ. Understanding this relation of church and Israel means, in Richard Hays's words, "seeing Israel and church as pilgrim people who stand in different times, different chapters of the same story, but in identical relation to the same gracious and righteous God."[10] Given this historical situation, how might we understand the language of "new covenant" so as to emphasize both the significance of Jesus Christ for all people and God's ongoing faithfulness to Israel? How might we do justice both to the unity of God's election and to the present disunity between Christians and Jews? The challenge is to restore the language of "new covenant" to its original context in Israel's election and thus to reframe the way it is heard and used in the church.

First, we must remember that "new covenant" is Israel's own language, arising from the prophecy of Jeremiah 31:31–34:

> The days are surely coming says the Lord, when I will make a new covenant with the house of Israel and the house of Judah. It will not be like the covenant that I made with their ancestors when I took them by the hand to bring them out of the land of Egypt—a covenant which they broke, though I was their husband, says the Lord. But this is the covenant that I will make with the house of Israel after those days, says the Lord: I will put my law within them, and I will write it on their hearts; and I will be their God, and they shall be my people. No longer shall they teach one another, or say to each other, "Know the Lord," for they shall all know me, from the least of them to the greatest, says the Lord; for I will forgive their iniquity, and remember their sin no more.

It is important to note that though there is something "new" about this "new covenant," it is neither a new people nor a new content. It is rather that God "will put [his] law within them, and . . . will write it on their hearts." The people of Israel will no longer need to be taught the ways of God, for those ways will have been inscribed on their very lives. They will freely live the covenant; they will incarnate the Torah. Novak stresses, and Christians must stress as well, that "in the redeemed future, whatever 'new covenant' there would be, that future would still be for the same people of Israel, past and present."[11] In fact, this particular passage in Jeremiah is followed by one of the most powerful affirmations of God's faithfulness to Israel in all of Scripture:

> Thus says the Lord,
> who gives the sun for light by day
> and the fixed order of the moon and the stars for
> light by night,
> who stirs up the sea so that its waves roar—
> the Lord of hosts is his name:
> If this fixed order were ever to cease
> from my presence, says the Lord,
> then also the offspring of Israel would cease
> to be a nation before me forever.
> Thus says the Lord:
> If the heavens above can be measured
> and the foundations of the earth below can be explored,
> then I will reject all the offspring of Israel
> because of all they have done,
> says the Lord. (Jer. 31:35–37)

God's faithfulness to Israel is as solid as the creation itself, and God's rejection of Israel is as impossible as the measuring of the heavens. Whatever the "new covenant" is, Scripture assures us it will not mean the rejection of God's people Israel. We will do well to keep this context in mind as we analyze the way "new covenant" gets picked up in the New Testament. I focus here on its use in 2 Corinthians 3 and the book of Hebrews; in Chapter 7 I consider its use in the tradition of the Lord's Supper (Luke 22:20; 1 Cor. 11:25).

In 2 Corinthians 3:1–4:6 Paul works out an elaborate defense of his ministry in relation to Moses and the written Torah. As part of this argument, he invokes the "new covenant" language of Jeremiah 31 to contrast his ministry of the Spirit with the ministry of the letter—with which he charges his opponents (2:17; 3:1; 3:6). He writes, "Now if the ministry of death chiseled in letters on stone tablets, came in glory so that the people of Israel could not gaze at Moses' face because of the glory of his face, a glory now set aside [καταργουμένην], how much more will the ministry of the Spirit come in glory?" (3:7–8). Reflecting on this verse, Hays helpfully notes, "In 2 Cor. 3:7 Paul's formulation means that the glory reflected on Moses' face (i.e., the glory of the old covenant) . . . turns out to have been impermanent not because it dwindled away but because it has now been eclipsed by the greater glory of the ministry of the new covenant."[12] In other words, Paul's critique of the old covenant is not that it was intrinsically flawed (for this would be a critique of God's own work) but that its glory could not compare with the glory revealed in the Spirit and written on the flesh of the community (a glory foretold in Jeremiah's prophecy).

Note also that it is not the covenant that is being nullified, or set aside, but its glory. What does this mean? Paul fleshes this out a few verses later when, drawing on the story of Moses' veiling his face (Ex. 34:29–35), he writes, "To this very day, when they [the people of Israel] hear the reading of the old covenant, that same veil is still there, since only in Christ is it set aside [καταργεῖται]" (3:14). In these verses Moses the man becomes Moses the writings, the Torah. Thus what is "set aside" or "nullified" (καταργεῖται) is not the Torah or the covenant but the veil. Once the veil over the old covenant is removed, that is, once the witness of Moses can be read clearly, the radiant glory of Christ shines forth. Paul's reflections are clearly shaped by Jeremiah, as they share the vision of the new covenant "written on the heart," "incarnated" in the lives of God's people (Jer. 31:33; 2 Cor. 3:2–3). What is "new" is not the identity of the people—they are still Israel, but they are an Israel whose character (from χαράττειν, "to engrave") has been transformed.

The language of "new covenant" also appears frequently in the letter to the Hebrews (Heb. 8:8,13; 9:15; 12:24). Unlike Paul's reading of Jeremiah 31, Hebrews uses this language in a deeply supersessionistic way, lending support to a replacement view of the "new covenant." The author of the letter speaks of Jesus' bringing a "better covenant" (7:22; 8:6) and glosses Jeremiah 31, saying, "In speaking of 'a new covenant,' he has made the first one obsolete. And what is obsolete and

growing old will soon disappear" (8:13). Given such rhetoric, what is actually remarkable about this letter is what it still affirms about Israel. For instance, the author makes clear in the invocation of Jeremiah 31 that the "new covenant" is
made with "the house of Israel" and "the house of Judah" (8:8). Further, in 11:40
the point of the new covenant is not to undo the promises of God or to call into
question the faithfulness of Israel—indeed the whole chapter is a recitation of
Israel's faithfulness—but rather to proclaim that the fulfillment of God's
promises to Israel miraculously awaited the inclusion of the Gentiles (not replacement by the Gentiles). Again in 2:16–17, the writer affirms that Jesus "did
not come to help the angels but the descendants of Abraham"—his sacrifice was
for *their* sins. Even if the author of Hebrews does stress the superiority of the new
covenant and the obsolescence of the old, the recognition that this new covenant
is still a covenant with Israel (understood as "the descendants of Abraham") sets
this epistle off somewhat from the church's later supersessionistic claims.

Because 2 Corinthians and Hebrews present divergent understandings of "new
covenant," we would do well to turn to the larger New Testament witness to con-
textualize our readings of these passages. A proper interpretation of this concept
will require us to provide a narrative account of God's economy, wherein Jews
and Christians are located within the story of God's creative and eschatological
purposes. Romans 9–11 is the obvious place to turn for such an account, as this
has become the *locus classicus* for discussing the relation of nonbelieving Jews to
the Jewish and gentile followers of Christ. These chapters represent the most extensive reflection on this topic in the New Testament and thus deserve a privileged place in the conversation.

Paul's reading of God's work among both Jews and Gentiles helps us understand
the "new covenant" not as a replacement or a parallel covenant but as a living
covenant that embraces two peoples in a relationship of tense reciprocity. Paul's affirmation, "It is not as though the word of God had failed" (9:6) lies at the heart of
these chapters. Any interpretation of them needs to show how this is the case, for
the very trustworthiness of Israel's God is at stake.[13] If God would go back on God's
word, then how can the followers of Christ trust his promises? Paul begins his discussion by trying to explain why God's own people seem to be left out of God's new
work in Christ. He asserts that "not all Israelites truly belong to Israel" (9:6), and
he carries this line of argument through the next two chapters. Even among the descendants of Abraham there was an electing and rejecting—Isaac instead of
Ishmael, Jacob instead of Esau. Paul uses these examples to remind his readers that
God's election has always been a matter of God's gracious freedom. He even cites
Exodus 33:19 to this effect, "I will have mercy on whom I have mercy, and I will
have compassion on whom I will have compassion" (9:15). Paul then invokes the
language of the remnant to explain why not all of Israel believes. In chapter 10 he
argues that those among Israel who have not believed in Christ have indeed heard
but have not understood—for they are being made jealous by another nation

(10:19, citing Isa. 65:1–2). Throughout chapters 9 and 10, Paul seems to be content to argue that God has maintained faith with *some* of Israel, described as a remnant (9:27), or as the Israelites who belong to Israel (9:6). But as chapter 11 begins, he takes up the hard question, What about the others? "I ask then has God rejected his people?" (11:1). "By no means!" Paul answers. "God has not rejected his people whom he foreknew" (11:2). Just as God has maintained a remnant in the past, so now "there is a remnant chosen by grace." Paul seems to be saying that God's faithfulness to this remnant constitutes God's faithfulness to Israel as such and thus God's word has not failed. Paul describes the rest of Israel as having been hardened, having stumbled over the stumbling block (11:7–9). But, we still wonder, what about those who stumbled—were they not chosen, too? What happens to them? Paul asks the question for us, "So I ask, have they stumbled so as to fall?" (11:11). Up until this point all that Paul has said would lead us to believe the answer is yes— God has chosen some and not others just as God has done in the past; God has maintained a remnant to whom God will be faithful; those who do not believe have been hardened and have fallen outside the covenant. But Paul unequivocally rejects this reading—μὴ γένοιτο, "By no means!"

Paul's adamant negation catches us up short and alerts us that a different way of reading the story is forthcoming. Paul argues that the resistance of some in Israel to the preaching of the gospel has resulted in the word's going out to the Gentiles, so that even Israel's hardening becomes part of God's elaborate plan to ingraft the nations into Israel's covenant. Paul uses the metaphor of Israel as an olive tree— some cultivated branches have been cut off and other wild shoots (Gentiles) have been grafted on (11:17ff.). The rejection of the gospel by some in Israel (the cutting off of branches) has made room for its acceptance among the Gentiles (the ingrafting). But even those branches of Israel that have been cut off, "if they do not persist in unbelief," will be grafted back on (11:23). This sounds again like the argument in chapters 9–10—believing Israel will be saved and the rest will fall away. But this seemed to be just what Paul denied in 11:11—the unbelievers did not stumble so as to fall. Does election finally rest on God's faithfulness or on human faith? Here is the crux of the issue, and Paul seems to have wavered up to this point.

Yet in verses 25ff. Paul gives a concise summary outline of how he understands this chapter of God's story to connect with what has gone before and what will come after. He does not support the early church's answer that God's promises now belong to the Gentiles because they believed and Israel did not. Rather, Paul says,

> I want you to understand this mystery: a hardening has come upon part of Israel, until the full number of the Gentiles has come in. And so all Israel will be saved; as it is written,

> "Out of Zion will come the Deliverer;
> he will banish ungodliness from Jacob."
> "And this is my covenant with them,
> when I take away their sins."

> As regards the gospel they are enemies of God for your sake; but as regards election they are beloved, for the sake of their ancestors; for the gifts and calling of God are irrevocable. Just as you were once disobedient to God but have now received mercy because of their disobedience, so they have now been disobedient in order that, by the mercy shown to you, they too may now receive mercy. For God has imprisoned all in disobedience so that he may be merciful to all. (11:25–32)

In the mystery of God's economy, part of Israel has been hardened for the purpose that the gospel would, in a sense, bounce off of them and go forth to the Gentiles. Yet even these disbelievers, Paul tells us, are beloved of God "for the sake of their ancestors; for the gifts and calling of God are irrevocable." Paul makes clear that God's electing grace will triumph finally over even Israel's disbelief. Together with "the full number of the Gentiles," then, "all Israel will be saved." The faithfulness of God to Israel's election and the ingrafting of the Gentiles into this eternal covenant forms the eschatological hope of Romans and of the Christian faith.[14] "Welcome one another, therefore, just as Christ has welcomed you, for the glory of God. For I tell you that Christ has become a servant of the circumcised on behalf of the truth of God *in order that he might confirm the promises given to the patriarchs, and in order that the Gentiles might glorify God for his mercy*" (Rom. 15:7–9, emphasis added).

This understanding of God's economy of election is echoed in Paul's letter to the Galatians: "And the scripture, foreseeing that God would justify the Gentiles by faith, declared the gospel beforehand to Abraham, saying, 'All the Gentiles shall be blessed in you'" (Gal. 3:8). Because God's election of Abraham was unconditional, that is, not based on Abraham's righteousness (an affirmation made in both Testaments: Gal. 3:17–18 and Deut. 7:7–8, 9:6–7), and because it included the eschatological hope of gentile inclusion, Paul draws on Abraham, both here and in Romans 4, to explicate the logic of God's ingrafting the Gentiles in Israel's covenant. Paul views this ingrafting, through Christ and the Holy Spirit, as one with an overarching economy of election that began with Abraham's call.[15] Paul thus represents what Novak and Wyschogrod have called a maximalist, or apocalyptic, perspective on Israel's redemption. Both the inclusion of the Gentiles and the transformation of the Torah (a chief concern in Galatians) are characteristic of such a position. Viewing Paul in this way helps remind us that as a Jew he was trying to narrate God's work in Christ and the Holy Spirit in such a way that it would cohere with the story of Israel that had come before. In a sense we could say that Paul was seeking to produce a "canonical narrative," a story that would unify the witness of Israel's Scripture with the new thing God was doing in the church.

Yet alongside Paul's reading of the "new covenant" we cannot forget the supersessionist tendencies of other New Testament writings, such as Hebrews, Matthew, and John. How can we acknowledge these texts while also framing their witness within the larger biblical narrative? First of all, we need to be aware that each of these texts contains ambiguities in its discussion of Israel. Even Matthew's depiction of the Jewish "people as a whole" shouting "his blood be on us and on our children" (Matt. 27:25) should not be read one-dimensionally as an indictment of all Jews as "Christ killers" (as it was in the *Adversus Judaeos* tradition). Rather, if Jesus' blood is the "blood of the covenant" (Matt. 26:28), then to be covered with his blood is to be a forgiven participant in the covenant.[16] There is, then, in the cry of Israel a telling echo of Exodus 24:28, "Moses took the blood and dashed it on the people, and said, 'See the blood of the covenant that the Lord has made with you in accordance with all these words.'" Read alongside this passage, the Jewish condemnation of Jesus in Matthew becomes a paradoxical plea for *inclusion* in Christ's covenant. In John's Gospel we find a similar ambiguity. For instance, the conviction that "salvation is from the Jews" (John 4:22) stands in critical tension with the later assertion that the Jews are from the devil (8:44). If the Jews are from the devil and salvation is from God, how can salvation be from the Jews? These ambiguities invite the reader to place these passages within a wider canonical framework that would not ignore their harsh indictments but might mitigate their rejection of Israel in light of the more determinative story of God's electing grace.

Trinity and Israel

As I have suggested above, such a frame story, or canonical narrative, can be found in the economy of God's triune election, God's determination to choose and form a people in and through whom the consummation of creation would be enacted. Although one must be careful not to read Trinity, as a doctrine, back into Scripture, what can be said is that the narrative of God's election and redemption of Israel and the Gentiles reflects in its basic structure the interworking of Father, Son, and Holy Spirit. Such a reading of the canon opens the door not only to rethinking election and ecclesiology but also to rethinking Trinity. For too long, Trinity was ghettoized as an irrelevant doctrine abstracted from the actual practice of Christian faith. Catherine Mowry LaCugna notes that the split between the immanent and economic Trinity, *theologia* and *oikonomia*, theology and soteriology, began as early as the fourth century.[17] As a matter of speculation about the inner life of God, God's identity as Trinity ceased to be viewed in terms of an ongoing, historically displayed connection with God's economy of salvation and consummation. Thus in modernity Trinity came to be seen as an increasingly archaic doctrine—infamously appended to the end of Schleiermacher's *Christian Faith* because it did not bear an intrinsic connection with the Christian life. Recently, however, a chorus of voices has called for a recovery of Trinity as foundational to Christian life and discourse. Although the twentieth-century recovery of this doctrine has moved the church in the right direction, this recovery has not taken into account the parallel movement to rethink Israel's place in Christian theology.[18]

LaCugna locates the heart of God's trinitarian identity in the fundamental story of Scripture. "The basic faith of Christians," she tells us, is that "in Jesus Christ, the ineffable and invisible God saves us from sin and death; by the power of the Holy Spirit, God continues to be altogether present to us, seeking everlasting communion with all creatures."[19] LaCugna does not give an argument for this formulation; rather, she takes it as a given that this shorthand description of God's economy sums up in an uncontentious way the central and determining features of God's engagement with creation. Yet this formulation continues to assume the "standard canonical narrative," that is, the summary framework that unifies the biblical witness around creation, fall, redemption, and consummation. Insofar as contemporary trinitarian reflection has sought to bring together this standard narrative of God's economy with God's eternal being, it remains grounded in a supersessionistic posture toward Israel. And in the end a supersessionistic doctrine of the Trinity will undermine itself. As we have seen above, summarizing the Christian faith in such a way that it displaces Israel and the covenant from their central place in God's economy leaves us unsure about whether God is ultimately faithful to God's promises. The doctrine of the Trinity, however, is precisely an attempt to ensure the conviction that the very nature of God corresponds to, is faithful to, the ways in which God engages the creation. Thus, a supersessionistic account of God's economy threatens the unity of person and act for which the doctrine of the Trinity strives. If, as Karl Rahner has put it, the immanent Trinity *is* the economic Trinity, then misdescribing God's economy will mean misdescribing God's identity. It is not sufficient to confess "God is Trinity" unless we mean by this "the God of Israel is Trinity."[20] The reemergence of trinitarian theology as a practical doctrine of the church needs to take its place alongside the end of Christendom and a renewed theology of Israel as a third element to be woven into a fresh description of the church's life and story.

Jesus Christ and the Visibility of Redemption

Even if one can give an account of the inclusion of the Gentiles in the covenant that avoids supersessionism, the question of Israel still evokes a timely challenge: "Where is this redemption you say has occurred in Jesus Christ?" As we saw, the early church's answer fluctuated between, "It is in the future," "It is invisible," and "It is in Rome." And though it may not be any clearer today where to locate redemption, perhaps there is yet another answer to be found by taking a closer look at the New Testament witness. In so doing we will begin to see more clearly the trinitarian shape of election, as Christ and the Holy Spirit together trace the outlines of Israel's redemption on the body of the church.

The Gospel of Luke opens by setting Jesus firmly within the horizon of Israel's expectations for redemption. In a series of speeches, the main characters of the story alert us to the central themes that are to arise in the pages to come. The angel Gabriel speaks to Mary, "Do not be afraid, Mary, for you have found favor with God. And now, you will conceive in your womb and bear a son, and you will name him Jesus. He will be great, and will be called the Son of the Most High, and the Lord God will give to him the throne of his ancestor David. He will reign over the house of Jacob forever, and of his kingdom there will be no end" (Luke 1:30–33). Mary replies, "[God] has helped his servant Israel, in remembrance of his mercy, according to the promise he made to our ancestors, to Abraham and to his descendants forever" (Luke 1:54–55). John's father, Zechariah, prophesies, "Blessed be the Lord God of Israel, for he has looked favorably on his people and redeemed them. . . . Thus he has shown the mercy promised to our ancestors, and has remembered his holy covenant, the oath that he swore to our ancestor Abraham, to grant us that we, being rescued from the hands of our enemies, might serve him without fear, in holiness and righteousness" (Luke 1:68, 72–73). At the sight of the newborn Jesus, Simeon praises God, saying, "Master, now you are dismissing your servant in peace, according to your word; for my eyes have seen your salvation, which you have prepared in the presence of all peoples, a light for revelation to the Gentiles and for glory to your people Israel" (Luke 2:29–32). The prophet Anna "began to praise God and to speak about the child to all who were looking for the redemption of Jerusalem" (Luke 2:38). In this medley of themes from Luke 1–2, the gospel is foretold. And it turns out to be a gospel of God's faithfulness to redeem the covenant with Israel through the work of the Holy Spirit and the life of Jesus, the Son.

In Matthew's Gospel Jesus' Israel-directedness is no less apparent. The Magi announce before Herod, the ruler of the age, that Jesus comes "to shepherd [God's] people Israel" (Matt. 2:6), and Jesus tells his disciples, "Go nowhere among the Gentiles, and enter no town of the Samaritans, but go rather to the lost sheep of the house of Israel" (Matt. 10:5–6). Later Jesus informs a Canaanite woman, a Gentile, "I was sent only to the lost sheep of the house of Israel" (Matt. 15:24), though his ultimate healing of her daughter represents a foretaste of the extension of Israel's covenant to include the nations. At this point in the story, however, Jesus' focus is on the gathering of the Jews, a gathering symbolically embodied in the Twelve Disciples, representing Israel's twelve tribes.

The gathering of the Jews is only the beginning of redemption. Jesus' life and ministry also usher in the radical new world of the messianic age. In Luke 4:18–19 Jesus reads from the Isaiah scroll (61:1–2; 58:6) in the synagogue, proclaiming that the redemption of Israel is present:

> The Spirit of the Lord is upon me,
> because he has anointed me to bring good news to the poor.
> He has sent me to proclaim release to the captives
> and recovery of sight to the blind,
> to let the oppressed go free,
> to proclaim the year of the Lord's favor.

Jesus returns to his seat, scandalously adding, "Today this scripture has been fulfilled in your hearing" (4:21). Jesus' work of healing, forgiving sins, seeking out the lost, eating with the outcast, proclaiming the reign of God, and calling Israel to obedience is the visibility of redemption. Jesus so embodies the reign of God that whenever he is present "the kingdom of heaven has come near" (Matt. 3:2; 4:17; 12:28). Sent in his name, the Twelve likewise carry with them the visible presence of God's reign (Matt. 10:17).

However, it is not only in Jesus' life and ministry that redemption becomes visible and the *shalom* of Israel becomes manifest. In his death on the cross, Israel is redeemed from sin, and Jesus, the Messiah, triumphs over Israel's enemies. Paul, along with other New Testament writers, reads the cross as a sacrificial offering for redemption, indeed, the final offering, because in it sin itself is put to death (Rom. 3:24–25; cf. 8:23; 1 Cor. 1:30; Heb. 9:12). Sin can no longer hold Israel in its grip. Likewise, in the cross Jesus triumphs over Israel's enemies. Of course, the cross looks less like a triumph than a grand defeat. Colossians, however, catches up the way in which the cross is indeed the triumph of Christ not only over sin but over Israel's visible, political enemies. "When you were dead in trespasses and the uncircumcision of your flesh, God made you alive together with him, when he forgave us all our trespasses, erasing the record that stood against us with its legal demands. He set this aside, nailing it to the cross. He disarmed the rulers and authorities and made a public example of them, triumphing over them in it" (Col. 2:13–15). What is telling is the way in which redemption from sin and redemption from enemies are held so closely together. Indeed, it seems that the forgiveness of sins is exactly what disarms the rulers and authorities, since their power is based on the logic of retribution rather than forgiveness. Christ's triumph over the enemies is thus a triumph of faithfulness— loving the enemy unto the end, forgiving others, and embracing God's peace even in the face of violence. The redemption from sin that makes love of enemies possible becomes the defeat of those enemies through love.

Given this close link between the cross and redemption, it becomes clear why Paul moves from his discussion of Israel, election, and the Gentiles in Romans 9–11 to an exhortation in Romans 12 that the redeemed community be conformed to the ways of Christ—presenting their bodies as a living sacrifice, blessing those who persecute them, repaying no one evil for evil, feeding and giving drink to the enemy (Rom. 12:1–21). This is the visibility of the redeemed life, and despite the ways in which the enemy still seems all too present, the triumph is there for those who are "predestined to be conformed to the image of [God's] Son" (Rom. 8:29).

Christ's faithfulness unto death on the cross transforms the expectations of covenant obedience. This is not to say that Torah is rendered obsolete, only that the Torah is now read through the lens of the cross. The covenant transformed in Christ still calls God's people to obedience (1 Pet. 1:2; Rom. 6:16–17; 10:16; 2 Thess. 1:8), even obedience to the law or the Torah (Matt. 5:17, Rom. 3:31, Gal.

6:2, 1 Tim. 1:8), but this Torah obedience is stamped by the cross of Christ, which becomes the definitive paradigm of faithfulness. Returning to 2 Corinthians 3, we see that the community of the "new covenant" that gazes upon the unveiled Moses (Torah) sees Christ and is transformed into his image (3:18). Although this is an image of glory (3:18), it turns out also to be an image of the cross (4:7–12). Being drawn into the new covenant means being drawn into the ministry of Christ, which Paul describes in this way: "We are . . . always carrying in the body the death of Jesus, so that the life of Jesus may also be made visible in our bodies. For while we live we are always being given up to death for Jesus' sake, so that the life of Jesus may be made visible in our mortal flesh" (4:10–11). The visibility of redemption is the mark of the cross.

The Holy Spirit and the Redeemed People

Despite the ways in which Jesus made redemption visible in his life and death, these ways were so tied up with his particular presence that after the crucifixion his disciples immediately despaired that Jesus was not, after all, the one to redeem Israel. The visibility of redemption seemed to vanish with him into the tomb. As we noted above, Luke's Gospel is introduced with the expectation that Jesus will be the one to redeem Israel (Luke 1:65; 2:38). This expectation turns out to frame the entire gospel, for it is just this issue that comes up again at the end of the story as two of Christ's followers make their way to Emmaus. The resurrected Jesus wanders up to them, but they do not recognize him, and they begin to recount to him his own story. "We had hoped he was the one to redeem Israel" (24:21), they lament. Once Jesus is in the grave, redemption seems to have died as well. There is nothing tangible to carry forward. But as Jesus reveals himself to them in the breaking of the bread and then again to the eleven in Jerusalem, their hopes are raised. Certainly now he is going to bring redemption. This hope ends the Book of Luke and begins the Book of Acts, where the same question appears. "So when they had come together, they asked him, 'Lord, is this the time when you will restore the kingdom to Israel?'" (Acts 1:6). Jesus' initial reply reflects the "not yet" of Christian eschatology: "It is not for you to know the times or periods that the Father has set by his own authority" (1:7).

What happens next, however, reflects the "already" of Christian eschatology, the present reality of the reign of God. Jesus has ordered them to stay in Jerusalem, to await the coming of the power of the Holy Spirit (1:4, 8). After his ascension the disciples, in Jerusalem, choose a twelfth to replace Judas, thus symbolically reconstituting the twelve tribes Jesus had gathered (1:12–26). On Pentecost the Holy Spirit descends upon the disciples and they begin to proclaim Israel's redemption to the Jews who have gathered in Jerusalem "from every nation" (2:5). No longer divided because of language, they all hear and understand the proclamation of "God's deeds of power" (2:11). Peter quotes from the prophet Joel to interpret the outpouring of the Holy Spirit as a sign that God's redemption of Israel has arrived (2:17–21). Three thousand believe, repent, and are baptized. Peter narrates this wondrous event as a fulfillment of God's promises: "For the promise is for you, for your children, and for all who are far away, everyone whom the Lord our God calls to him" (2:39). In so doing Peter recalls both the trustworthiness of God's election ("I will establish my covenant between me and you, and your offspring after you throughout their generations"; Gen. 17:7) and the expansiveness of God's redemption ("Peace, peace, to the far and the near, says the LORD; and I will heal them"; Isa. 57:19). The community that arises from this miraculous work of the Spirit is characterized in this way: "All who believed were together and had all things in common; they would sell their possessions and goods and distribute the proceeds to all, as any had need. Day by day, as they spent much time together in the temple, they broke bread at home and ate their food with glad and generous hearts, praising God and having the goodwill of all the people. And day by day the Lord added to their number those who were being saved" (2:43–47). The redemption that was made visible in Jesus' life, ministry, death, and resurrection is now extended to the community gathered by the Holy Spirit in his name. There is still an "already" and "not yet" character to this redemption, but it is clear in Acts that God the Holy Spirit is fulfilling the hopes of Israel. Jews from every nation of the world are being gathered in Jerusalem into a community of peace and plenty, and God is preparing to graft in the Gentiles to share in the blessings. Israel's redemption is made both visible and present, not through the violent politics of empire, which would take the kingdom by force (Matt. 11:12), but through the peaceful politics of election. Such a politics is the calling of the Christian community to live in peace and love of enemies, to share the plenty of God's earth, and to witness to the unity and reconciliation between Jews and Gentiles made possible through Christ and the Holy Spirit.

After reconstituting a community of Israel that would embody the ways of redeemed life, the Spirit moves to draw the Gentiles into the elect community. It happens first when Peter visits Cornelius, a gentile God-fearer to whom he is sent by the Spirit. As Peter proclaims the story of Christ, "the Holy Spirit fell upon all who heard the word. The circumcised believers who had come with Peter were astounded that the gift of the Holy Spirit had been poured out even on the Gentiles, for they heard them speaking in tongues and extolling God. Then Peter said, 'Can anyone withhold the water for baptizing these people who have received the Holy Spirit just as we have?' So he ordered them to be baptized in the name of Jesus Christ" (Acts 10:44–48). Upon hearing this report, the church at Jerusalem, initially skeptical, "praised God, saying 'Then God has given even to the Gentiles the repentance that leads to life'" (11:18). As more Gentiles are gathered into the promises of Israel, the church finds it necessary to hold a council at Jerusalem to discuss the terms of gentile inclusion. There Peter again points to the work of the Holy Spirit, "And God, who knows the human heart, testified to them by giving them the Holy Spirit, just as he did to us" (15:8). After hearing the testimony from Peter, Barnabas, and Paul, James stands up and narrates these events into Israel's story, using the words of Amos (9:11–12). He proclaims,

> Simeon has related how God first looked favorably on the Gentiles, to take from among them a people for his name. This agrees with the words of the prophets, as it is written,
>
> > After this I will return,
> > and I will rebuild the dwelling of David, which has fallen;
> > from its ruins I will rebuild it, and I will set it up,
> > so that all other peoples may seek the Lord—
> > even all the Gentiles over whom my name has been called.
> > Thus says the Lord, who has been making these things
> > known from long ago. (15:14–18)

Through the witness of the Holy Spirit, James sees that these events reflect the eschatological ingathering of the nations into the covenant.

By attending more closely to the role of the Holy Spirit in God's work of election, covenant, and redemption, we reclaim the communal and historical dimensions of these doctrines. The gnostic redescription of election is thus held at bay and Israel's place as the elect people is once again highlighted for Christian theology. A fully trinitarian understanding of election reclaims just those communal and material aspects of Israel's life that were jettisoned in early Christian formulations. This historicizing of election also means that redemption is risked on a particular gathered community. God chooses to be present in the world not as a cosmic force or a transcendent principle but through a people. And thus God's witness in the world relies on this people. So it has always been with Israel. God could have chosen to reveal God's ways apart from Israel, apart from the lived lives of a people, apart from the risk that this people would fail in its calling. But God did not. We see, for instance, in Ezekiel 36 that Israel's sin profanes God's name and leads the nations to call God's character into question (36:20). Yet even still God does not choose to make an end run around Israel in order to be revealed in some way that would not have to rely on human participation. Rather, God decides,

> I will sanctify my great name, which has been profaned among the nations, and which you have profaned among them; and the nations shall know that I am the Lord, says the Lord God, when *through you* I display my holiness before their eyes. I will take you from the nations, and gather you from all the countries and bring you to your own land. I will sprinkle clean water upon you, and you shall be clean from all your uncleannesses, and from all your idols I will cleanse you. A new heart I will give you, and a new spirit I will put within you; and I will remove from your body the heart of stone and give you a heart of

flesh. I will put my spirit within you, and make you follow my statutes and be careful to observe my ordinances. (Ezek. 36:22–26, emphasis added)

The remarkable thing about this passage (which nicely parallels Jeremiah 31) is that God is determined to reveal God's holiness and to sanctify God's name before the nations *through Israel*. God is resolved to work through the risky means of calling and forming a people for obedience so that the world will know God and God's ways.

So likewise in Acts did God entrust the visibility of redemption to the gathered communities, upon whom the Holy Spirit had come and in whom the redeemed life of peace and plenty was being lived. But in so doing God took a risk. God chose not to make redemption self-evident apart from a people who would witness to its evidence among them. God chose to hazard redemption on those followers of Christ, Jew and Gentile, gathered and transformed by the Holy Spirit— a people more often disobedient than not, a people who have again and again belied God's redemption with violence and oppression.

The church was thus intended to be the place where the eschatological pilgrimage of the nations to Zion would begin, the place where swords were beaten into plowshares, where humankind and animals lived in harmony, where the peaceable kingdom found a beachhead. Yet as the conflict between synagogue and church turned from family rivalry to bitter persecution, as the church lost its grounding in Israel's stories and Israel's hope, as Rome tempted Christians with power and dominion, the redeemed life of peaceful communion between Jew and Gentile was lost sight of. It proved far easier to spiritualize God's reign or to abdicate responsibility to those with the power to enforce a new social order through violence.

So today if unbelieving Jews and Gentiles do not see that God's redemption in Christ through the Holy Spirit is both visible and present, it is because God's people in the church have fled from the high calling to make this redemption visible in their midst. Indeed, it is no wonder that the people of Israel still look at the church and ask, "Where is the redemption you say has come in Christ?" Over the centuries since Constantine, it is in fact arguable that the people of Israel, with their diaspora faithfulness to the politics of the covenant, have been the ones most clearly witnessing to the peaceful ordering of God's coming reign. Paul's anticipation that the church would make Israel jealous has been ironically, and at times tragically, reversed. The calling of the church today, post-Christendom and post-Holocaust, is to embody again the politics of the redeemed people of God, a politics of peace and plenty, of fellowship between Jew and Gentile.

Summing Up the Story

Given this account of the church's witness to God's triune election and redemption, we are left with the task of at least pointing toward how this story might be caught up in a summary formulation (in Soulen's terms, a "canonical narrative") that would guide us in reading the canon as a unified witness to God's economy of election. The above reading of Paul, the Gospels, and Acts showed a story of the church and Israel, covenant and redemption, in which God's triune identity is affirmed and in which Israel is neither displaced nor rendered indecisive in God's economy. This narrative substructure also rises to the surface in several other New Testament texts. What we find are numerous short formulations of God's economy of trinitarian election that could be read as protocanonical narratives (or, one might say, protocredal structures). Again, I do not mean that we find in the New Testament anything like a full-blown trinitarian doctrine or credal standard. Rather, what we find is a summary story reiterated in several New Testament passages of how Father, Son, and Holy Spirit work together toward the end of calling and sanctifying a holy people according to the cruciform image of Christ. Because this "canonical narrative" explicitly points to the interworking of Father, Son, and Holy Spirit, it suggests an economy of election that corresponds to the church's traditional claims about the trinitarian nature of God.

The blessing that opens the epistle to the Ephesians provides an excellent summation of this triune economy of election:

> Blessed be the *God and Father* of our *Lord Jesus Christ,* who has *blessed us in Christ* with every spiritual blessing in the heavenly places, just as he *chose us in Christ* before the foundation of the world to be holy and blameless before him in love. He *destined us* for adoption as his children *through Jesus Christ,* according to the good pleasure of his will, to the praise of his glorious grace that he freely bestowed on us in the Beloved. In him we have *redemption through his blood, the forgiveness of our trespasses.* . . . *[God]* has made known to us the mystery of his will, according to his good pleasure that he set forth *in Christ, as a plan* [οἰκονομίαν] *for the fullness of time, to gather up all things in him,* things in heaven and things on earth. *In Christ* we have also obtained an inheritance, having been *destined* according to the purpose of him who accomplishes all things according to his counsel and will, so that we, who were the first to set our hope on *Christ* might live for the praise of his glory. In him you also, when you had heard the word of truth, the gospel of your salvation, and had believed in him, were marked with the seal of *the promised Holy Spirit:* this is the pledge of our inheritance toward *redemption as God's own people,* to the praise of his glory. (Ephesians 1:3–14, emphasis added)

In this remarkable passage the fullness of God's plan, God's economy [οἰκονομία], is described in terms that are not only trinitarian but that make election the center of God's work in the world.[21] The Father chooses and destines a people (vv. 4–5), who are chosen in Christ (vv. 3, 10, 11, 13), who is himself chosen (v. 4) to embody the holiness of the covenant and to redeem by his blood (vv. 4, 7). The Holy Spirit seals the promise and is the foretaste, the pledge, of the coming fullness of redemption (vv. 13–14), when the Father will gather up all things in Christ (v. 10).

This blessing in chapter 1 of Ephesians leads to further reflection on the nature of God's electing work in chapter 2, which presents a stunning witness to the unity of church and Israel in God's covenant:

> So then, remember that at one time you *Gentiles by birth* . . . were . . . without Christ, being *aliens from the commonwealth of Israel,* and *strangers to the covenants of promise,* having no hope and *without God* in the world. But now *in Christ Jesus* you who once were far off have been brought near *by the blood of Christ.* For *he is our peace;* in his flesh he has made both groups into one and has *broken down the dividing wall,* that is, the hostility between us. He has abolished the law with its commandments and ordinances that he might create in himself one new humanity in place of the two, thus *making peace,* and might *reconcile both groups to God in one body through the cross,* thus putting to death that hostility through it. So he came and proclaimed *peace to you who were far off and peace to those who were near;* for *through him both of us have access in one Spirit to the Father.* So then you are *no longer strangers and aliens,* but you are *citizens with the saints* and also members of the household of God. (Ephesians 2:11–19, emphasis added)

This passage makes clear that in Christ and through the Holy Spirit, God the Father is redeeming Israel and gathering the Gentiles into the chosen people, thus making peace and inaugurating the eschatological consummation. In the first place, the image of the ingathering of the Gentiles into the people of Israel is pervasive. The Gentiles are no longer "strangers and aliens" but have been brought near to Israel; the wall of division has been broken down. As in Romans, so here there is only one covenant people, Israel. The Gentiles participate in the promises of God by being united with this people through Christ in the Holy Spirit (2:18, 22). They are thus called "fellow heirs" with Israel—not replacement heirs or heirs alone but heirs *alongside* the original heirs of the covenant. Second, the language and images are unapologetically political. Paul used the agricultural metaphor of ingrafting in Romans 11, whereas here the political image of citizenship appears. Joining with the commonwealth of Israel through Christ is to have one's citizenship changed; it is to have a new political status. Third, the ingathering of the Gentiles echoes Israel's redemptive hopes expressed in Isaiah 57:19 (and echoed in Acts 2:39)—"Peace, peace, to the far and the near, says the Lord." Finally, here as throughout the New Testament, this electing activity has a distinctly trinitarian shape. Christ Jesus, in his flesh and by his blood, has united Jews and Gentiles and reconciled both to God the Father in the unity of the Holy Spirit (2:13, 16, 18).[22]

Turning to 1 Peter, we find another epistle that is resolutely shaped both by Israel's story and by a trinitarian understanding of the electing work of God. The epistle is addressed "to the exiles of the Dispersion . . . who have been *chosen and destined by God the Father* and *sanctified by the Spirit* to be *obedient to Jesus Christ* and to be *sprinkled with his blood*" (1:2).[23] In this opening salutation the author sets forth an understanding of election that combines a trinitarian subject with an Israel-like view of the church as the chosen people.[24] One finds in this brief summary of God's work what became the classic patristic formula *a Patre ad Patrem*: Election is by the Father through the Son in the Holy Spirit. Corresponding to this, the rest of the letter presents the story of God's people as being made holy in the Spirit, through conformity to the Son, unto the reign of the Father.[25]

God the Father chooses and destines the elect (1:2, 11, 20; 2:4, 6, 9; 5:13) and thus is the source as well as the goal of the people of God. This electing activity is directed both toward the church and toward Jesus Christ, the Son. As the elected one, Christ is "destined before the foundation of the world" to be a sacrificial lamb for God's people and to open the way for Peter's gentile readers to "come to trust in God" (1:18–21).[26] Through Christ, the "chosen" living stone, the people of God have been quarried and built into "a spiritual house, to be a holy priesthood" (2:5). The Son's role in election includes embodying the model of covenant faithfulness through his own obedience in the midst of suffering. "If you endure when you do right and suffer for it, you have God's approval. For to this you have been called, because Christ also suffered for you, leaving you an example, so that you should follow in his steps" (2:20–21). Although this exhortation is directed particularly to slaves, its general applicability to the sufferings of the people is made clear later, when Peter writes, "Since therefore Christ suffered in the flesh, arm yourselves also with the same intention" (4:1; cf. 3:17–18; 4:13). Likewise, the plea for a nonviolent response to evil found in 3:9, "Do not repay evil for evil or abuse for abuse; but, on the contrary, repay with a blessing," flows out of Christ's own enactment of covenant obedience in 2:23, "When he was abused, he did not return abuse; when he suffered he did not threaten." Jesus' suffering and nonviolent response to evil gives Christian obedience (1:2) a distinctly cruciform shape. Such suffering is bearable because God's election will not fail and God's restoration of the people is sure (5:10).

Election is not only from and toward God the Father, by means of the election, sacrifice, and obedience of the Son, but it is also through the sanctifying work of the Holy Spirit (1:2). The Spirit brings the good news of God's election for salvation (1:12) and actively shapes the community in holiness. Focusing on 2:5—"like living stones, let yourselves be built into a Spiritual house, to be a holy priesthood, to offer Spiritual sacrifices acceptable to God through Jesus Christ"[27]—John Hall Elliot stresses the importance of the Spirit in God's electing work. "It is the activity of the Spirit which accounts for the inner unity of these descriptions of the believing community in v.5. And because of this sanctifying action of the Spirit the factor of holiness assumes an important position here. The elect people of God is the people whom the Spirit sanctifies on the basis of this people's faith in Jesus as the Christ. Election and holiness are correlates in the Divine economy."[28] As in Israel, election is for the sake of holiness. It is for the end of sanctifying a people for God. "I will be your God, and you will be my people" means also and always,

"You shall be holy, for I the LORD your God am holy." In 1 Peter the Holy Spirit is named as the chief actor in this fulfillment of election.

If the subject of election in 1 Peter is the triune God, then the object is just as surely the chosen people of God, understood in terms of the life and stories of Israel. Notably, the passages from Israel's Scripture that are cited or alluded to in this letter include those most central to its identity as the covenant people. In 2:9 Peter writes, "But you are a chosen race, a royal priesthood, a holy nation, God's own people, in order that you may proclaim the mighty acts of him who called you out of darkness into his marvelous light." This bold assignation alludes to and conflates several passages from Israel's Scripture that paradigmatically describe the identity of the chosen people. Most notable is Exodus 19:5–6: "Now therefore, if you obey my voice and keep my covenant, you shall be my treasured possession out of all the peoples. Indeed, the whole earth is mine, but you shall be for me a priestly kingdom and a holy nation" (cf. Mal. 3:17, Deut. 7:6; 26:18–19). Also, one hears echoes of Isaiah—"the people whom I formed for myself so that they might declare my praise" (Isa. 43:21). The church shares with Israel a primal calling and vocation to praise God through their formation as God's people. This vocation to holiness is found in 1 Peter 1:15 and is drawn directly out of Leviticus 19:2, "You shall be holy, for I the LORD your God am holy."

Election for holiness means that God's faithfulness is often displayed in God's judgment. Amos's words to Israel, "You only have I known of all the families of the earth; therefore I will punish you for all your iniquities" (Amos 3:2) are echoed in Peter's conviction that "the time has come for judgment to begin with the household of God" (4:17). Although judgment does eventually extend to all, the chosen ones of God are given priority in judgment just as they are given priority in service and grace. But as in the Old Testament, so here God's judgment works within the context of faithfulness toward the elect. Thus 1 Peter applies the promise of God's faithfulness in Hosea to the newly ingrafted Gentiles, "Once you were not a people, but now you are God's people; once you had not received mercy, but now you have received mercy" (2:10; cf. Hos. 1:9; 2:23).

Finally, the church's life, like that of the people of Israel in Babylon, is understood in 1 Peter as an existence in exile. In the salutation Christians are identified as "exiles of the Dispersion." This exilic identity is not just a statement of Christian alienation in the Roman culture (identified as "Babylon" in 5:13), but indeed it provides a lens through which to understand the nature of the life of the church until Christ's return. "Beloved," Peter writes, "I urge you as aliens and exiles to abstain from the desires of the flesh that wage war against the soul. Conduct yourselves honorably among the Gentiles, so that, though they malign you as evildoers, they may see your honorable deeds and glorify God when he comes to judge" (2:11–12). It is precisely as exiles, as aliens, that is, in their distinctive otherness, that Christians are called upon to influence the world. Though the language is not used here in 1 Peter, the image of Israel as a light to the nations is not far off. Insofar as the church participates in the election of Israel, it, too, by its unique existence shines as a witness to God's reign in the world.

Finally, 1 and 2 Thessalonians give significant examples of a formulaic testimony to trinitarian election:

> We always give *thanks to God* for all of you and mention you in our prayers, constantly remembering before our *God and Father* your work of faith and labor of love and steadfastness of hope *in our Lord Jesus Christ.* For we know, brothers and sisters beloved by God, that *he has chosen you,* because our message of the gospel came to you not in word only, but also in power and *in the Holy Spirit* and with full conviction. . . . And you became *imitators of us and of the Lord,* for in spite of persecution you received the word with *joy inspired by the Holy Spirit.* (1 Thess. 1:2–6, emphasis added)

> We must always give *thanks to God* for you, brothers and sisters, beloved by *the Lord,* because *God chose you* as the first fruits for salvation *through sanctification by the Spirit* and through belief in the truth. For this purpose he called you through our proclamation of the good news, so that you may *obtain the glory of our Lord Jesus Christ.* (2 Thess. 2:13–14, emphasis added).

Here again we have a formulaic witness to trinitarian election as a way of summarizing the canonical story. The basic structure is this: Those whom God the Father chooses are transformed by the power of the Holy Spirit in order to be conformed to the Son—both in his suffering and in his glory (which turn out to be one and the same, as in 2 Cor. 3). Frank Matera has noted the particular significance that this understanding of election and communal vocation has for the Thessalonian correspondence, and indeed Paul's entire theology:

> 1 Thessalonians—and to some extent 2 Thessalonians—provides an outstanding example of New Testament paraenesis that makes extensive use of "election theology" to encourage and console the Thessalonian community. In both letters Paul reminds the members of his congregation that they are God's elect (1 Thess. 1:4; 2 Thess. 2:13), who have been called (1 Thess. 2:12; 4:7; 5:24; 2 Thess. 1:11; 2:14) and destined (1 Thess. 3:3; 5:9) by God to live in a manner worthy of their election. Because this election theology, with its summons to sanctification, underlies Paul's ethical thought, it provides an excellent entrée to his moral teaching.[29]

All of the above passages are significant both in their attempt to tell in summary form the story of God's economy and in their surprising unanimity concerning the centrality of trinitarian election.[30] If we were to try to set forth in brief span the canonical narrative that arises from these passages, it would run something like this: God created the world for the sake of consummating the creation in a relationship of covenant. Israel is that people called first by the Father into the covenant and formed into a holy nation. Although sin and evil threaten God's plan, through the Son the people of Israel are gathered and redeemed, from their enemies and from their sin, and eschatological covenant obedience is revealed in the image of the crucified Christ. By the Holy Spirit the Gentiles are called and grafted into Israel's covenant, being united with the Jewish flesh of Jesus and conformed to his likeness. This Spirit works in and through God's people to bring about a community of peace and plenty and to direct all the creation to its good end, that is, the gathering up of all things into the covenant of Israel. This account of the economy of triune election attempts to draw out of these New Testament passages a summary canonical narrative that both witnesses to the trinitarian identity of God and retains a determinative place for Israel in God's eschatological plan.

It should not be overlooked that most of the New Testament references to trinitarian election appear in doxological contexts. It is no accident that Ephesians 1:3–14 takes the form of a Jewish blessing, "Blessed be the God and Father of our Lord Jesus Christ" or that the passages cited in 1 and 2 Thessalonians are words of thanksgiving. Nor should it surprise us that Paul ends his extended reflection on God's electing grace in Romans 11 doxologically: "O the depth of the riches and wisdom and knowledge of God! How unsearchable are his judgments and how inscrutable his ways! . . . For from him and through him and to him are all things. To him be the glory forever. Amen" (11:33, 36). Because the doctrine of election is, as Barth tells us, "the sum of the gospel," it is at its heart a witness to the gracious faithfulness of God. As such it arises out of and gives rise to thanksgiving. It recalls us to the theological axiom *lex orandi, lex credendi*—the rule of prayer is the rule of faith. Proclaiming the doctrine of election is an act of gratitude, and it returns us to praise as the only appropriate response to the triune God who has chosen to gather even us into God's own people.

6

The Freedom of Election

Identifying the church as the chosen people in and with the Jews creates the possibility of imagining political alternatives to the voluntarism and violence of modernity. Though my focus in what follows is on the church, the politics of election names a vocation largely shared by Christians and Jews. As Novak emphasizes,

> With the demise of the old characterization of Western civilization as Christendom, in either the political or the cultural sense, both Jews and Christians must ask the ancient question, "How do we sing the Lord's song in a strange land?" (Psalms 137:4). For secularity has threatened them both quite similarly. A common threat has created a new common situation. It is thus inevitable that historically perceptive Jews and Christians should be rediscovering one another. As Jakob J. Petuchowski put it so well, "Neither Jews nor Christians can really afford to be isolationists. In this pagan world of ours, we *together* are the minority 'people of God.'"[1]

Novak's reference to Psalm 137, "How do we sing the Lord's song in a strange land?" recalls the context of exile as a context of threat, a context in which Israel struggled to live faithfully on foreign soil, to embody the polity of Jerusalem in the midst of Babylon. In the present context, only as Jews and Christians learn to engage in this struggle for faithfulness together will we begin to witness to the politics of election, a politics that Christians believe has been made visible through God's redeeming work.

As I noted in the previous chapter, the New Testament witnesses to the church's life as a life of exile, "for here we have no lasting city, but we are looking for the city that is to come" (Heb. 13:14). Even more so than the Jews, who continue to live the tension between land and landlessness, Christians are a displaced people, whose calling is to scatter among the nations in mission until Christ returns (Matt. 28:19). Such dispossession not only names a certain kind of freedom, grounded in the assurance of election, but it also maps the path to peace. For without the dominion, the domain, of Christendom, the church is set free for peace, since it need no longer defend a place in order to be a people. This is a lesson learned from Israel and made possible by being ingrafted into Israel's covenant. It is also a mode of life made present and visible by communion in Christ and the indwelling of the Holy Spirit.

Gerhard Lohfink reminds us that election, being God's people, has always implied a distinct political identity in contrast to the nations: "In the Bible the people of God is always understood as a contrast-society. People of God is . . . the Israel which knows itself to be chosen and called by God in its entire existence— which includes all of its social dimension. . . . That God has chosen and sanctified this people in order to make it a contrast-society in the midst of other nations was for Jesus the self-evident background of all his actions."[2] What might it look like to be such a people today, to sing the Lord's song so that it might be heard above the cultural cacophony? To do this would require embodying election as a communal vocation and a foretaste of salvation. This is not a retreat from the world but a distinct calling in and for the world.

As we have seen, one of the underlying tensions in the modern liberal polity is the struggle between freedom and peace, for just to the extent that people are "free," understood in voluntaristic terms, their freedom threatens to encroach on the peace of the other. Such freedom leads to struggle and violence. Peace becomes the casualty of freedom. The commendable goal of modern democratic polity is its attempt to forge a middle way such that freedom and peace alike can be maintained, even if always in an unstable tension. On the one hand, the maintenance of peace comes at the cost of limiting freedom and thus countering violence with the greater threat of violence. On the other hand, the preservation of freedom comes at the cost of peace, just insofar as freedom in a liberal polity names the freedom to pursue one's interests through competition with others for scarce resources. The politics of election articulates a different kind of freedom, grounded in the assurance of God's gracious covenant, and thus it makes possible a peace that is not the containment of violence through violence but rather the inauguration of the messianic reign of Christ made visible and present through the indwelling of the Holy Spirit.

The politics of election challenges the modern construction of freedom as abstract choice and alternatively construes Christian freedom as the capacity to live faithfully. Thus, election is not a denial of freedom, as many mistakenly assume, but the basis of freedom. Christian freedom, understood as a goal of God's election of Israel, names a quality of communal and personal life resulting from faithful participation in the covenant. There is a kind of circularity here, for only by faithful participation in covenant life will one acquire freedom, which in turn creates the capacity to participate in the covenant faithfully. This, however, is not a vicious circle that has no entry but a benign circle that may be entered at any point—for freedom is both a gift and a calling, both a given and a goal.

In the context of election and covenant, freedom as the capacity to live faithfully entails the dual foci of freedom from sin and self-determination and freedom for risky engagement with the reign of God. Such an understanding of freedom is grounded in the witness of Israel and thus is accessible for Christians only as we open our ears to Jewish voices. Indeed, I suspect it is precisely these "outside" voices that can best lead Christians beyond our own long-held disagreements about freedom, election, and grace.

The Idolatry of Voluntarism

As noted in Chapter 1, freedom has long enjoyed the status of unquestioned good in the moral and political discourses of modernity. We have counted on freedom to hold together our vast differences by the slender thread of choice. We have assumed that as long as we affirm each person's freedom to choose, our differences need not divide us. Yet this thread wears thin. For some, the contemporary moral debates surrounding abortion and euthanasia have undermined their confidence that freedom alone names a moral good. For others, the pursuit of freedom has meant divorce, abandonment, and loneliness. It is simply no longer clear that maximizing options represents an undisputed good.

The triumph of choice has not only defined the parameters of moral and political discourse in the modern state, but it also has transformed the way we think about church and the Christian faith. Peter Berger describes this shift as the rise of "the heretical imperative." The multiplication of options combined with a suspicion of tradition has turned even religion into a matter of consumer preference. "There comes to be a smooth continuity between consumer choices in different areas of life—a preference for this brand of automobile, for this sexual life-style as against another, and finally a decision to settle for a particular 'religious preference.'"[3] In this way heresy (from the Greek αἵρεσις, meaning "choice" or "opinion"), is made an imperative—one not only *may* but *must* choose beliefs for oneself. The modern person is condemned to be a *bricoleur* of religion, piecing together fragments of once coherent traditions in order to construct her or his own "personal faith."[4] In modernity heresy becomes the norm rather than the exception, and freedom becomes our fate.[5]

Even God cannot escape commodification. We are told now that we must choose God as we choose a church, choose a religion, and choose a peanut butter. But to be able to choose God in this sense would mean placing oneself in a position of judging the rightness or wrongness of God's ways, the truth or falsity of God's truth. This would require, moreover, making a determination about God based on some criteria other than God, criteria that thereby would remain more determinative than God's own story. Yet this has become the typical move in modern theology, as well as in much evangelical piety. One chooses Christianity because Christian truth seems to match up with how one has already come to understand the world or because Christianity grounds the morality that one has already judged good or because following Jesus will make one's life more meaningful. To make God the object of one's decision in this way, however, is to arrogate to oneself the task of judging whether or not God lives up to some standards (truth, morality, or meaningfulness) determined on prior grounds. Bruce Marshall notes the problems with such a position:

> For many theologians, since, say, Locke, the Christian community must decide about the truth of its own most central convictions by seeing how well these comport with other beliefs (perhaps, for example, those currently dominant in this or that corner of high culture). But this seems incoherent, and therefore impossible. If a community holds true the identification of God as Father, Son, and Holy Spirit only insofar as that identification fails to conflict with some other beliefs, then those other beliefs, not the trinitarian identification, will be the ones this community is least willing to give up. Therefore that community will not, supposing our location of the church's central beliefs is correct, be church.[6]

What Marshall says of the community holds true all the more for the individual. This means, in the end, that the individual who chooses God from a position of neutrality (thus objectifying God as a commodity) retains a uniquely modern detachment from this decision, since the grounds for choosing God always stand apart from God's claim on one's life. One remains detached enough from one's own choices to undecide, to take back one's decision and try another religious, or nonreligious, option, since such determinations are fundamentally arbitrary. One's ability to persevere in the Christian life, then, depends on one's ability to maintain a certain subjective state of personal commitment and conviction.[7] Such freedom turns out to be but another name for slavery, since even our knowing and loving of God is not free from the compulsion of self-determination.

Thus arises the need for a theological response to the triumph of voluntarism. But differences among Christians have historically kept the churches from finding a united voice on this matter. From the early arguments between Augustine and Pelagius, the question of human freedom has divided Christian theology. Indeed, it has divided entire ecclesial traditions. Martin Luther's writings on the bondage of the will were opposed by the Council of Trent's affirmations of human merit and cooperation with God. The Calvinist convictions on total depravity and predestination were met by Wesleyan affirmations of free will and Christian perfection. These debates drove a wedge between the sufficiency of God's grace (always threatening to become an overpowering determinism) and the role of human freedom (always threatening to become a self-sufficient claim to righteousness). God's electing grace and human freedom were assumed to be related in an inverse ratio—as one increased, the other necessarily decreased. With the rise of modernity, the free-will camp proved unable to resist being co-opted by modern Enlightenment notions of freedom. On the other side, there was a retrenchment in which God's sovereign grace receded further and further into the darkness of the "hidden counsels" and thus receded from Christ, the Spirit, and the true freedom of the Christian life.[8]

Despite these historical differences about what Christians should affirm, there has emerged in postmodernity a broad consensus about what we should deny. We find, for instance, John Paul II arguing in *Veritatis Splendor* that "freedom itself needs to be set free."[9] The need to free freedom from its bondage to abstract individual autonomy has been an important theme throughout the pope's ministry. As early as 1964 Karol Wojtyla, then a bishop at Vatican II, "criticized the draft of the declaration on religious freedom because it did not sufficiently emphasize the connection between freedom and truth. 'For freedom on the one hand is for the sake of truth and on the other hand it cannot be perfected except by means of truth.'"[10] In *Veritatis Splendor* he affirms that any claims to freedom are illusory if this freedom does not arise from and serve the truthful law of God. He writes, "Certain currents of modern thought have gone so far as to *exalt freedom to such an extent that it becomes an absolute. . . .* The individual conscience is accorded the status of a supreme tribunal of moral judgment which hands down categorical and infallible decisions about good and evil" (32). Conceived in this way, "freedom is exalted almost to the point of idolatry" (54). Lacking any clear moral direction, modern liberal democracy teeters on the brink of totalitarianism as it reduces morality to a matter of majority opinion (101, 113).

Alongside this Catholic critique we find a similar argument from the Lutheran theologian Robert Jenson. He cites the Supreme Court ruling in *Planned Parenthood v. Casey:* "The heart of liberty is the right to define one's own concept of existence, of meaning, of the universe, and of the mystery of human life." Such liberty is supposed to "define the attributes of personhood."[11] Jenson, though, recognizes that such a definition implies the rejection of the God of Abraham, Isaac, and Jacob. "Those with any knowledge of Jewish or Islamic or Christian theology will instantly recognize this supposed liberty to define existence, meaning, the universe, and human life as the freedom these theologies ascribe uniquely to their God."[12] He adds, "The God of Abraham is . . . *a se.* That is, he is free to begin with himself, and so is free to choose also his world and his creatures and his and their meanings. *Per contra,* there could be a deity whose very function was to support us in our choices, to assuage the burden we assume when we declare ourselves *a se.*"[13] According to Jenson, it is this latter deity who has won the day once we assume ourselves free to be self-creators. Such freedom turns out to be but a new form of idolatry.

Not only do we find Catholics and Lutherans but also the Calvinists and the Wesleyans voicing a common critique. William Placher, a Reformed theologian, notes that in a liberal, capitalist society

> I am most free when I can do whatever I want. Sail to Tahiti, feed the hungry, make a fortune in the stock market, drink myself to oblivion—after all, it is my life. Society can justly require only that I not interfere with the freedom of others. But communal ideals that require self-sacrifice or a sense of vocation that somehow limits my choices—these seem unwarranted interference with freedom. I am left to do whatever I want, in a context where my very freedom guarantees that there be no right

answer as to what I should do. And then I find it odd that it should be so hard to find meaning or purpose to life.

Christian liberty is different: it is freedom *for* a life of service, and it is such because it is freedom *from* sin and the law.[14]

Although we might not find it surprising that a Reformed theologian has some suspicions about unbounded freedom, the Methodist theologian Stanley Hauerwas levels an equally strong critique. He writes, "The modern conception has made freedom the content of the moral life itself. It matters not *what* we desire, but *that* we desire. Our task is to become free, not through the acquisition of virtue, but by preventing ourselves from being determined, so that we can always keep our 'options open.' We have thus become the bureaucrats of our own history, seeking never to be held responsible for any decisions, even for those we ourselves have made."[15] This litany of voices arises from divergent traditions that have historically been at odds with one another over the issue of freedom. But a common crisis has produced a common critique in which the arbitrary freedom of modern liberalism is unmasked as slavery to the self and to the desires of the moment. Or as Paul might put it, it is slavery to the powers of sin: "I do not do the good I want, but the evil I do not want is what I do" (Rom. 7:19). It is a slavery that is all the more pernicious for being called freedom.

The tragic results of this modern idolatry of choice are highlighted in the story of Jessica Dubroff, a seven-year-old girl who died in her 1996 attempt to be the youngest pilot ever to cross the country. The tragedy is not just her death but even more so the way her parents narrated her flight and her loss. Her father, who died with her in the crash, maintained, "This is just another experience that Jess has selected for herself." One wonders in what sense a seven-year-old can be said to have the capacity to select such a course for herself. To what extent was she free from her parents' ambitions on her behalf? Her mother, after the crash, waxed philosophical, "I don't want this to mean that you hold your children down, you don't given them freedom and choice. And God, that's what her beauty was. She got to choose."[16] Choice as an empty good provides us with the ultimate deferral of responsibility, since even the tragic or the terrible can be narrated as good by virtue of being chosen.

If this is not true freedom, then what is? Despite the common theological critique, we do not find such agreement when it comes to positive theological affirmations. I would suggest, however, that Jaroslav Pelikan points us in the right direction when he traces the roots of the Augustinian-Pelagian controversy over freedom and grace to what he calls "the 'de-Judaization' of Christianity." He writes, "The course taken by the development of the Augustinian tradition has been affected by the loss of contact with Jewish thought, whose refusal to polarize the free sovereignty of God and the free will of man has frequently been labeled Pelagian. But the label is not appropriate, for Judaism has a Pelagian doctrine of nature but an Augustinian doctrine of grace."[17] If we were to follow

Pelikan's guidance and listen again to Israel's witness, we might find precisely the language we need to articulate an ecumenical alternative to the modern distortions of freedom.

The Witness of Israel: Freedom in Covenant

Israel's understanding of the covenant provides a theological description in which both the priority of God's electing grace and the human response of freedom are embraced. For Israel, God's graciousness and human freedom are not understood as a zero-sum game. The increase of one does not mean the decrease of the other. Rather, it is precisely in and through God's electing grace that Israel is made free for faithfulness. Grace and freedom are complementary, not conflicting. The closer one is bound to the grace of the covenant, the freer one becomes. The farther one flees from covenant grace, the farther into slavery one falls. Similarly, freedom and law are not separated as antitheses, since freedom grows out of covenant obedience. One might say that freedom is not doing what you want but being who you are. This is not to be confused with the empty appeal to "be yourself," since this generally means simply "doing what you want." Rather, *being* who you are is made possible by first *knowing* who you are—that is, being narrated into the story of God's election. Only after knowing who you are as a covenant partner of the God of Israel can one begin to live into this identity and thus live in freedom.[18]

Jeremiah's prophecy to an exiled Israel provides resources for rethinking freedom as a correlate of God's election. Jeremiah voices God's judgment upon a people who have taken refuge in a false and destructive autonomy:[19]

> For my people have committed two evils: they have forsaken me, the fountain of living water, and dug out cisterns for themselves, cracked cisterns that can hold no water. Is Israel a slave? Is he a homeborn servant? Why then has he become plunder? . . . Have you not brought this upon yourself by forsaking the Lord your God, while he led you in the way? . . . For long ago you broke your yoke and burst your bonds, and you said, 'I will not serve!' Yet I planted you as a choice vine, from the purest stock. How then did you turn to degenerate and become a wild vine? . . . Have I been a wilderness to Israel, or a land of thick darkness? Why then do my people say, 'We are free, we will come to you no more'? Can a girl forget her ornaments, or a bride her attire? Yet my people have forgotten me, days without number. (Jer. 2:13–14, 17, 20–21, 31–32)

In their turning away from God and the covenant, the people of Israel cry out "I will not serve!" and "We are free!" They determine to hew their own cisterns rather than rely on God's plentiful living water. The Israelites have been deceived into thinking that self-determination, freedom *from* God and the covenant, is true freedom. But God reveals to them that they have actually turned from freedom to slavery; they have been plundered like slaves; they have become like a wild vine; they have, indeed, hewn their own cisterns, but these cisterns do not hold water.

God shows them that true freedom is to bear God's yoke, to be led in God's way, and to be cultivated by God's hand. Freedom within the covenant means faithfulness to one's identity before God. Apart from God Israel does not know who it is and thus does not know what it would mean to be free. "Can a girl forget her ornaments, or a bride her attire? Yet my people have forgotten me, days without number." Israel without God is a bride without a gown. They have lost the very identifying marks that make them who they are, and to have no identity is not to be free but to be lost.

Freedom and identity for Israel are not to be found in abstraction from the life and claims of others. This is why the narratives of Exodus (Israel's liberation) and Sinai (the giving of the Torah) are interwoven in the Jewish Scripture. In God's story there is no liberation without covenant, no freedom apart from the faithful service of God, no identity apart from the common life of the chosen people. This stands in contrast to contemporary readings of the politics of Exodus and liberation, which tend to ignore the covenant at Sinai. Jon Levenson points out this confusion:

> For many people today liberation means in essence an expansion of choices: the more options you have, the freer you are. Concentration on the movement out of bondage in Egypt can leave the impression that the Torah, too, endorses the modern Western agenda of self-determination in its various forms, just as concentration on covenant, a form of contractual relationship, can leave the false impression that the Torah endorses the currently popular idea that the only obligations that persons have are those they have voluntarily assumed, there being no morality independent of human will. But . . . the biblical story of the exodus is not couched in the vocabulary of freedom at all. Rather, it serves to undergird a set of obligations to the divine sovereign, who is Israel's king, their lord in covenant, and the deity to whose service they have been dedicated and consecrated.[20]

God calls the people of Israel forth for the distinct purpose that they may serve and worship their God (Exod. 3:12; 7:16; 9:1, 13; 10:3; Lev. 25:55). Such service, however, is not the negation of freedom but its condition and completion. So the rabbinic tradition can affirm, "When Torah came into the world, freedom came into the world."[21] Freedom so understood is the capacity to live in faithfulness to the God who has created and redeemed us. Van Buren calls Christians back to Israel's witness on this point: "The logic of a Gentile theology that moves directly from the Exodus to the general statement that God is a God of the liberation of the oppressed, is too simplistic for Israel. To be freed from slavery is not in itself freedom. . . . Torah is the content of liberation. A Christian theology of the people Israel . . . is obliged to point out to the church that it has failed to listen to the witness of Israel on this matter of the substance of election. The content or substance of Israel's election is life lived according to God's Torah. That is freedom."[22] What Christians need to recover is the sense that God's sovereign and gracious election along with giving of the Torah are not threats to freedom but pathways to freedom. The law reflects God's ordering of creation toward the end of covenant life. To walk in God's ways is to walk in happiness, for blessed are those "whose delight is in the law of the Lord" (Ps. 1:1–2).

As we move from the Old Testament to the New this covenantal understanding of freedom remains intact. By affirming Israel's understanding of freedom, we do not contradict Paul's resolute conviction that the consummation of the covenant is not a *reward* for having kept the law—as if God's election were based on anything but God's gracious promise (Gal. 2:16; Deut. 7:6–9). Rather, having been claimed for this good end by God's election, the people of God are free to walk the path in faithfulness, as the path turns out to be the training necessary to participate joyfully and freely in God's coming reign (Gal. 5:13–14; 6:2).

Echoing the themes of Jeremiah, Jesus' counsel in John 8:31–32 distinguishes clearly between the liberal freedom of self-creation and the covenantal freedom created by disciplined participation in the life of Christ. "If you continue in my word, you are truly my disciples; and you will know the truth, and the truth will make you free." In modernity we have assumed that the exact opposite is true. We are taught to begin with the assumption that we are always already free. Exerting this freedom, we choose our own truth, in light of which we may decide to listen to the guidance of a like-minded individual. But Jesus' promise inverts this modern order. He tells us one must first hear his word, and not only hear it but "continue in it." The path to freedom, one sees already, is going to require perseverance. Through the training of discipleship, these followers come to know the truth, and only then can they be said to be free. Freedom is not the neutral starting point but the end goal of the journey with Christ. The beginning of this journey, as Jesus emphasizes a few chapters later, is the electing grace of God. "You did not choose me," he tells his disciples, "But I chose you. . . . I have chosen you out of the world" (John 15:16, 19). Those whom the Son has chosen have been given to him by the Father (John 17:2–24), and they will not be lost (John 17:12). "My sheep hear my voice. I know them, and they follow me. I give them eternal life, and they will never perish. No one will snatch them out of my hand. What my Father has given me is greater than all else, and no one can snatch it out of the Father's hand. The Father and I are one" (John 10:27–30). The assurance of divine election and the call to discipleship do not rob human beings of freedom; they make freedom possible.

Freedom from Sin and Self-Determination

How might we describe the nature of this covenant freedom after the coming of Christ? First of all, it is a freedom from sin and self-determination. As both Jesus and Paul remind us, freedom from sin is the most determinative liberation the Christian knows. In John 8:34 Jesus warns, "Very truly, I tell you, everyone who commits sin is a slave to sin." But as Paul assures us, in Christ those who were enslaved to sin are set free to be servants of righteousness (Rom. 6:18, 7:25). One of the most pernicious forms sin takes is the human desire for self-determination, the desire to reject God's creative work and become a self-creator—that is, to "be like God" (Gen. 3:5). Yet God's election sets one free from this mistaken drive to secure one's own life and salvation through the assertion of will. The good news declares that one's future is no longer in question, one's final goal is no longer in jeopardy. The end of the story, the coming of God's reign, does not depend on our decisions but rather on God's decision to write us into the story of grace. Our stories are no longer our own, and thus they are made safe within the covenant. Election relieves us of the heretical imperative, the burden of having to create a faith or a life ex nihilo. Only in this light can we begin to see why election was such a comforting doctrine for Calvin, why he called it "a very sweet fruit" and affirmed that "we shall never be clearly persuaded, as we ought to be, that our salvation flows from the wellspring of God's free mercy until we come to know his eternal election."[23]

The freedom of this great assurance rings out in the closing moments of the magnificent film *Babette's Feast*. Lorens Loewenhielm, once part of a small Lutheran religious community in Denmark, chooses as a young man to pursue fame and honor on the battlefield. He turns his back on the community and on the woman he loves, telling her, "I am going away forever and I shall never, never see you again. For I have learned here that life is hard and cruel and that in this world there are things that are impossible." He journeys to France and promises himself, "I will forget what happened on the Jutland coast. From now on I shall look forward not backward. I will think of nothing but my career, and, some day, I will cut a brilliant figure in the world of prestige." Loewenhielm embodies the modern assumption that freedom means self-creation through escape from any given narrative or community. Yet as he leaves, the dean of the church reminds them all, "God's paths run beyond the sea and the snowy mountain peaks where the human eye sees no tracks."

And so it is that years later Loewenhielm returns as a decorated general to share a meal, a feast, with this people on the coast of Denmark. Coming back to the place to which he had promised never to return, Loewenhielm is transformed by the feast, rich in eucharistic imagery, and stands to speak to the gathered community:

> Mercy and truth have met together. Righteousness and bliss shall kiss one another. Man, in his weakness and shortsightedness, believes he must make choices in this life. He trembles at the risks he takes. We do know fear. But no! Our choice is of no importance. There comes a time when your eyes are opened and we come to realize that mercy is infinite. We need only await it with confidence and receive it in gratitude. Mercy imposes no conditions. And, lo! Everything we have chosen has been granted to us. And everything we rejected has also been granted. Yes, we even get back what we rejected. For mercy and truth are met together and righteousness and bliss shall kiss one another.

That which he once rejected, the companionship of this community and this woman, that which he once thought impossible, he has received back.

Loewenhielm articulates for us the good news that the choices by which we give up that which we should save, the choices that determine our lives in ways that we cannot predict or control, the choices that lead us beyond the sea and snowy mountain peaks, even these God takes up and redeems. Seen in this light, his rejection of God's people recalls Peter's denial of Christ. For even as Peter's threefold renunciation could not sever him from the call and claim of God, so Loewenhielm's search for power and fame could not break the tie that bound him to God's mercy; "we even get back what we rejected." The everlasting character of God's covenant relieves one of the need to determine one's own destiny, and thus it frees one from the peculiarly modern anxiety that arises from having to be a self-creator. The covenant people is made able to risk without fear, for "mercy imposes no conditions," and human choice cannot nullify the goodness of God.

Freedom for the Risk of God's Reign

Election and covenant in Christ thus create not only a freedom from sin and self-determination but also a freedom for risky engagement with the reign of God. Jesus ushers in the messianic age and thereby frees his followers to risk boldly in the service of God's kingdom. He invites his disciples to "consider the lilies of the field, how they grow; they neither toil nor spin, yet I tell you even Solomon in all his glory was not clothed like one of these. . . . Therefore do not worry, saying 'What will we eat?' or 'What will we drink?' or 'What will we wear?' For it is the Gentiles who strive for all these things. . . . But strive first for the kingdom of God and his righteousness, and all these things will be given to you as well" (Matt. 6:28–33). Just insofar as God's people are *free from* the need to ensure their own well-being, they are set *free for* the single-minded pursuit of God's reign. Worrying about what to eat and drink and wear is to live like the Gentiles, those who do not know themselves chosen and thus safe in God's future.

Within the context of covenant life, Christians are free to release control of our destiny, and thus space is opened for risky engagements—for throwing in our lot with the poor and the outcast, for befriending the sinner. Jesus embodied such risky freedom in his own life and ministry, placing himself in the rejected margins where human existence was most fragile. His command in the Sermon on the Mount, "Give to everyone who begs from you, and do not refuse anyone who wants to borrow from you," can be lived seriously only if one has been freed from the need to secure one's own life.

This kind of freedom for risk can be seen in the work and witness of Dorothy Day and the Catholic Worker Movement. Through her ministry of serving the poor in New York City, Day came to learn that the precariousness of voluntary poverty creates a kind of freedom through dispossession. As she puts it, "Giving liberates the individual not only spiritually but materially. For, in a world [of] enslavement through installment buying and mortgages, the only way to live in any true security is to live so close to the bottom that when you fall you do not have far to drop."[24] The conviction that sustained her was not just that rock bottom wasn't far off but that God's promises to secure our lives are trustworthy. "If we do give in this way, then the increase comes. There will be enough. Somehow we will survive. . . . At the same time we must often be settling down happily to the cornmeal cakes, the last bit of food in the house, before the miracle of increase comes about."[25] Jesus' call to live in service of the "least of these" rests on the assurance that our lives are secured already in God's election.

God's covenant fidelity frees us for other risky engagements as well, such as lifelong commitments to marriage and holy orders. Such commitments can be sustained only if they are viewed within a larger story that relieves them of their arbitrariness. Otherwise they risk being reduced to the level of all other choices, made and unmade at will. What is widely lacking today is any coherent account of life that raises these commitments above the continuous flux of personal preference. Without such an account, one can only fear a lifelong commitment, since there is no assurance that such a decision will not ruin one's life. God's faithfulness allows us to risk these lifelong commitments precisely because their success does not rest solely on our capacity to make things work out rightly. Rather, it rests on the assurance that our lives are caught up in God's covenant, by which our covenants are sustained and our failings are redeemed.

The freedom to risk living God's reign includes also the freedom to embrace the law as God's gift. Again here is a place where Christians can learn from the witness of Israel. God's law need not be antithetical to freedom. In fact, the command of God is but the form given to the grace of election. Yet as the apostle Paul warns us, openness to God's law is risky because it creates the possibility for both self-righteousness and despotic enforcement. C. S. Lewis attempts to understand and Christianly embrace the Jewish delight in the law as he reflects on Psalm 119. "It may be the delight in Order, the pleasure in getting a thing 'just so'—as in dancing a minuet," he writes. "The Order of the Divine mind, embodied in the Divine Law, is beautiful. What should a man do but try to reproduce it, so far as possible, in his daily life? . . . This is not priggery nor even scrupulosity; it is the language of a man ravished by a moral beauty. If we cannot at all share his experience, we shall be the losers."[26] Just as the beauty of a dance requires training and precision, so the life lived in faithfulness to God's covenant requires guiding one's steps according to the path laid out by God's gracious command. Learning such steps proves to be the path to freedom, not its hindrance, for the dance so learned opens to door to unlimited improvisation. Freedom, Christianly understood, requires training in the steps of faith, apprenticeship in the movements of charity. The unfree person is the one unable to move to the music of creation in harmonious partnership with others. To shift metaphors, delight in the law is "a delight in having touched firmness; like the pedestrian's delight in feeling the hard road beneath his feet after a false short cut has long entangled him in muddy fields."[27] The command of God is the map that directs God's people on the joyous journey toward the consummation of the covenant. The risks of the journey are made bearable by the assurance of God's electing grace.

In the liturgy Christians remind themselves again and again of this incongruous unity of service and freedom, of law and grace. We pray, for instance,

> Help us so to know you
> that we may truly love you,
> so to love you
> that we may fully serve you,
> whose service is perfect freedom.[28]

And we sing hymns such as:

> Make me a captive, Lord, and then I shall be free
> Force me to render up my sword, and I shall conqueror be
> ...
> My will is not my own till Thou hast made it Thine
> If it would reach a monarch's throne, it must its crown resign.[29]

The affirmation that God's service is freedom appears paradoxical, but this is so only insofar as we have accepted the myth that freedom means autonomous self-rule. If in fact freedom is the ability to be faithful to covenant identity, the power to be who one truly is, then such language simply represents the peculiar speech necessary to sustain Christians in their risky witness to God's reign.

This freedom to risk living with and for others without the fear of losing the self mirrors the very identity of God in triune relation. God's life is not a life detached from others, and thus God's freedom is not an abstract freedom of arbitrary will. Rather, it is the freedom of the triune God to live in a communion of love and to share that love by risking a relationship with the creature. Barth points to the way in which God's trinitarian life of covenant models a life of attachment and thus a freedom that is not aloof isolation or self-assertion but rather faithfulness to one's true identity in covenant relationship:

> God's freedom is not merely unlimited possibility or formal majesty and omnipotence, that is to say empty, naked sovereignty. Nor is this true of the God-given freedom of man. If we so misinterpret human freedom, it irreconcilably clashes with divine freedom and becomes the false freedom of sin, reducing man to a prisoner. . . . In God's own freedom there is encounter and communion. . . . God's freedom is the freedom of the Father and the Son in the unity of the Spirit. Again, man's freedom is a far cry from the self-assertion of one or many solitary individuals. It has nothing to do with division and disorder. God's own freedom is trinitarian, embracing grace, thankfulness, and peace. . . . God's freedom is essentially not freedom *from*, but freedom *to* and *for*.[30]

Human identity and freedom, as God's gracious gifts to and through the elect community, imitate the divine dance of God's trinitarian indwelling. It is a freedom for life in communion with God and God's people. It is a substantive freedom that names the formation of a body in correspondence to the Christ-shaped Torah. It is not a freedom *from* others, as modern individualistic accounts would have it, but is a freedom *with* others. Thus, one is free just to the extent that one belongs to God and thus to God's people.

In answer to those who would say that free will requires the possibility of sinning, St. Augustine appeals to the eschatological goal of human life. "Now the fact that they will be unable to delight in sin [in the City of God] does not entail that they will have no free will. In fact, the will will be the freer in that it is freed from a delight in sin and immovably fixed in a delight in not sinning. The first freedom of will, given to man when he was created upright at the beginning, was an ability not to sin, combined with the possibility of not sinning. But this last freedom will be more potent, for it will bring the impossibility of sinning; yet this also will be the result of God's gift, not of some inherent quality of nature."[31] The telos of freedom is not to have the choice of sin or faithfulness eternally set before one but rather to be freed from such a choice and for eternal faithfulness to one's covenant identity. Some might retort that this really does not sound like freedom at all, since it excludes the possibility of choosing to be *un*faithful. But Augustine quickly retorts, "Certainly God himself cannot sin; are we therefore to say that God has no free will?"[32] God is supremely free, so the fact that God cannot sin only serves to show that sin is not a necessary component of freedom but rather is antithetical to it. Augustine even argues that in God's reign freedom will no longer be considered an individual possession but will be shared communally. "In the Heavenly City then, there will be freedom of will. It will be one and the same freedom in all, and indivisible in the separate individuals."[33] All will participate in the same freedom because all will participate in God's freedom of eternal charity.

The Witness of Baptism

How might Christians recover this understanding of freedom and resist the modern idolatry of choice? One way is to draw on the liturgical rites and practices that inscribe covenant freedom upon our lives, for instance, the sacrament of baptism. This sacrament functions as a crucial moral and political practice, as it is here that the redefining of freedom within a communal identity is paradigmatically enacted. It is not a coincidence that the politically charged affirmation "Jesus is Lord!" (Rom. 10:9) most likely began as a baptismal confession.[34] Baptism is a social, and thus political, reorientation of identity. As the initiation into covenant membership, baptism parallels circumcision, with the obvious though notable difference that it is a ritual of inclusion for both men and women. Thus, the author of Colossians can write, "In [Christ] also you were circumcised with a spiritual circumcision, by putting off the body of the flesh in the circumcision of Christ; when you were buried with him in Baptism, you were also raised with him through faith in the power of God, who raised him from the dead" (Col. 2:11–12). The passive voice in these verses highlights that baptism is God's action on our behalf, calling us and grafting us into the covenant. As one baptismal service affirms: "In baptism God claims us, and seals us to show that we belong to God. God frees us from sin and death, uniting us with Jesus Christ in his death and resurrection. By water and the Holy Spirit, we are made members of the church, the body of Christ, and are joined to Christ's ministry of love, peace, and justice."[35] These words emphasize the deep connection between God's electing claim on our lives and the resulting freedom in Christ. Baptism challenges any understanding of freedom as detachment from God or others, since the freedom of baptism at once unites us with Christ, makes us members of the church, and sends us on a mission to the world. Baptism enacts the freedom from sin and death and the freedom for a risky life in the ministry of love, peace, and justice.

Baptism makes clear both the priority of God's election and the necessity of human response. "Through baptism we enter the covenant God has established. Within this covenant God gives us new life, guards us from evil, and nurtures us in love. In embracing the covenant we choose whom we will serve, by turning from evil and turning to Christ."[36] And so the question is asked, "As God embraces you with the covenant, I ask you to reject sin, to profess your faith in Christ Jesus, and to confess the faith of the church, the faith in which we baptize."[37] The covenant that God has established arches over the twin movements of embracing—the candidates embrace the covenant in an act of freedom that is itself made possible because they have already been embraced by God's freedom. The interworking of God's action and human action here is reminiscent of Paul's exhortation, "Work out your own salvation with fear and trembling, for it is God who is at work in you, enabling you both to will and to work for his good pleasure" (Phil. 2:12–13). The prior embrace of God's covenant enables us to renounce evil and turn to God. The conviction that this is indeed made possible in baptism was the root of Luther's memorable refrain in times of temptation. "I have been baptized!" he would shout at the devil, hurling his inkwell against the wall. In this declaration he was naming the truth that because God had claimed him for the covenant, the powers of sin could neither claim him nor terrorize him any longer.

The practice of baptizing infants, for all its history of complicity in the church's Constantinian captivity, nonetheless stands as a particularly vivid witness to the fact that God's electing grace precedes and makes possible any human freedom to live in the covenant. It reminds us that we do not begin life as individuals with something called free will; rather, we begin life as those called into covenant with God, and thus along with the whole covenant people (Israel and church) we are set on a path that will lead to true freedom in faithfulness.

Freedom in Death: Martyrdom Versus Euthanasia

The deep differences between liberal freedom (choice) and covenant freedom (faithfulness) are highlighted when we confront death, for death is the enemy that seems to portend the final defeat of freedom. Here the questions are posed in all their starkness. How can freedom be maintained when one's own abilities cannot alter the inevitable end? What might it look like to die in freedom?

For a liberalism in which freedom equals choice, a free death can mean only a chosen death. When human fulfillment is understood as autonomy, suffering becomes the great evil that conquers the will and plunders the self. Suffering, through illness or oppression, brings about just that enforced passivity that is the defeat of all one's self-assertion. In such a situation, courage requires finding a way to assert one's freedom, even if the only way to do this is through taking one's own life. Such an act becomes a desperate attempt at defiance in which one ironically protects one's self by killing oneself. One robs the forces of death only by becoming their partner.

It is not surprising, then, that the current debate about physician-assisted suicide is couched in the language of freedom and rights. Indeed, for some, the ability to end one's life is the ultimate act of personal autonomy. Echoing John Locke's conviction that one's self is one's most basic piece of property,[38] the columnist Walter Williams has argued for the right to die precisely because, as he puts it, "I cherish private property rights." He imagines the Supreme Court's taking up the case of his own right to die:

> First, the Court should determine just who owns Williams. The evidence will show that while some of my ancestors were owned, my mother and father were not. Since Williams has attained 21 years of age, it would seem that he owns himself.
>
> That finding of self-ownership would make the Court's task easy. Their 9–0 decision would read: Though the thought of Williams ending his precious life is distasteful and while the loss of his insightful weekly columns will be a great loss to society, nonetheless, we find he owns himself and has the right to dispose of his life in any manner consistent with the safety of others.[39]

The ultimate ability to secure one's self against external threat turns out to be the ability to bring about one's own death.

One of the significant contributions of *Veritatis Splendor* is its description of true freedom as self-giving love and thus of martyrdom as an act of pure freedom. Following John Paul's lead, we may juxtapose martyrdom with euthanasia as alternative paradigms of dying in freedom. "Jesus . . . is the living, personal summation of perfect freedom in total obedience to the will of God. His crucified flesh fully reveals the unbreakable bond between freedom and truth, just as his Resurrection from the dead is the supreme exaltation of the fruitfulness and saving power of a freedom lived out in truth" (87). As an act of pure self-giving in conformity to Christ, martyrdom reflects the freedom to remain faithful to

God's law and truth even in the face of the darkest coercion and violence (87, 90–93). Freedom names a substantive capacity for faithfulness rather than an empty capacity for choice. The freedom to be faithful in the face of death stands in sharp contrast to the freedom to choose death. Martyrdom is not an act of choice and should never be sought, for this would be both to will the sin of another and to think too little of one's own life. However, as the possible tragic result of faithfulness, it is a witness to the irrevocability of true Christian freedom, which cannot be taken away, even by the power of the sword.

This account of freedom as displayed in martyrdom shares certain features in common with Stanley Hauerwas and Charles Pinches's account of courage. They note that in contrast to the tradition of civic courage, in which courage is paradigmatically displayed by the soldier in war (found in Aristotle, Machiavelli, Jean-Jacques Rousseau, and contemporary America), Aquinas provides an account of Christian courage that is paradigmatically displayed in martyrdom.[40] They write,

> The good that life is for, and therefore the good for which it can be courageously sacrificed, is not for Aquinas the common good of the nation but rather friendship with God. This good, interestingly, is beyond the power of human beings to effect; they must learn to accept it as a gift. Yet this is also the source of their strength, for they trust that God will bring to completion the work He has begun in them even in the face of death itself.
>
> It follows that *Christians are freed from the anxiety of having to secure the meaning of their lives in the mode of their death.* . . . The martyr's acceptance of her death as a continuing part of her service to God demonstrates how fortitude can infuse our lives and remain even as we die in our weakness. Martyrs, in effect, have to be ready to lose to their persecutors, dying ingloriously. They can do so only because they recognize that neither their life not their death carries its own (or anyone else's) weight of meaning; rather that is carried by the God who supplies it.[41]

That Pinches and Hauerwas associate such courage with a certain kind of freedom is not accidental. For courage is but a way of naming the freedom to be faithful in the face of danger. I would suggest, however, that increasingly in American society the paradigmatic instance of courage, and thus of freedom, is, tragically, not the glory of the battlefield but the despair of the deathbed. Physician-assisted suicide represents in a liberal polity that act which fundamentally expresses both the autonomy and the isolation of the individual. Our elderly have begun to see it as both their duty and their right to remain independent as they age. They fear being a burden on family, friends, church, or society. Having lived in such a way that their lives are not dependent on others, they seek to die that way as well— both for their own good, since they have come to believe that such independence is dignity, and also for the good of others, whose time and resources they believe they have no right to claim. Suicide comes to be seen as an act of courage because it affirms one's own autonomy while relieving others of the burden of one's dependency. Sadly, such courage is made both necessary and intelligible by a society that gives people no greater good to hope for than that even their own deaths will be self-determined.

What, then, of the Christian who dies not the death of a martyr but the unheralded death of old age, heart failure, cancer, Alzheimer's, or accident? For most of us, this is the death we are given, neither glorious nor treacherous but perhaps all the more difficult for being commonplace. I would suggest that the freedom of the martyr is but a paradigm of the freedom every Christian possesses in the face of death, and as such every Christian death can be the death of a witness ("martyr" comes from the Greek μαρτυρέω, "to bear witness"). Freedom in covenant with God and God's people is a freedom in the face of death, precisely because such communion cannot be destroyed by death ("I believe in the communion of saints, the forgiveness of sins, the resurrection of the body, and the life everlasting"). Christians need not fear that suffering will defeat the self, since one's self is determined not by the ability to make a willful choice but by God's promise to take one's story up into the story of God's people and thus protect it through all the unexpected turns of life. This is not to say Christians will not suffer but that in the face of suffering and even death, when our own powers are diminished or gone, our freedom is not lost. We are free to remain faithful to the covenant because the God of the covenant remains faithful to us.

7

The Peace of Election

The rise of liberal democratic polities, based on maximizing the free choices of individuals, has produced societies that are battlegrounds of private and group interests. Nation-states have come to function as giant interest groups, turning international politics into a constant struggle to secure national advantage. In the twentieth century alone, from the Marne to the Holocaust to the dropping of the atomic bomb, warfare has escalated beyond what could have been imagined just a hundred years ago. As Anthony Giddens has noted, "The combined spread of industrialism and of the nation-state system has served to ensure that virtually every state across the globe now possesses armed strength far in excess of that of any traditional empire."[1] Violence seems to be pervasive, and many simply accept it as a necessary part of world politics. Peace is sustained, at best if at all, by a global balance of threat and power.

As we saw in Chapter 1, the political model of the polis is no less buttressed by force and struggle. The citizen of the polis strives within himself to rule his unruly passions by the power of reason. The citizens struggle against one another for the honor and resources necessary to become self-sufficient men of virtue.[2] The polis as a whole guards its borders tightly against the threat of the barbarians. Like the nation-state, the polis fundamentally presupposes conflict.

Election and Violence

Where is the alternative by which the violence of the nation-state and the polis alike are called into question? Where is the story, where is the community, in which peace is more than just the violent restraint of violence? For many, an appeal to election is immediately suspect on this count, since it often seems to be nothing more than a justification for the arrogant oppression of the outsider. It is true that the claim to have a special calling from God can easily be translated into denigration of the nonelect. This, in turn, can breed violence and hatred. There is no doubt that many Palestinians today interpret Israel's claims to election in this way. So, too, must many Native Americans have heard the United States' rhetoric of "Manifest Destiny" in the nineteenth century. The history of

135

using election to justify empire building and violence toward the enemy is dark and tragic. But the proper response to this history is not to ignore election, for this would be to acquiesce in its abuse, but to recover the doctrine as a call to the people of God to witness to the ways of peaceful blessing.

The first assumption that must be challenged is that the election of God's people necessitates the creation of an opposing category of the "rejected." As we saw in Chapter 2, Jewish understandings of election have not been grounded on this dualism to the same extent as Christian accounts have. If God's election of Israel had the Gentiles in its purview from the beginning, and if the telos of election is "to gather up *all things* in [Christ], things in heaven and things on earth" (Eph. 1:10, emphasis added), then there is no group that is a priori excluded from the covenant. Indeed, we cannot set any limits on the extent of God's ingathering of the creation. We might even say that the logic of the trinitarian economy of election points toward a full inclusion of all creation in God's eschatological reign. However, we dare not become presumptuous with God's grace, claiming election as our due rather than receiving it as a gift.[3] Understood as an open-ended calling and gathering, election need not, indeed cannot, serve to divide people into opposite camps of the elect and the reprobate.

Diaspora Identity

Daniel Boyarin has struggled with the challenge of how to construct and sustain particularist identities "without falling into ethnocentrism or racism of one kind or another."[4] How can one make a claim like election without turning such a claim into a justification for domination? Or again, how can a community maintain its distinctiveness while also maintaining a wider vision that would include concern for the other? If universalism might tend toward coercion, particularism might tend toward indifference. Boyarin argues that both the reign of Christendom and to a lesser extent the current practices of the modern Jewish state wed the worst features of particularism and universalism. "The most pernicious aspects of both of these hermeneutic systems are in an unholy alliance with each other, so that ethnic/racial superiority has been conjoined with spatial, political domination and the constraint towards conformity in the discourse of nationalism and self-determination. For five hundred years we have seen the effects of such a conjunction in the practices of Christian Europe, and now we see its effects *mutatis mutandis* in many of the practices of the Jewish state."[5] Boyarin identifies precisely the concern that many have when they hear talk about election. How can a people who claim to be genealogically (in the case of the Jews) or ecclesiologically (in the case of Christians) set apart not become racially or religiously oppressive toward the outsider? How can election avoid becoming another appeal to *Blut und Boden*, blood and land?

Boyarin suggests the answer lies precisely in the social situation in which the particularist claim is made. If, on the one hand, it is made by those who wield power, it serves to consolidate and justify their domination. If, on the other hand, this claim is made by subordinate groups, minority voices, it becomes a form of resistance and an embodied alternative to the dominant forces.[6] "In order, then, to preserve the positive ethical, political value of Jewish genealogy as a mode of identity, Jews must preserve their subaltern status."[7] As an example of how political dominion entirely transforms the meaning of communal practices, Boyarin notes that the legitimate diaspora concern "for the feeding and housing of Jews and not 'others'" becomes in today's Israel "a monstrosity, whereby an egregiously disproportionate portion of the resources of the State of Israel is devoted to the welfare of only one segment of the population."[8]

Boyarin calls attention to the fact that the Jewish Bible preserves two primary discourses of Jewish identity, one that ties it to the land and another that ties it to the body. The first trajectory suggests that Jewish identity has to do with being a people indigenous to a certain place that defines them. The second trajectory locates Jewish identity not in the land but in Jewish flesh. Boyarin urges Jews (and, by analogy, Christians) to foreground the prophetic voice of exile and no-madic (bodily) identity. As noted in Chapter 2, it is significant that the Jews have preserved the stories of a time when someone else dwelt in their land. In fact, the biblical account of Abraham's election mitigates against making the land the de-termining factor in Jewish identity. Israel was a people before it had land, and thus the Jews have been able to sustain their identity in diaspora. The rabbinic con-struction of Jewish identity in diaspora not only responded to but—and here Boyarin challenges the tradition—*required* dispossession of the land, "because in an unredeemed world, temporal dominion and ethnic particularity are . . . im-possibly compromised."[9] It is bodies and not land that provides the material bond of Jewish identity. Diaspora, then, becomes the necessary correlate of a strong cul-tural and genealogical identity, if such an identity is going to avoid coercion or contempt of the other.

Isaac Bashevis Singer echoed the significance of diaspora peace for Judaism when, upon receiving the Nobel Prize for literature in 1977, he responded, "The high honor bestowed upon me by the Swedish Academy is also a recognition of the Yiddish language—a language of exile, without a land, without frontiers, not supported by any government; a language which possesses no words for weapons, ammunition, military exercises, war tactics; a language that was despised by both gentiles and emancipated Jews."[10] The Jews, by virtue of their election and thus their ability to sustain peoplehood in diaspora, have been a remarkable witness to the peaceful sustaining of a visible community apart from weapons and war.

Whether or not Boyarin's position finds support among Jews, it remains quite instructive for Christians. Seeking to reclaim a strong ecclesial identity in the post-Christendom world, Christians must attend to his reminder that the politics of election is not a politics of domination or power (the Christendom model) but a politics of dispossession in exile, awaiting (while embodying) the coming reign of God. Indeed, this is more determinatively so for Christians than for Jews, since the Christian calling is not to gather in Jerusalem but to scatter into the world and "make disciples of all nations" (Matt. 28:19). In this time between the times, the need is not to reclaim the political clout and territorial focus of the Christendom partnership but to emphasize the bodily material unity by which Christians embody the politics of the messianic age through a nomadic dispersion of witness.

Messianic Peace

There are other distinct differences as well in the ways Jews and Christians think about peace, politics, and identity. The most basic is that Christians believe Christ has ushered in the messianic age. This claim has deep political and communal implications that distinguish Christian readings of our present political possibilities from Jewish ones. Read through the stories of Jesus, messianic peace can be understood as the telos of a narrative that begins with God's decision to bring forth from Sarah's womb a new kind of people. This people would be defined not by their opposition and struggle with the nations but by their calling to bless the nations. The eschatological horizon of this election was the vision of the peaceful reign of God. But in the time following these early promises, the people of Israel were enslaved in Egypt, did battle with the Canaanites, were overthrown by the Assyrians, and faced exile in Babylon. Ten tribes were "lost" and the remaining tribes of Judah and Benjamin were dispersed. Each time the promise seemed near fulfillment, another threat arose. Though traditionally Jews have believed God's peaceful redemption to lie somewhere in an unknown future, their present covenantal life was to represent a foretaste of that coming reign of God. This is not to say that for the Jews the messianic kingdom will be a mere extension of covenant existence. As we saw in Chapter 2, both Novak and Wyschogrod agree that Israel's redemption will be in certain ways discontinuous with present reality. Wyschogrod, though, does believe that the chosen people, insofar as they walk in the ways of Torah, have begun already in a limited way to embody God's redemption. That war between Jews remains unthinkable is a sign that "the messianic vision of the abolition of war is already realized in the community of Israel."[11] For Novak, in contrast, the absence of redemption means that in the present time "our testimony to the nations of the world is not positive but negative."[12] Israel can only witness to the unredeemed character of the world, and thus, for Novak, the fundamental political stance of the elect people should be a rejection of utopian pseudomessianism in favor of a political realism that understands that often all we can do is the lesser evil.[13]

For its part, the church claims that the redemption of Israel and the world has been inaugurated in Jesus Christ and the Holy Spirit. This creates for the church a political calling that is neither utopian nor realist.[14] Although for Israel there remains a theological rationale for the "realistic" politics of an unredeemed world, for the church the vocation to unbounded messianic peace has arrived in

Christ's redemption. Michael Goldberg states this difference bluntly: "While pacifism is a Christian virtue, it is not a Jewish one. Self-defense is."[15] Such a conviction must be heard over against the equally true assertion, "While Judaism is not a pacifist religion, it has, nonetheless, a significant nonviolent strain within it, one so constant that no understanding of Judaism is possible without it."[16] The theologic of pacifism is not as clearly defined for Jews as for Christians, since only the church claims that the Jewish messianic peace has been made present through the Holy Spirit in its midst.

Eucharist and Peace

If the church is the place where Christ has established his reign of messianic peace, then where is it? We seem to be back again to the Jewish challenge: "Where is this redemption you say has occurred in Jesus Christ?" The church of Christendom, the church of place and dominion, certainly did not carry forward this witness in any clear way (though this is not to deny that there have been many powerful Christian witnesses to peace, especially the martyrs). Nonetheless, in this time between the times, when even the church awaits the fullness of peace at Christ's return, the Christian embodiment of the messianic reign is enabled and sustained by the practice of the Eucharist.

As we saw in Chapter 5, the story of the "new covenant" is the story of the extension of the covenant to the Gentiles and the embodying of redemption in cruciform obedience. But "new covenant" is not just a story; it is a people sacramentally gathered at the Lord's table.[17] It is propitious that the language of "new covenant" has remained central to the churches' eucharistic celebrations. In Luke's narrative of the Last Supper, Jesus takes "the cup after supper, saying 'This cup that is poured out for you is the new covenant in my blood'" (Luke 22:20). Luke's is the only one of the synoptic Gospels that includes the "new" (though textual variants, perhaps reflecting the language of early eucharistic practice, include it in both Matt. 26:28 and Mark 14:24), but it is this version that is picked up in the liturgy of the early church as attested in Paul: "In the same way he took the cup also, after supper, saying 'This cup is the new covenant in my blood. Do this, as often as you drink it, in remembrance of me'" (1 Cor. 11:25).

It is here at the Lord's table that the central themes of "new covenant" are brought together. First, the eucharistic celebration is a remembrance of the Passover. It is thereby an act that continues to remind the church of its deep connection with Israel and the Jewish story. Second, in the Eucharist Christians are trained to resist the temptation to read election through a gnostic lens, for here the emphasis is not on the individual but on the community, not on some spiritual escape but on our fleshly life together, not on a dualism between the elect and the rejected but on a community sent into the world in peace. Third, with the eating of Christ's body and blood, this new covenant is quite literally enfleshed. Just as Jeremiah envisioned a time when the Torah would become part of the very flesh of the Jews, so in the Eucharist the one who embodies cruciform Torah obedience becomes part of the flesh of Jew and Gentile alike. Or rather, their flesh becomes part of his. As Augustine and Aquinas have taught us, eucharistic food is not consumed by the body, but rather it consumes the body.[18] Eucharist thereby becomes the place where God's corporeal election of Israel is extended to the Gentiles. For the Gentiles are united in the Lord's Supper to the flesh of the Jewish Jesus. By participating in Christ through Eucharist, they are made to participate in the covenant God made with Jewish flesh. The celebration of the Lord's Supper is thus made scandalous because not only are Gentiles eating with Jews, they are eating a Jew. And as his body consumes theirs, they are grafted into Israel, not just spiritually but by having their own bodies transformed into Jewish flesh. This practice makes visible the new life of the covenant, and so it is here, if anywhere, that the practice of peace can be nurtured and sustained even in the face of the church's resistance to its calling. It is here that even when the church is fragmented by violence, the Messiah is present in the flesh to call the people to peace in the redemption of the Holy Spirit.

If we turn our attention back to the story of Jesus and his disciples at the end of Luke and the beginning of Acts, we remember that the disciples were intently questioning Jesus about the coming redemption. They did not yet see Israel's redemption, and thus they were unsure if Jesus was really the Messiah. Significantly, each time the disciples ask Jesus, "Where is the redemption of Israel?" he reveals it to them to the breaking of the bread. In the first instance he reveals *himself* as Israel's redemption at the table on the road to Emmaus ("their eyes were opened," Luke 24:31); in the second it is revealed to them by the Spirit who gathers them into a community of peace and plenty through the breaking of bread and sharing of possessions (Acts 2:46). Acts 1–2, therefore, holds together as a unit, beginning with the disciples' question, "Lord, is this the time when you will restore the kingdom to Israel?" (1:6) and ending with the description of the gathered and redeemed people of God (2:37–47). Somehow in "the breaking of the bread" the redeemed ways of God are both enacted and enabled; that is, Israel's redemption is made visible. The description of the gathered people in 2:42–47 provides the proleptic answer to the disciples' question about redemption in 1:6—a proleptic answer because they still await Jesus' return and do not "know the times or periods the Father has set" (1:7, 11). The Lord's Supper, then, as a community-forming practice, takes on a distinctly political character in Acts.

This is hinted at also in Luke's Gospel. For instance, it is just after the Last Supper that the question arises among the disciples about power and authority, the question of "which one of them was to be regarded as the greatest" (Luke 22:24). Jesus responds by contrasting the politics of "the kings of the Gentiles" who "lord it over them" (Luke 22:25) with the politics of his community of the new covenant—"not so with you; rather the greatest among you must become like the youngest and the leader like one who serves" (22:26). It is as if Jesus (and Luke) wanted to make clear the contrast between the rule of the nations and the politics of the Lord's Supper, where Jesus had just served them his own flesh and blood. In the face of the church's failure to sustain communities of peace and plenty or to bring reconciliation between Jew and Gentile, the Lord's table has become a place both of judgment and hope. Insofar as we continue to celebrate the Eucharist in churches divided by wealth and poverty, divided from the Jews, and divided by the sword, we continue to eat and drink God's judgment upon ourselves (1 Cor. 11:17–34). The political dangers of such division are highlighted in the history of South Africa. Few people realize that the regime known as apartheid had its roots in the decision of the Dutch Reformed Church in 1857 to allow separate celebrations of the Lord's Supper for European and African Christians.[19] An entire epoch of oppression was built on this divided table.

Still, the Lord's table can also be a place where the redeemed life of God's elect is recalled, embodied, and anticipated. This is the case because Christians who feast at the Eucharist are made one with Christ. As such, to arise from the table and do violence to one another is not only a self-destructive act; it is destructive of Christ himself. It is to crucify Christ anew. Calvin understood this decisive communal aspect of the Lord's Supper:

> We shall benefit very much from the Sacrament if this thought is impressed and engraved upon our minds: that none of the brethren can be injured, despised, rejected, abused, or in any way offended by us, without at the same time, injuring, despising, and abusing Christ by the wrongs we do; that we cannot disagree with our brethren without at the same time disagreeing with Christ; that we cannot love Christ without loving him in the brethren; that we ought to take the same care of our brethren's bodies as we take of our own; for they are members of our body; and that, as no part of our body is touched by any feeling of pain which is not spread among all the rest, so we ought not to allow a brother to be affected by any evil, without being touched with compassion for him.[20]

Given such a passionate declaration of the power of the Lord's Supper, one could in no way justify rising from the table and killing one's sister or brother, for, following Calvin's logic, one could not kill a sister or brother without killing Christ himself. What this means for the politics of the elect and redeemed community, is that there can be no justification for a Christian in America to rise from the Lord's table and kill a Christian in Baghdad, Moscow, or Nagasaki. The Eucharist is a sacrament of peace, whereby Israel's redemption is made present by the Holy Spirit in the body of Christ.

This recalling of the church to its vocation as God's redeemed people is why frequent celebration of the Eucharist is so important. Calvin urged a return to the practice of the early church (as did Luther and Wesley) where "it became the unvarying rule that no meeting of the church should take place without the Word, prayers, partaking of the Supper, and almsgiving"[21] (citing Acts 2). This at least weekly partaking of the Supper was needed for the church to be able to sustain its common life together. Calvin had no question but that the Eucharist profoundly enabled the church's peaceful witness. "For as often as we partake of the symbol of the Lord's body, as a token given and received, we reciprocally bind ourselves to all the duties of love in order that none of us may permit anything that can harm our brother, or overlook anything that can help him."[22] Christians are shaped by the Eucharist into a peaceful people, among whom there can be no violence, no harm, because their bodies have been conformed to the peaceful sacrifice of the cross. Celebration of the Lord's Supper, then, is not only a way of sustaining the peace of God's people in their covenant life together; it is also a way of resisting the politics of the world that would call Christians to serve the violence of the nation. Because God has inaugurated Israel's redemption, and because the church partakes in that redemption through feeding on Christ, Christians are enabled to defy the call of the nation to kill brothers and sisters in the name of the United States, Ireland, or Korea.

In addition to making for peace, the Eucharist also enables the church to embody the plentitude of redemption. God promised through Zechariah not only that "there shall be a sowing of peace" but also that "the vine shall yield its fruit, the ground shall give its produce, and the skies shall give their dew" (Zech. 8:12). In other words, in God's redemption peace and plentitude go hand in hand. Both of these characteristics of the coming reign are invoked and embodied in communion. It is no accident that Paul used the term *koinonia* (communion, fellowship) to describe the fellowship of the elect (1 Cor. 1:9), the eucharistic participation in Christ (1 Cor. 10:16), and the offering for the poor in Jerusalem (2 Cor. 9:13; Rom. 15:26). This intimate relation between the Eucharist and economic sharing is what leads Paul to such harsh condemnation of the Corinthians in 1 Corinthians 11. Those who are well off are apparently eating the food of the common meal before "those who have nothing" arrive. Some in the community are going hungry while others are getting drunk. So Paul warns that those who eat and drink of the Lord's Supper "without discerning the body, eat and drink judgment against themselves" (1 Cor. 11:29). Indeed Paul goes so far as to say, "For this reason many of you are weak and ill, and some have died" (11:30).

Whatever else "discerning the body" may imply, it means at least that "as long as one Christian anywhere in the world is hungry, the eucharistic celebration of all Christians everywhere is incomplete."[23] To leave some Christians hungry while others eat is to leave Christ himself hungry and to risk facing the judgment, "I was hungry and you gave me no food, I was thirsty and you gave me nothing to drink. . . . Truly I tell you, just as you did not do it to one of the least of these, you did not do it to me" (Matt. 25:45). In the Eucharist, where Christ's body is broken and multiplied, the church is reminded and empowered to live as the redeemed people of God, to participate in the plentitude of God's reign, to embody the politics of election. In so doing, perhaps we can learn again from Luke's vision something of what such a community ought to look like: "There was not a needy person among them, for as many as owned lands or houses sold them and brought the proceeds of what was sold. They laid it at the apostles' feet, and it was distributed to each as any had need" (Acts 4:34).

The Lord's Supper, however, is not only about peace and plenty within the body of Christ. It is a foretaste of the heavenly banquet, a living into the end time toward which we trust God is bringing us. Eucharist looks forward with expectation to the coming feast of God's kingdom, where "many will come from east and west and will eat with Abraham and Isaac and Jacob in the kingdom of heaven" (Matt. 8:11). This is the "not yet" of God's redemption of Israel. In this time between the times, the church knows that God's redemption is assured, and thus it is able not only to exhibit peace in its own life but to wait patiently for God's peace to gather all nations to Zion. Augustine urges the church to exhibit such patience even toward enemies, for "she must bear in mind that among these very enemies are hidden her future citizens; and when confronted with them she must not think it a fruitless task to bear with their hostility until she finds them confessing the faith."[24] God's election of Israel carries with it the promise to bring peace through the ingathering of the nations. As those who have tasted of this redemption, Christians are called to patient nonviolence in the face of their enemies, since these enemies, too, are called into God's covenant. Because Christians know that redemption is assured in Christ, they are made able to wait in faithfulness and good hope, knowing that God's providential guidance of the world aims to extend the eucharistic foretaste of peace to all creatures. Only in the confidence of God's redemption and providence can Jesus' call to "love your enemies and pray for those who persecute you" (Matt. 5:44) be conceivable as a Christian practice.

At the heart of the church's witness to its identity as God's redeemed people is the ability to live at peace and to make the goods of God's earth plentiful to those in need. Without such an embodiment of redemption, the church will rightly continue to be called into judgment by Israel's question: "Where is this redemption you say has begun in Christ?" Never can we forget that even for Christians such redemption in its fullness remains an eschatological hope, and thus synagogue and church alike wait for the Messiah. But the challenge of living into its redemption sets before the church in this time between the times the alternative of hallowing God's name or profaning it. God has taken the risk of being known through God's people. Insofar as Christians fail to embody the redeemed life made possible by the Holy Spirit, and they do so often, they belie Christ's redemption and profane God's name. But in the sharing of the eucharistic meal, the church is recalled and restored to its identity as the redeemed people of God. As such it is given hope and strength to conform its life, by the power to the Holy Spirit, to the cruciform character of the new covenant.

Eucharist and Land

To put this another way, the church is enabled to embody a politics that does not require the violent defense of place precisely because the church is given a place in the Eucharist. This means that the centrality of Lord's Supper for the church's redeemed life parallels the centrality of the land for Israel's restoration. It does not *replace* the land, for the church still looks forward to dwelling with Israel in the New Jerusalem (Rev. 21:2, 10). Exactly what kind of city this will be is not clear, but there is no a priori reason to reject Justin Martyr's, Irenaeus', and Tertullian's expectation that it will be a tangible restoration of the land of Israel. The Eucharist is not a replacement of Israel's landed hopes. Rather, Christ's body itself has become the beachhead of God's restoration of the land.

In the Sermon on the Mount, Jesus cites Psalm 37:11, saying, "Blessed are the meek, for they shall inherit the land [τὴν γῆν]" (Matt. 5:5). The common translation "they shall inherit the earth" deceptively shifts the focus from the land of Israel to a universal hope that is more easily detached from the particularities of the promised land and the Jewish people.[25] Inheriting the land recalls the promise as given to Abraham (Gen. 15:17) and passed on to his descendants (Deut. 1:8). Jesus' invocation of this phrase connects his ministry with the tangible hope of Israel's restoration. But who are the "meek" (πραΰς)? As one reads on through Matthew, one discovers that Jesus himself is the only one called "meek." Matthew interprets Jesus' entry into Jerusalem as a fulfillment of the words of Zechariah,

> Tell the daughter of Zion,
> Look, your king is coming to you,
> humble (πραΰς) and mounted on a donkey. (21:5)

Elsewhere Jesus tells his disciples, "Take my yoke upon you, and learn from me; for I am gentle (πραϋς) and humble in heart, and you will find rest for your souls" (11:29). Jesus' language here evokes both the land and Torah obedience. The chosen ones (11:27) who take up Christ's yoke—a common rabbinic metaphor for Torah obedience (e.g., Jer. 6:16),[26] will experience rest—a hope associated with entering the promised land (Ps. 95:11; Heb. 4:1–11), for Christ is the meek one, the inheritor of the land.

Both W. D. Davies and Walter Brueggemann help us see that the New Testament gathers up the promise of the land in the person of Jesus. Davies writes, for instance, "The centre of gravity of Paul's ministry has shifted away from geographic eschatology. The real centre of his interest has moved from 'the land,' concentrated in Jerusalem, to the communities 'in Christ.'"[27] He adds that this ecclesiological focus "led [Paul] not so much to look away from the land of his fathers as to discover his inheritance 'in Christ'—the land of Christians, the new creation, if we may so express the matter."[28] Brueggemann affirms similarly, "Jesus embodies precisely what Israel has learned about land: being without land makes it possible to trust the promise of it, while grasping land is the sure way to lose it. The powerful are called to dispossession. The powerless are called to power. The landed are called to *homelessness*. The landless are given a *new home*. Both are called to discipleship, to be 'in Christ,' to submit to the one who has become the embodiment of the new land."[29] The body of Jesus becomes the material site of redemption, and his dispossession of wealth and power shifts the focus of land from a territory to defend to a bodily location where covenant faithfulness can be risked.[30] Boyarin's call for an identity based on body rather than land is here enacted for Christians in the body of Christ, which is also, mysteriously, the very land of promise.

Land, Christ, and redemption are thus linked through the Eucharist. For if Christ is the embodiment of the landed hopes of Israel—not a replacement but a foretaste in the flesh—then to eat his flesh, to participate in his body, is to participate in the promise of the land. Insofar as the church does this it is called into the peaceful plentitude of Israel's hopes—not by inhabiting a particular piece of earth but by carrying Christ's broken body throughout the earth. This means that even in the Eucharist the church never ceases to be a people without place and thus a peaceful people who have no "place" to defend. Here Milbank is especially insightful, and I quote him at length, for he illuminates the way in which Eucharist is both the site of peaceful communion and yet not a "site" at all but a gift of memory and a promise. He argues that we should not

> envisage the church in spatial terms—as another place, which we might arrive at, or as *this* identifiable site, which we can still inhabit. How could either characterize the Church which exists, finitely, not in time, but as time, taken in the mode of gift and promise? Not as a peace we must slowly construct piecemeal, imbibing our hard-learned lessons, but as a peace already given, superabundantly, in the breaking of bread by the raised Lord, which assembles the harmony of peoples then and at every subsequent eucharist. But neither as a peace already realized, which might excuse our labor. For the body and blood of Christ only exist in the mode of gift and they can *be* gift (like any gift) only as traces of the giver and promise of future provision from the same source. . . . Therefore the short answer to where is the Church? . . . might be, on the site of the eucharist, which is not a site, since it suspends presence in favour of memory and expectation, "positions" each and every one of us only as fed—gift from God of ourselves and therefore not to ourselves—and bizarrely assimilates us to the food which we eat, so that we, in turn, must exhaust ourselves as nourishment for others.[31]

The gift of eucharistic peace is a siteless participation in God's coming redemption. For just as God has promised to "dwell in the midst of Jerusalem" (Zech 8:3), God has also promised to dwell in the bread and wine of the Lord's Supper. In this fleshly gift, this body that is the soil of God's redemption, Christians taste peace and are made into peaceful citizens of God's holy land.

Seeking the Peace of the City: Ad Hoc Engagements

What, then, of the world's peace? Does this politics of election imply a withdrawal from the world, an attempt to nurture small pockets of community while consigning the rest of the world to its own violent end? To ask this question is already to have missed the ways in which the church's own faithfulness to God's redemption is in and with, not without, the world. From the start God's election was to be a blessing to the nations, and God's redemption in Christ through the Holy Spirit the extension of the covenant to the world. So for the church to attend to its own life as a witness to redemption politics is for it to be the leaven of peace that bears witness to God's reign through its nonviolent patience. This means that the church's first political service to the nation and the world is to embody fresh political alternatives. Barth saw this clearly. "The decisive contribution which the Christian community can make to the upbuilding and work and maintenance of the civil [community]," he wrote, "consists in the witness which it has to give to it and to all human societies in the form of the order of its own upbuilding and constitution."[32] To sing the Lord's song, to remember Jerusalem (Ps. 137) is already to engage in a truly "public work," a *leitourgia*, a liturgy of God's electing grace.[33] This is not a retreat from the world but a faithful embodiment of God's future at the heart of the world.

Yet the church finds itself, as Israel has so often, not at the world's center but scattered in exile. Indeed, exile is the church's permanent state until Christ returns to usher in the fullness of God's reign. Jeremiah, speaking God's word to an exiled people, calls Israel to what seems initially to be a peculiar mission. "Seek the welfare [*shalom*, 'peace'] of the city where I have sent you into exile, and pray to the Lord on its behalf, for in its welfare [*shalom*] you will find your welfare [*shalom*]" (Jer. 29:7). Now Jeremiah harbors no illusions about the goodness of Babylon. The point is not that they somehow *deserve* Israel's prayers or God's blessing. Indeed, Jeremiah makes clear that once the Babylonians have served their role in God's judgment on Israel, they, too, will be punished for their iniquity (25:11–12). Nonetheless, while in exile, God's chosen people have a calling on behalf of Babylon that recalls God's promise that Abraham's offspring would be a blessing to *all* the families of the earth.

This aspect of the politics of election is paradigmatically embodied in the lives of Israelites such as Joseph, Daniel, and Esther—Jews who found themselves in positions of power in foreign lands and, without denying their commitment to God and God's people, were able to contribute to the good of even Israel's enemies. For the church to embody such a role today would obviously look very different, but we could perhaps imagine an analogous participation in the life of the nations. What would be called for are ad hoc engagements with the world's powers in order to achieve goods such as feeding the hungry, caring for the orphan, and welcoming the stranger. These could include working with government agencies or receiving government funding for projects that serve the community. It could also mean advocating for structures in civil society that would be somehow analogous to the church's own life and polity. This is again to take Barth seriously when he writes, "Among the political possibilities open at any particular moment [the church] will choose those which most suggest a correspondence to, an analogy and a reflection of, the content of its own faith and gospel."[34]

An example of advocating such analogous structures might be Beiner's proposal of an economic vision similar to the Jewish kibbutz movement. He suggests, for instance, that economic justice might be approximated by making sure that the highest income in a society is no more than five times the lowest income.[35] Thus, if the street sweeper makes $25,000 a year, then the CEO, the corporate lawyer, and Michael Jordan all make no more than $125,000. Beiner writes that such "regulation, by the collective decision making of the society as a whole, of tolerable margins of relative income . . . would be in some way analogous to the collective regulation within the kibbutz."[36] His proposal has analogues as well with the redeemed community in Acts. It must be noted, of course, that in Acts the sharing of resources as need arose, the unlimited liability within the community, was made possible precisely by that which the state does not share, that is, the *koinonia* of Christ, the participation in God's redeemed covenant community. The church cannot expect the unconverted powers of the world to be able to embody such a polity. Nonetheless, churches can advocate for something analogous in the state. Such advocacy need not reduce churches to special interest groups. Nor should it become an excuse for them to redirect their efforts away from the hard work of creating within their own midst communities of economic justice. Rather, it is an imaginative attempt to forge an analogical structure in society that parallels the church's own politics of election.

Any such ad hoc engagements would have to weigh carefully the tension that often arises between effectiveness and faithfulness. That is, they would always have to maintain their ad hoc, tactical character. Like Esther, Joseph, and Daniel, the church is called to participate with the powers of the world insofar as this can bring a blessing to the nations. But just as Esther courageously claimed her Jewish identity and thwarted the king's planned pogrom, just as Joseph resisted the advances of Potiphar's wife that he might not sin against God, just as Daniel prayed openly to the Lord in defiance of King Darius, so the church must actively maintain its identity and mission even if this brings it into conflict with the powers and threatens its partnerships. For if the church's service in and with the world does not have this ad hoc detachment from the state's interests, it will quickly revert to the role of chaplain to the civic order.

Stephen Carter has warned us that any ecclesial engagement with the state can easily become a "Faustian bargain"—a partnership where the church comes to rely so much on government assistance that it is willing to compromise its own mission in order to maintain the partnership.[37] Carter suggests, for instance, that the special tax exemptions churches enjoy and the government aid sometimes used to support church programs can become just such a temptation. "Churches . . . have become addicted to government aid, even through the indirect form of tax exemptions and charitable deductions. But addictions carry costs, not the least of which is the sad fact that, in the end, the supplier always controls the addict—something to ponder, surely, as one contemplates how to avoid the trivialization of religious faith in America. One way might be to put the religions beyond the power of government not only to regulate, but to purchase; and the only way to stay beyond the reach of the government's power to purchase obedience is to remain beyond the long arm of government assistance."[38] The temptation to make such Faustian bargains exists not only in the arena of special tax status and the concomitant requirement that the church police its political speech, but also in the church preschool that receives state funds and thus cannot sing songs about Jesus and in the soup kitchen that cannot pronounce a blessing over God's bounty. The challenge for any ad hoc partnership lies in discerning how to serve in and with the world without abandoning the very convictions that make such service an intelligible Christian practice.

In a recent edition of the *Catholic Worker* newspaper, a small headline—"We Are Not Tax-Exempt"—appeared next to an appeal for donations. Such an admission was obviously not meant to entice people to give. But the short article read in part, "As a community, we have never sought tax-exempt status, believing that we are bound by conscience, not by government regulations, rewards, or privileges."[39] This decision to resist any structural partnership with the ruling powers, to be free from the strings attached to government assistance, allows the *Catholic Worker* to maintain the ad hoc distance necessary to carry out its unrestricted ministry in and for the world.

The Way Forward

The church, as God's chosen people with Israel, is called to embody a politics of election—faithfulness to the Christ-shaped Torah and to the Holy Spirit's redemption of Israel. In contrast to the politics of both modern liberalism and the ancient polis, such a communal life witnesses to God's election of Israel as the founding act of all true politics. Standing in this story, the church is called to stand against voluntarism and violence. Through the Eucharist, which in this light becomes a formative political act, the gathered people of God are united with the holy soil of Christ's flesh and made into a community capable of sharing the peace and plenty of God's redemption.

By embodying this radical political alternative, the church is set free to reach out in blessing to the nations. Sometimes this blessing will take the form of a firm no—standing against the world on behalf of the world, as the Confessing Christians did in Nazi Germany. Sometimes this blessing will take the form of a qualified yes—encouraging the nations to witness, perhaps unwittingly, to the Lordship of God, as did Cyrus in the Old Testament. But always the church's political calling and highest blessing will be in its witness to the New Jerusalem that is coming and indeed now is, among those who have been chosen to embody God's reign on earth.

Notes

Introduction

1. By "supersessionism" I mean primarily the claim that the church has replaced Israel as God's people chosen for the salvation and blessing of the world. I discuss further nuances of supersessionism in later chapters.

2. *Nostra Aetate*, sec. 4, in Austin Flannery, ed., *Vatican Council II: The Conciliar and Post Conciliar Documents*, new rev. ed. (Collegeville, MN: Liturgical Press, 1992), pp. 739–740.

3. Cited in Norbert Lohfink, *The Covenant Never Revoked: Biblical Reflections on Jewish-Christian Dialogue* (New York: Paulist Press, 1991), p. 5.

4. General Assembly of the Presbyterian Church (USA), "A Theological Understanding of the Relationship Between Christians and Jews," in World Council of Churches, ed., *The Theology of the Churches and the Jewish People* (Geneva: WCC Publications, 1988), p. 110.

5. Ibid., p. 114.

6. See the other documents collected in Helga Croner, ed., *Stepping Stones to Further Jewish-Christian Relations: An Unabridged Collection of Christian Documents* (New York: Stimulus Foundation, 1977) and Helga Croner, ed., *More Stepping Stones to Jewish-Christian Relations: An Unabridged Collection of Christian Documents, 1975–1983* (New York: Stimulus Foundation, 1985).

7. I continue to use the terms "Old Testament" and "New Testament," though with real reservations, when speaking of these writings within the Christian canon. In using them I do not mean to imply in any way that "old" means superseded. When speaking of the Jewish Bible, I usually refer to "Israel's Scripture." The currently popular academic designation, "Hebrew Bible," seems inadequate and even misleading, since it implies a certain context of interpretation that includes neither the Jewish oral Torah nor the Christian New Testament. This is to say that "Hebrew Bible" is not a description arising out of the reading practices of either the synagogue or the church. Since my concern is to understand readings from within these particular communities, this is not in the end a helpful description. Paul van Buren and Kendall Soulen have come up with commendable proposals for replacing the language of "Old" and "New" Testaments. In his *Theology of the Jewish-Christian Reality*, vol. 1, *Discerning the Way* (San Francisco: Harper and Row, 1980), p. 23, van Buren refers to the "Apostolic Writings" and the "Scriptures." Soulen, in *The God of Israel and Christian Theology* (Minneapolis: Fortress Press, 1996), p. 179, n. 32, argues for the use of "Apostolic Witness" and "Scriptures." Soulen writes, "Because the terms *Old Testament* and *New Testament* are bound up with the logic of the canonical narrative criticized in this book, I refer to the parts of the Christian canon as the Scriptures (or, for clarity's sake, the Hebrew Scriptures) and the Apostolic Witness respectively. The *Scriptures* recommends itself as an alternative to *Old Testament* because it follows the usage of Jesus

and the first Christians (see Mark 12:24; Acts 17:2; Rom. 1:2). *Apostolic Witness* seems a suitable alternative to *New Testament* inasmuch as it identifies the characteristic that the church deems the writings to possess that endows them with an authority equal to that of the Scriptures." Although I find Soulen's argument cogent and in many ways persuasive, I am concerned that this way of naming these collections of writings implies that the New Testament is somehow not "scripture" in the same way as the Old Testament. Because "scripture" is a functional term, and because the whole Christian Bible functions as scripture for the Christian community, I am not happy with limiting this designation to one part of the canon.

8. By the term "liberal," I do not mean the left wing of the Democratic party as opposed to the right wing of the Republican party. I hope my usage becomes clear in what follows, but it may be helpful to say briefly up front that I use "liberal" to refer to a distinct project of modern democratic social thought grounded in the dominance of a certain kind of "freedom" (*liber*). This freedom is primarily understood as a lack of restraint and authority, allowing the individual to pursue her or his own autonomous choices without interference from another to the extent that she or he does not infringe on another's freedom to do the same. Any simple definition such as this is bound to be inadequate due to the complexities of liberal social practice, but it does begin to point out certain features emphasized in liberal theory and embodied in liberal societies. In *What's the Matter with Liberalism?* (Berkeley: University of California Press, 1992), Ronald Beiner provides a helpful description: "Liberalism is the notion that there is a distinctive liberal way of life, characterized by the aspiration to increase and enhance the prerogatives of the individual; by maximal mobility in all directions, throughout every dimension of social life (in and out of particular communities, in and out of socioeconomic classes, and so on); and by a tendency to turn all areas of human activity into matters of consumer preference" (p. 22).

9. It is noteworthy that in several recent theological overviews, the doctrine of election is being given renewed attention. These brief but significant reflections represent gestures toward rethinking the doctrine of election along the lines I am proposing here; that is, they attend more to Israel and Trinity than has previously been the case. See, for instance, Douglas John Hall, *Confessing the Faith* (Minneapolis: Fortress Press, 1996), pp. 322–331; Daniel Migliore, *Faith Seeking Understanding* (Grand Rapids, MI: Eerdmans, 1991), pp. 74–79; Dietrich Ritschl, *The Logic of Theology* (Philadelphia: Fortress Press, 1987), pp. 124–138; and Robert W. Jenson, "The Holy Spirit," in Carl E. Braaten and Robert W. Jenson, eds., *Christian Dogmatics*, vol. 2 (Philadelphia: Fortress Press, 1984), pp. 134–139.

10. David Novak, *The Election of Israel: The Idea of the Chosen People* (Cambridge: Cambridge University Press, 1995), p. 108.

11. Ibid., pp. 14–21.

12. General Assembly of the Presbyterian Church (USA), "A Theological Understanding," p. 108.

Chapter One

1. Walker Percy, *Love in the Ruins: The Adventures of a Bad Catholic at a Time Near the End of the World* (New York: Ballantine Books, 1971), p. 3.

2. Ibid., p. 48.

3. Ibid., p. 49.

4. Alasdair MacIntyre, *After Virtue: A Study in Moral Theory*, 2nd ed. (Notre Dame, IN: University of Notre Dame Press, 1984), pp. 1–5. Alongside MacIntyre, philosophical critiques of modern liberalism that seek to recover a classical alternative include Martha C. Nussbaum, *The Fragility of Goodness: Luck and Ethics in Greek Tragedy and Philosophy* (Cambridge: Cambridge University Press, 1986); Martha C. Nussbaum, *The Therapy of Desire: Theory and Practice in Hellenistic Ethics* (Princeton, NJ: Princeton University Press, 1994); and Bernard Williams, *Shame and Necessity* (Berkeley: University of California Press, 1993). I draw primarily on MacIntyre's work both because he specifically engages the theological aspects of the recovery of the Greek tradition (especially as traced through Augustine and Aquinas) and because of the influence he has had on Milbank and Hauerwas.

5. MacIntyre, *After Virtue*, pp. 109ff., 263.

6. I am aware that by choosing to focus on only two negative aspects of the modern liberal project, I am creating something of a caricature. However, just as the point of a caricature is to highlight certain features and show how they are characteristic of the whole, so here I hope to show how these two features constitute the unstable foundation of the liberal ethos.

7. MacIntyre, *After Virtue*, pp. 11–12.

8. Ibid., p. 21.

9. See Stanley Hauerwas, *Christian Existence Today: Essays on Church, World and Living in Between* (Durham, NC: Labyrinth Press, 1988), p. 29. As Ronald Beiner points out, "Every society has an ethos. One that didn't would not just fail to be a moral community, it would fail to be a society at all. So liberal society does have an ethos. Under the liberal dispensation, the ethos is—lack of ethos; individuals in this society are habituated to being insufficiently habituated. That is the liberal paradox. Incoherent as it may appear, it goes to the core of what liberalism is and what it attempts to be" (Beiner, *What's the Matter with Liberalism?* [Berkeley: University of California Press, 1992], p. 22).

10. MacIntyre describes the resulting character of political debates in modern societies: "On the one side there appear the self-defined protagonists of individual liberty, on the other the self-defined protagonists of planning and regulation, of the goods which are available through bureaucratic organization. But in fact what is crucial is that on which the contending parties agree, namely that there are only two alternative modes of social life open to us, one in which the free and arbitrary choices of individuals are sovereign and one in which the bureaucracy is sovereign, precisely so that it may limit the free and arbitrary choices of individuals. Given this deep cultural agreement, it is unsurprising that the politics of modern societies oscillate between a freedom which is nothing but a lack of regulation of individual behavior and forms of collectivist control designed only to limit the anarchy of self-interest" (MacIntyre, *After Virtue*, pp. 34–35).

11. Beiner, *What's the Matter with Liberalism?* p. 8.

12. Ibid., p. 25.

13. Alasdair MacIntyre, *Whose Justice? Which Rationality?* (Notre Dame, IN: University of Notre Dame Press, 1988), pp. 336–338.

14. Robert Bellah, Richard Madsen, William M. Sullivan, Ann Swidler, and Steven Tipton, *Habits of the Heart: Individualism and Commitment in American Life* (New York: Harper and Row, 1985), p. 23.

15. Friedrich Nietzsche, "On the Genealogy of Morals," in *Basic Writings of Nietzsche*, ed. and trans. Walter Kaufmann (New York: Random House, 1968), p. 467.

16. Friedrich Nietzsche, *The Gay Science*, sec. 335, cited in *After Virtue*, p. 114.

17. Nietzsche's concession to the givenness of violence does not necessarily make his position a celebration of violence in itself. As Gregory Jones reminds us, "While Nietzsche wants to stress the inescapability of violence, the importance of the will to power, and the dangers of a weak-willed celebration of pity, he also emphasizes in several places, the significance of gift-giving. . . . Nietzsche's account of gift-giving is significant in its distinction of power from violence. Gift-giving uses the strength of power as a way of minimizing, though never escaping, the reality of violence. From such a perspective, life is sustained by the effective utilization of power, which requires a recognition that violence is inescapably part of how things really are in the world; even so, we ought also to recognize that gift-giving can be a power that is generous in its very being. This reading of Nietzsche moves away from the Nazi glorification of predatory violence to a more sustained ethical and political concern" (L. Gregory Jones, *Embodying Forgiveness: A Theological Analysis* [Grand Rapids, MI: Eerdmans, 1995], p. 80). See also Romand Coles, "Storied Others and Possibilities of *Caritas:* Milbank and Neo-Nietzschean Ethics," *Modern Theology* 8, 4 (October 1992): 331–351.

18. Robert Jenson astutely traces the prevailing Nietzschean alternatives: "As soon as choice is enthroned as the supreme value of life, it becomes apparent that a life merely so lived is empty; choice must have some content or it is nothing. And the 'value' with the least and so most tolerable content is love-as-sentiment. Having tried naked choice as our only meaning, we find that we are not up to such Nietzschean rigor, and fall back a half step on 'loving' choice. . . . The horribly clear-sighted Nietzsche saw two death-dealing specters at the nihilist end: the glorious superman and the feeble 'last man.' In the end we prove incapable of the superman's ghastly courage, and grasp instead the last man's sentimentality" (Robert W. Jenson, "The God-Wars," in Carl E. Braaten and Robert W. Jenson, eds., *Either/Or: The Gospel or Neopaganism*[Grand Rapids, MI: Eerdmans, 1996], pp. 33–34).

19. Thomas Hobbes, *Leviathan: or the Matter, Forme and Power of a Commonwealth Ecclesiasticall and Civil,* ed. Michael Oakeshott (New York: Macmillan, 1962), p. 100.

20. Ibid.

21. This account of modernity is admittedly neither original nor uncontested, but my concern is not to provide yet another extensive diagnosis of modernity's ills. Rather, I am seeking to draw on a growing consensus about the weaknesses and dangers of the dominant liberal polity as a way of helping the church think critically about what kind of *ressourcement* is necessary to nourish a faithful ecclesiology in a culture that is not only postmodern but rapidly becoming post-Christian.

22. MacIntyre first poses this question in *After Virtue*, pp. 109–120.

23. Ibid., p. 263.

24. Ibid., pp. 191, 219.

25. Ibid., pp. 186–187.

26. Ibid., p. 187.

27. MacIntyre's distinctions between what are and are not practices do seem to have an element of arbitrariness to them. On this see Stanley Hauerwas and Paul Wadell's review of *After Virtue* in the *Thomist* 46, 2 (April 1982): 319–320. For instance, despite what MacIntyre says about bricklaying, Hauerwas continues to consider it a practice—see "The Politics of Church: How We Lay Bricks and Make Disciples" in *After Christendom? How the Church Is to Behave if Freedom, Justice, and a Christian Nation Are Bad Ideas* (Nashville, TN: Abingdon Press, 1991), pp. 93–112. What MacIntyre does seem to have right here,

even if particular instances can be argued, is that technical skills, in order to produce virtue and achieve internal goods, must be caught up in the larger activity of a practice through which these skills are directed to some goal, and in which this goal is fluid enough to require redescription and rediscovery over time as the practice is passed on *(After Virtue,* pp. 193–194, 273).

28. MacIntyre, *After Virtue,* p. 188.

29. Ibid., pp. 201ff. I do not address all the complexities or problems involved in MacIntyre's account of narrative. On this point, see L. Gregory Jones's helpful treatment in "Alasdair MacIntyre on Narrative, Community, and the Moral Life," *Modern Theology* 4, 1 (1987): 52–69.

30. MacIntyre, *After Virtue,* pp. 220–221.

31. Ibid., p. 221.

32. Ibid., p. 216.

33. In subsequent works, most notably *Three Rival Versions of Moral Enquiry* (Notre Dame, IN: University of Notre Dame Press, 1990), MacIntyre has begun to speak more clearly out of a certain Thomistic tradition. However, even here his philosophical posture keeps him from giving the strong theological account that would be necessary to display a specifically Thomistic take on the good end for humankind.

34. MacIntyre, *After Virtue,* p. 219.

35. Ibid., p. 258.

36. Percy, *Love in the Ruins,* p. 5.

37. Ibid., p. 154.

38. Consider the following excerpt from a church newsletter, printed in honor of Flag Day:

> "If you want your father to take care of you, that's PATERNALISM.
> If you want your mother to take care of you, that's MATERNALISM.
> If you want Uncle Sam to take care of you, that's SOCIALISM.
> If you want your comrades to take care of you, that's COMMUNISM.
> BUT—if you want to take care of yourself, that's AMERICANISM!"

That a mainline Protestant church could so glibly affirm the myth of individual self-sufficiency says more than we may like about the ways in which the churches in America have appropriated the nation's ideals. What ought to be surprising (but unfortunately is not) is that this church seems to perceive no tension between these Americanist assertions of individual autonomy and the call to be the body of Christ.

39. This language of protection and containment is drawn from John Milbank, *Theology and Social Theory: Beyond Secular Reason* (Cambridge, MA: Blackwell, 1990), pp. 1–2, 105–106, 123, 223, 227, 229, 245, 268.

40. William T. Cavanaugh, "'A Fire Strong Enough to Consume the House': The Wars of Religion and the Rise of the State," *Modern Theology* 11, 4 (October 1995): 403.

41. Ibid., p. 405.

42. Milbank, *Theology and Social Theory,* pp. 121, 234.

43. John Locke, *A Letter Concerning Toleration,* in *Political Writings of John Locke,* ed. David Wootton (New York: Penguin Books, 1993), pp. 396, 429.

44. Philip D. Kenneson, "Selling [Out] the Church in the Marketplace of Desire," *Modern Theology* 9, 4 (October 1993): 341.

45. Bellah et al., *Habits of the Heart,* p. 72.

46. Ibid.

47. Kenneson, "Selling [Out] the Church," p. 345, n. 11.

48. MacIntyre, *After Virtue*, p. 263.

49. Milbank, *Theology and Social Theory*, p. 412.

50. Ibid., p. 411.

51. Milbank, *Theology and Social Theory*, p. 352.

52. Stanley Hauerwas and Charles Pinches, *Christians Among the Virtues: Theological Conversations with Ancient and Modern Ethics* (Notre Dame, IN: University of Notre Dame Press, 1997), p. 67.

53. Ibid., p. 69.

54. Milbank, *Theology and Social Theory*, pp. 369, 373. Subsequent references to this work are noted parenthetically in the text by page number.

55. The status of Jesus, however, is drastically relativized in Milbank's theology. Jesus' significance lies in his role as founder of the church and his "exemplary practice" of non-violence (*Theology and Social Theory*, p. 396). His identity is thus located not in the particularity of the character whose life is narrated in the biblical stories (contra Hans Frei); indeed his "identity does not actually relate to his 'character', but rather to his universal significance for which his particularity stands, almost, as a mere cipher" (John Milbank, "The Name of Jesus," in *The Word Made Strange: Theology, Language, and Culture* [Cambridge, MA: Blackwell, 1997], p. 149). "A cipher for what?" one might ask. Milbank suggests that the Gospels "can be read, not as the story of Jesus, but as the story of the (re)foundation of a new city, as new kind of human community, Israel-become-the-Church. Jesus figures in this story simply as the founder, the beginning, the first of many. There is nothing that Jesus does that he will not enable the disciples to do," including making atonement ("Name of Jesus," pp. 150–151). Thus, the call to remember "the name of the founder [Jesus] is really an instruction to remember every name, including that of the founder, as worthily as possible, and to learn from every 'Christian' example" ("Name of Jesus," p. 156). So Christ turns out to be a cipher for the exemplary practice of nonviolence (through forgiveness of sins), which is carried forward in infinite, nonidentical repetition in the church's life. My hunch is that Milbank's relativizing of Jesus' significance parallels his relativizing of Israel, just insofar as all claims to radical particularity are subsumed by his overarching ontology.

56. Milbank, "Name of Jesus," p. 155. This passage, along with Milbank's emphasis on relating the part to the whole, is also reminiscent of James Gustafson, who writes, "[Christianity] continues to provide the basis for the enlargement of vision, the alteration and expansion of the order of the heart, and the motivation to participate in the ordering of all things in a manner appropriate to their relations to God" (James Gustafson, *Ethics from a Theocentric Perspective*, vol. 1, *Theology and Ethics* [Chicago: University of Chicago Press, 1981], p. 324). I suspect that the commonality here comes from a shared reliance on both Friedrich Schleiermacher and Spinoza. On Schleiermacher's relation to Spinoza, see Julia A. Lamm, *The Living God: Schleiermacher's Theological Appropriation of Spinoza* (University Park: Pennsylvania State University Press, 1996). Her description of Schleiermacher sounds remarkably like Milbank. "Schleiermacher's appropriation of Spinoza was filtered through the revival of Spinoza in late-eighteenth-century Germany, which means that it was essentially aesthetic in character; Spinoza's uncompromising monism is thus translated into an aesthetic monism that allows for genuine individuality, novelty, beauty, and goodness. It is most especially in this sense that Schleiermacher's Spinoza is a Platonized Spinoza. In his Christian dogmatics, the aesthetic becomes the re-

demptive" (p. 9). Such a Spinozistic monism, filtered through Romanticism, need not lead to a reductionistic materialism but "could correlate an experience of nature as dynamic with the biblical notion of a living God who operates through the powers of nature and history. For Schleiermacher, it also allows for a higher unity that includes a genuine plurality" (p. 161). Like Spinoza, Schleiermacher denies the attributes of intellect and will to God, since this would imply that there is some division in God. However, unlike Spinoza "[Schleiermacher] can . . . be said to be anthropocentric in that the one 'goal' of the divine decree is the Kingdom of God, or the 'planting and extension of the Christian Church'" (p. 224, cf. pp. 216–217). Such a "divine decree" cannot be understood to be an act of volition, since God has no "will" that could choose between alternatives; rather, it is a way of naming the unifying purpose and telos of creation, preservation, and redemption—which are all one and the same thing (pp. 223–224). When Schleiermacher's relation to Spinoza is analyzed in this way, one begins to see the deep similarities between his project and Milbank's.

57. Milbank, "Name of Jesus," p. 166, n. 13.

58. David Novak, *The Election of Israel: The Idea of the Chosen People* (Cambridge: Cambridge University Press, 1995), pp. 23–24.

59. Milbank, "Name of Jesus," p. 156.

60. Michael Wyschogrod, *The Body of Faith: God in the People Israel* (San Francisco: Harper and Row, 1983), p. 226.

61. Such messianic peace took root, for instance, in the small French village of Le Chambon during World War II. André Trocmé, a pastor in the village, organized his parishioners to hide Jewish children. This was not only an act of compassion but an act of faithfulness to Christ's way of nonviolence. Trocmé was convinced that "Christian nonviolence is not a part of the fabric of the universe. . . . Rather, it has a temporary character. It is tied to the delay God grants men because of the voluntary sacrifice of the messianic King. By deriving nonviolence not from a philosophy of the universe . . . but from His sacrifice on the cross, Jesus gives it historical precision and a much greater impact" (André Trocmé, *Jesus and the Nonviolent Revolution* [Scottdale, PA: Herald Press, 1973], p. 66, cited in Stanley Hauerwas, "Remembering as a Moral Task: The Challenge of the Holocaust," in *Against the Nations: War and Survival in a Liberal Society* [Notre Dame, IN: University of Notre Dame Press, 1992], p. 88, n. 37).

62. Hauerwas and Pinches, *Christians Among the Virtues*, p. 68.

63. See Hauerwas and Pinches's favorable appraisal of Bernard Williams's move to recover the Socratic question as central to ethics (ibid., p. 56).

64. Stanley Hauerwas, *The Peaceable Kingdom: A Primer in Christian Ethics* (Notre Dame, IN: University of Notre Dame Press, 1983), p. 116.

65. Stanley Hauerwas, *A Community of Character: Toward a Constructive Christian Social Ethic* (Notre Dame, IN: University of Notre Dame Press, 1981), p. 125. See the same or similar points in Hauerwas and Pinches, *Christians Among the Virtues*, pp. 15–16, and Stanley Hauerwas, "Constancy and Forgiveness: The Novel as a School for Virtue," in *Dispatches from the Front: Theological Engagements with the Secular* (Durham, NC: Duke University Press, 1994), pp. 55–56. For a very early example of Hauerwas's work on character, which emphasizes free choice and self-determination, see "Toward an Ethics of Character," in *Vision and Virtue: Essays in Christian Ethical Reflection* (Notre Dame, IN: University of Notre Dame Press, 1982), pp. 48–67.

66. This point is not lost on Hauerwas. He writes elsewhere, "Discipleship is quite simply extended training in being dispossessed. To become followers of Jesus means that we

must, like him, be dispossessed of all that we think gives us power over our own lives and the lives of others. Unless we learn to relinquish our presumption that we can ensure the significance or our lives, we are not capable of the peace of God's kingdom" *(Peaceable Kingdom,* p. 86). It is not by chance that here, where Hauerwas is speaking the language of "discipleship," he emphasizes not "making our lives our own" but rather recognizing our lives as God's own.

67. L. Gregory Jones, *Transformed Judgment: Toward a Trinitarian Account of the Moral Life* (Notre Dame, IN: University of Notre Dame Press, 1990), p. 18.

68. See, for instance, Stanley Hauerwas, *In Good Company: The Church as Polis* (Notre Dame, IN: University of Notre Dame Press, 1995), p. 8.

69. Richard B. Hays, *The Moral Vision of the New Testament: Community, Cross, New Creation* (San Francisco: HarperSanFrancisco, 1996), p. 196.

70. For instance, in *A Community of Character,* Hauerwas affirms "(1) that the self is a gift and (2) that we need a story that helps us accept it as a gift" (p. 148). He goes on, "What we require is . . . a true story. Such a story is one that provides a pilgrimage with appropriate exercises and disciplines of self-examination. Christians believe scripture offers such a story. . . . We are possessors of the happy news that God has called people together to live faithful to the reality that he is the Lord of this world. All men have been promised that through the struggle of this people to live faithful to that promise God will reclaim the world for his Kingdom. By learning their part in this story, Christians claim to have a narrative that can provide the basis for a self appropriate to the unresolved, and often tragic, conflicts of this existence" (p. 149). This account of the self, arising as it does out of the biblical witness to Israel, stands at least in some respects in tension with the accounts he gives when he is using the language of virtue. Nonetheless, the very attention Hauerwas pays to the "self" may be a result of his Aristotelian influences (or perhaps a lingering liberalism). It is significant that such attention to the "self" is not characteristic of Jewish thought.

71. *In Good Company,* pp. 6, 26–28, 209, 226, 233. There are in the index twice as many references to "Israel" and "Jews and Judaism" as there are to "polis."

72. In *Christians Among the Virtues,* Hauerwas and Pinches follow Milbank in critiquing MacIntyre on just this point. "In effect, the ancient world knew no peace, it knew only the absence of conflict in an exclusive *polis* where the virtuous life always took its meaning and direction from heroism in war. Indeed, *conquering* was pervasive, if not Athens of Sparta, then reason of the appetites, or masters of slaves" (p. 65).

73. Hauerwas, *In Good Company,* p. 28.

74. Ibid., pp. 30–31. He expresses the same conviction a few pages later, "Just to the extent Christians are tempted to tell our story separately from the story of Israel, we become something less than God's body" (p. 38). And elsewhere, "No conversation over differences is more important than that between Israel and the church. For it is from Israel that we learn of the God who is present to us in the life, cross, and resurrection of Jesus. It is from Israel's continuing willingness to wait for the Messiah that we learn better how we must wait between the times. The church and Israel are two people walking in the path provided by God; they cannot walk independently of one another, for if they do they both risk becoming lost" (*The Peaceable Kingdom,* p. 107).

75. For instance, "The crucial question for Christians is not the justification of democracies but our relation to the Jews. For it is the Jews who rightly insist that salvation is not knowledge, is not a gnosis, but fleshly. To be saved is to be engrafted into a body that reconstitutes us by making us part of a history not universally available" ("The Democratic

Policing of Christianity," in *Dispatches from the Front*, p. 106). See also the sermon "Jews and the Eucharist," in "The Church's One Foundation Is Jesus Christ Her Lord, or in a World Without Foundations All We Have Is the Church," in *In Good Company*, pp. 34–38. One of Hauerwas's thickest theological discussions of Israel comes in *The Peaceable Kingdom*, pp. 76–87, where he attends to Israel and Jesus as embodiments of the kingdom of God.

76. Hauerwas and Pinches, *Christians Among the Virtues*, p. 62.

77. This is Oliver O'Donovan's felicitous phrase from *The Desire of the Nations: Rediscovering the Roots of Political Theology* (Cambridge: Cambridge University Press, 1996), p. 25.

78. Percy, *Love in the Ruins*, p. 341.

79. Ibid., pp. 5–6.

80. This point is noted in Sarah Freedman's astute thesis, "Some Views of the Jews in the Fiction of Walker Percy" (M.T.S. thesis, Duke University, 1992).

81. This conversation comes in Walker Percy, *The Thanatos Syndrome* (London: Andre Deutsch, 1987), p. 126, which is the sequel to *Love in the Ruins*.

82. Ibid., p. 123.

83. My references to "Constantine" and "Constantinianism" are not intended to refer primarily to the *person* of Constantine. Rather, as John Howard Yoder puts it, "our concern is not with Constantine the man—how sincere his conversion was, what he believed, how he intended to use the church. Nor do we suggest that the year 311 represented an immediate reversal without preparation or unfolding. The great reversal certainly began earlier and took generations to work itself out. Nonetheless, the medieval legend which made of Constantine the symbol of an epochal shift was realistic: he stands for a new era in the history of Christianity" (Yoder, "The Constantinian Sources of Western Social Ethics," in *The Priestly Kingdom: Social Ethics as Gospel* [Notre Dame, IN: University of Notre Dame Press, 1984], p. 135).

84. The dating of the end of Christendom will necessarily appear somewhat arbitrary, as are all such datings. O'Donovan would locate it in 1791 with the passage of the First Amendment to the Constitution (*The Desire of the Nations*, p. 195), whereas Hauerwas, for one, sights its demise much later. Indeed, Hauerwas and William Willimon somewhat facetiously locate Constantine's overthrow on "some Sunday evening in 1963" when the Fox movie theater opened in Greenville, South Carolina—serving notice to the church that it would no longer be granted a privileged status (*Resident Aliens* [Nashville, TN: Abingdon Press, 1989], pp. 15–16). This difference in dating the end of Christendom represents a deeper contrast in these positions. The question is whether one sees continuity or discontinuity between early-modern liberalism and the later forms of liberalism in which church and state are more radically dissociated. As we will see in Chapter 4, O'Donovan wishes to reject late-modern liberalism (post-1791) by recovering certain features of an earlier liberalism that embodied the legacy of Christendom. Hauerwas and Willimon, in contrast, wish to critique late-modern liberalism as part of a much longer history of Christian compromise. The difference, in short, is whether the mistakes in the church's relation to civil powers began in 313 or in 1791.

85. George Lindbeck, "The Church," in *Keeping the Faith*, ed. Geoffrey Wainwright (Philadelphia: Fortress Press, 1988), p. 190.

86. Richard B. Hays, *Echoes of Scripture in the Letters of Paul* (New Haven, CT: Yale University Press, 1989), p. 53.

87. Paul van Buren, *A Theology of the Jewish-Christian Reality*, vol. 2, *A Christian Theology of the People Israel* (San Francisco: Harper and Row, 1983), p. 19. The Jewish writer Michael Wyschogrod makes a similar point: "Although God is both the creator and ruler of the universe, He reveals Himself to man, not as the conclusion of the cosmological or teleological proofs, but as the God of Abraham who took the people of Israel out of the land of Egypt and whose people this nation remains to the end of time. He thus remains inaccessible to all those who wish to reach Him and, at the same time, to circumvent this people" (Michael Wyschogrod, "Israel, Church, and Election," in *Brothers in Hope*, ed. John M. Oesterreicher [New York: Herder and Herder, 1970], pp. 79–80).Booknotes from

Chapter Two

1. Novak and Wyschogrod explicate Israel's identity as the elect people in ways that are complementary though certainly not identical. Where necessary I note the differences between them; however, I do not focus on these and even less do I presume to resolve them. Rather, I concentrate on those aspects of their proposals where they are in agreement.

2. On the sources of this movement, see Peter Ochs, "A Rabbinic Pragmatism," in Bruce D. Marshall, ed., *Theology and Dialogue: Essays in Conversation with George Lindbeck* (Notre Dame, IN: University of Notre Dame Press, 1990), pp. 214, 241, n. 7.

3. By focusing on these two figures as representatives of Judaism, I am making a theological decision, though not an arbitrary one. Nonetheless one may ask: Do two Jews make a Judaism? And are these perhaps idiosyncratic perspectives just insofar as both Novak and Wyschogrod are involved in Jewish-Christian dialogue? In answer to this question, Novak makes the following points: "(a) Both Wyschogrod and I draw heavily on the Biblical-Rabbinic tradition, to whose teaching authority we are both personally committed. As such, I don't think we can be dismissed as heretical or idiosyncratic. (b) Wyschogrod and I are the only two contemporary Jewish thinkers who have attempted to theologically constitute this core Jewish doctrine [election] with philosophical (contra apologetic) sensitivity. That means that he and I are the only ones who have been willing to 'take on' Spinoza *et al.* (c) If theology is a normative (as distinct from a descriptive) endeavor, then one is going to have to read the tradition in a noninductive way. In other words, any normative reading of a tradition is going to have to make selective judgments regarding priorities (and very much *sub specie durationis* as befits anything situated in a narrative). The fact that both Wyschogrod and I have been in deep dialogue with Christian thinkers means that we both (*mutatis mutandis*) see that as theologically important for Jews at this juncture in history" (David Novak, personal correspondence, August 16, 1996, used by permission).

4. David Novak, *The Election of Israel: The Idea of the Chosen People* (Cambridge: Cambridge University Press, 1995), pp. 1–5.

5. David Novak, "Jewish Theology," *Modern Judaism* 10 (1990): 322.

6. Ibid..

7. Novak, *Election*, p. 2.

8. Ibid., p. 4. On the ways in which "race" and thus the possibility of "racism" is a construction of enlightenment notions of science and philosophy, see Cornel West, "A Genealogy of Modern Racism," in *Prophesy Deliverance!* (Philadelphia: Westminster, 1982), pp. 47–65. Of course, Novak's point does not mean that biology counts for noth-

ing, only that the way in which Jews constitute a "family" gains its significance not from biology but from the historical and theology reality of divine election.

9. Novak, *Election*, p. 5.

10. Ibid., p. 19.

11. Ibid., pp. 4–5.

12. This is notwithstanding the fact that there have been many social instantiations of this Israel and many variant visions of living the covenant. Jacob Neusner reminds us of this when he writes of the "many Judaisms" in the first century. See his *Jews and Christians: The Myth of a Common Tradition* (Philadelphia: Trinity Press International, 1991), pp. 25–26.

13. I therefore use the terms "Israel" and "Jews" interchangeably throughout the book as a way of reminding us that there is no ideal "Israel" that floats above or could be detached from the actual *people* of Israel, the Jews, past and present.

14. Novak, *Election*, p. 10.

15. Ibid.

16. Ibid., p. 23.

17. Compare Louis Jacobs's summary description of Judaism: "Judaism affirms that God, the Creator of the world and all that is in it, has chosen the Jewish people [election] to live according to his will as revealed through the Torah [covenant] and eventually to lead all men to His service [redemption]" (Jacobs, *The Jewish Religion: A Companion* [New York: Oxford University Press, 1995], p. 3).

18. All Scripture quotations in this chapter come from the Jewish Publication Society, *Tanakh* (Philadelphia: Jewish Publication Society, 5748/1988), unless otherwise noted.

19. Novak comments, "Election is primarily generic and only secondarily individual. Abraham is elected as the progenitor of a people. Every member of this people is elected by God and every member of this people is called upon to respond to his or her generic election" (*Election*, p. 117).

20. Michael Wyschogrod, *The Body of Faith: God in the People Israel* (San Francisco: Harper and Row, 1983), p. 254.

21. Cited from C. G. Montefiore and H. Loewe, eds., *A Rabbinic Anthology* (New York: Schocken Books, 1974), p. 106. All further citations from this volume are given parenthetically in the text as "M&L," followed by the page number.

22. Wyschogrod, *Body*, p. 253.

23. Ibid., p. xv; cf. pp. 57–58, 174–177, 184.

24. This quotation serves as Wyschogrod's epigraph to *The Body of Faith*.

25. Ibid., p. 213. "The term *Hashem* means 'The Name' and has long been used by Jews to refer to God by reference to the ineffable name of God, whose pronunciation is both unknown and forbidden. The term *God* is a neutral one. It is used by many religions to refer to the being or object worshiped and thus presupposes a class of Gods, as in the biblical exclamation 'Who among the gods is like you, Hashem?' The term *God* therefore has a built-in tendency toward the abstract because it focuses on the characteristics gods have in common rather than on the uniqueness of the God of Israel. To speak of Hashem is to speak of the one who is related to the people of Israel" (Wyschogrod, *Body*, p. 92).

26. Novak, *Election*, p. 31.

27. Ibid., p. 189.

28. This is not unlike the Donatist controversy faced by Christians in North Africa in the fourth century. The Donatists claimed that the efficacy of the sacraments was vitiated by the sin of the presider, specifically, the presider who had apostatized by handing over

the Bible to Roman soldiers during persecution. In a position similar to that of Rashi, Augustine voiced the judgment that God's gracious work in the sacraments could not be negated even by the sin of the priest. This judgment was based on Augustine's deep conviction about God's electing grace. Such grace is unconditional and thus God's covenant is irrevocable—it is neither determined by nor contingent upon the faithfulness of the human response, though it always seeks to evoke and create such faithfulness (Jaroslav Pelikan, *The Christian Tradition*, vol. 1, *The Emergence of the Catholic Tradition (100–600)* [Chicago: University of Chicago Press, 1971], pp. 308–313).

29. Novak, *Election*, p. 191.

30. As Novak puts it in *Jewish Social Ethics* (New York: Oxford University Press, 1992), p. 35, "For humans, the covenant is coeval with life. 'To love the Lord your God and to listen to his voice and to cleave unto him: that is your life and the length of your days. . . . ' (Deuteronomy 30:20)."

31. This same twist occurs in the New Testament at the end of the hymnic fragment cited in 2 Timothy 2:11–13.

> If we have died with him, we will also live with him;
> if we endure, we will also reign with him;
> if we deny him, he will also deny us;
> if we are faithless, he remains faithful—
> for he cannot deny himself. (NRSV)

32. Wyschogrod, *Body*, p. 64.

33. Novak traces the roots of this modern turn to Spinoza's reformulation of election. "The power of [Spinoza's] rejection is that it was not a simple dismissal of the doctrine. Instead, it was a radical inversion of its traditionally accepted meaning, a deconstruction of it, if you will. In the traditional version of the doctrine, it is God who elects Israel and institutes the covenantal relationship with her. Spinoza, conversely, inverts this relationship and asserts that in truth it was Israel who elected God and instituted the covenantal relationship with him" (Novak, *Election*, p. 22; see further pp. 22–49).

34. Ibid., pp. 12, 31.

35. One is reminded here of Karl Barth's well-known formulation: The covenant is the internal basis of creation, and creation is the external basis of the covenant. Or as he also puts it, "The covenant is the goal of creation and creation the way to the covenant" (Karl Barth, *Church Dogmatics*, ed. G. W. Bromiley and T. F. Torrance [Edinburgh: T. & T. Clark, 1958], III/1, p. 97; see also pp. 42–44, 94–98, 228–232).

36. Wyschogrod, *Body*, p. 102.

37. Ibid., pp. 102–103.

38. Ibid., p. 103.

39. Ibid., p. 220.

40. Novak, *Election*, p. 121.

41. Ibid., pp. 121–126.

42. Ibid., pp. 135–136.

43. Ibid., p. 136.

44. Ibid., p. 23.

45. Ibid., p. 164. "The factor of human freedom in the covenant between God and Israel, which . . . was considerably developed in Rabbinic Judaism, does not extend, however, to the freedom to leave the covenant" (ibid., p. 189).

46. See ibid., pp. 182–183.

47. Rabbi Avdimi bar Hama bar Hasa did suggest that God threatened to drop Mount Sinai on the Israelites if they did not accept the Torah. Rabbi Aha bar Jacob, however, makes the point that this would be "a great indictment of the Torah," since an agreement made under compulsion is not valid (B. Shabbat 88a, cited in Novak, *Ethics*, pp. 27–28; cf. *Election*, pp. 166–167).

48. For the following, see Novak, *Election*, pp. 167–169.

49. Wyschogrod, *Body*, p. 13.

50. Ibid., pp. 61–62.

51. Novak, *Ethics*, p. 35.

52. Jon Levenson, *Creation and the Persistence of Evil* (Princeton, NJ: Princeton University Press, 1988), p. 141.

53. This rabbinic way of preserving the mutuality of the relation between God and Israel is perhaps something like what Thomas Aquinas was trying to do when he conceived of the human will as being free even when it is moved by God. Aquinas affirms quite explicitly, "We must come at length to this, that man's free-will is moved by an extrinsic principle, which is above the human mind, to wit by God" (Aquinas, *Summa Theologica*, trans. Fathers of the English Dominican Province [Allen, TX: Christian Classics, 1948], I-II, 109, 2). But how is such an external movement still free? Commenting on Philippians 2:13, "It is God Who worketh in us both to will and to accomplish," Aquinas makes the case that because God is the creator, God can direct and move the human will to its true end (which God knows even better than the fallen human being does), without contradicting the true nature of the person. Since "the cause of the will can be none other than God" (I-II, 9, 6), God can move the will externally without denying its freedom. This is because God does not move the will coercively against its nature but rather moves it to do freely what is, in fact, most natural to it. "God so moves [the will], that He does not determine it of necessity to one thing, but its movement remains contingent and not necessary, except in those things to which it is moved naturally. ... That is natural to a thing which God so works in it that it may be natural to it: for thus is something becoming to a thing, according as God wishes it to be becoming" (I-II, 10, 4).

The understanding of God as a "cause" is admittedly problematic here insofar as the God of Israel is never a "cause" in either the Aristotelian or Neoplatonic senses (see Novak's critique of Maimonides's use of Aristotle, *Election*, pp. 225–240). However, what we find in Aquinas is one of the most helpful Christian attempts to hold together God's action and human action as complementary rather than as exclusive alternatives. Although his reliance on Aristotle may leave him far from a traditional Jewish conceptuality here, his attempt nonetheless moves in the right direction. In Aquinas's terms, one might say that the Jewish desire for God and love of God remains free even though it is itself instilled and evoked by God and thus God's election cannot be refused. Chosenness is, in Aquinas's sense, "natural" to the Jews—that is, it names a quality intrinsic to Jewish identity—by virtue of God's election, and thus to respond to God's electing love with love is both free and the natural outcome of God's prior electing. Because, as Novak puts it, "essence in biblical theology follows from existence, but existence is never derived from essence" (*Election*, p. 126), the very existence of the people of Israel, by virtue of God's election, determines their essence as those who return God's love in obedience to the covenant. To refuse God's covenant can only be a denial of existence—a choice not of freedom but of self-contradiction. True freedom can only mean choosing to live in accordance with reality, that is, in accordance with one's true nature as God's elect.

54. Novak, *Election*, p. 12. Of course, Novak is well aware of the ways in which marriage is itself, especially for Jews and Christians, a serious political act.

55. Novak, "Jewish Theology," p. 322.

56. Novak, *Election*, p. 145.

57. Wyschogrod writes, "Israel attempts to sanctify national existence in obedience to the divine election, which is a national election. And it is a national election precisely because the nation is most remote from God and is therefore commanded to be the most proximate. To believe that the individual can be lifted out of his nation and brought into relation with God is as illusory as to believe that man's soul can be saved and his body discarded" (Wyschogrod, *Body*, p. 68).

58. Raphael Jospe argues this point nicely in "The Concept of the Chosen People: An Interpretation," *Judaism* 43, 2 (1994): 127–148.

59. Novak, *Election*, p. 86.

60. Ibid., p. 143.

61. Wyschogrod, *Body*, p. 205.

62. In this way Torah may be seen as the paradigmatic cultural-linguistic framework in George Lindbeck's sense of "comprehensive interpretive schemes, usually embodied in myths or narratives and heavily ritualized, which structure human experience and understanding of self and world" (George Lindbeck, *The Nature of Doctrine: Religion and Theology in a Postliberal Age* [Philadelphia: Westminster, 1984], pp. 32–33).

63. Novak, *Election*, p. 150. Compare p. 151, n. 27: "While not denying that the commandments have their good consequences, the emphasis of rabbinic teaching is that they are ends in themselves as responses to God's commanding presence."

64. Ibid., p. 151.

65. Ibid., p. 147, emphasis omitted.

66. Wyschogrod, *Body*, p. 211. Wyschogrod goes on to add, "The Torah is not a demand that exists apart from the being of Israel." Here we find a disagreement between Wyschogrod and Novak, who argues, "The Torah in toto is concerned with more than Israel, but also with the elementary norms that the creator has enabled all humans to discover with intelligence and good will in their own social nature" (*Election*, p. 253, cf. pp. 241–248). In terms of relating the people of Israel and the Torah of Israel, Novak charges that Wyschogrod subordinates Torah to people as part of his overall emphasis on grace over merit. Novak argues for a more dialectical relationship: "The Jewish people is at least as much for the sake of the Torah as the Torah is for the sake of the Jewish people" (p. 246). Novak fears that Wyschogrod's (over)emphasis on God's gracious election and his subordination of Torah to peoplehood threaten antinomianism, especially in Israel's relation with those outside the covenant. Here Novak draws on the Noahide commandments (the traditional seven laws God gave to Noah, which are to be followed by all people—as opposed to the 613 laws of the Torah given only to the Jews) to argue for a natural law that binds both the nations and the people of Israel, thus placing them on equal footing in certain matters. Novak clearly fears that without a natural law that embraces Israel as well as the nations, and without an equality between Israel and Torah (gracious election and meritorious response), there will not be sufficient checks on the course the people of Israel might pursue in service of their own ends. "It would seem that one has to search the tradition for a view of the Torah that applies equally, even if only on certain points, to both Israel and the nations of the world. Only such a discovery can save us from confusing—God forbid—the idea of the chosen people with the odious idea of a *Herrenvolk* [master

race], an idea whose adherents are directly responsible for our greatest agony in history" (p. 248). In short, whereas Novak's theology of creation and Torah includes a form of natural law as a check on Israel's self-serving appeals to chosenness, Wyschogrod relies on Torah as an internal argument for Israel's proper relation to the nations.

67. Wyschogrod, *Body*, p. 183.

68. Ibid., p. 244.

69. Novak, *Election*, pp. 134–135.

70. Jacobs, "Redemption," in *Jewish Religion*, p. 414.

71. Novak, *Election*, p. 253.

72. Zechariah's inclusion of the animals in God's redeemed Jerusalem finds support in other biblical images, such as the peaceable kingdom in Isaiah 11. The implications of this for how Christians, as God's redeemed community, should relate to the wider animal world need more exploration. For a start, see Charles Pinches and Jay B. MacDaniel, eds., *Good News for Animals? Christian Approaches to Animal Well-Being* (Maryknoll, NY: Orbis Books, 1993), especially Stanley Hauerwas and John Berkman, "A Trinitarian Theology of the 'Chief End' of 'All Flesh,'" pp. 62–74.

73. Gershom Scholem, *The Messianic Idea in Judaism* (New York, 1971), pp. 1–2; cited in Robert Wilken, *The Land Called Holy: Palestine in Christian History and Thought* (New Haven, CT: Yale University Press, 1992), p. 22.

74. Wyschogrod, *Body*, p. 256.

75. Novak, *Election*, p. 23.

76. Ibid., p. 103.

77. Wyschogrod, *Body*, p. 230.

78. Ibid., pp. 103–104. As Novak puts it, "The Jewish people as members of the everlasting covenant community hope for the final inclusion of all humankind into their covenant with God. . . . The inclusion of the non-Jewish world in that covenantal love will be the result of God's bringing them into the covenant at the endtime of redemption" (Novak, *Election*, pp. 103, 106).

79. Wyschogrod, *Body*, p. 224.

80. For what follows, see Novak, *Election*, pp. 152–162, 252–255; Wyschogrod, *Body*, pp. 254–256.

81. Jacobs, *Jewish Religion*, p. 343; Wyschogrod, *Body*, p. 255.

82. "For the minimalist, the Torah as we know it will remain in force in the messianic era. For the maximalist, everything, including the Torah, will change in messianic times" (Wyschogrod, *Body*, p. 255; cf. Novak, *Election*, pp. 154–156).

83. Novak, *Election*, p. 154; *Ethics*, p. 38.

84. Novak, *Election*, p. 154.

85. Ibid., p. 155.

86. Ibid., p. 156.

87. Wyschogrod, *Body*, p. 178.

88. Ibid., pp. 219, 243.

89. Novak, *Election*, p. 162.

90. Novak, *Ethics*, p. 18.

91. Novak, *Election*, p. 160; *Ethics*, p. 18.

92. Novak, *Ethics*, p. 19.

93. The echoes of Reinhold Niebuhr here make for an interesting parallel. Both Novak's emphasis on ethical humility and doing "the lesser evil" as well as his attack on any overly

optimistic utopianism are themes central to Niebuhr's project (see, for instance, Niebuhr's *Interpretation of Christian Ethics* [San Francisco: Harper and Row, 1963]). Of course, Novak's stress on the unredeemed status of the world corresponds to Jewish eschatology in a way that Niebuhr's similar affirmations conflict with traditional Christian claims about the redemption that has already begun in Christ. Nonetheless, both Novak's Elijah, who stands outside of history in an eschatological future, and Niebuhr's Jesus, who stands at the edge of history in an idealistic transcendence, threaten to underwrite the existing political order just insofar as any real alternative remains inaccessible in this age. For example, both find ways to make their religious communities relevant to American democracy by distancing them from those more radical (eschatological) parts of the tradition that might call the American project into question. Thus, Novak sees Niebuhr as an ally, who "still has much to teach all of us about how biblical theism can be seen as the most adequate foundation for democracy without making it a 'theocracy'" (p. 236). If Novak's work parallels Niebuhr on the Protestant side, it also parallels John Courtney Murray on the Roman Catholic side. Novak has understood himself as attempting to do for the American Jews what Murray did for American Roman Catholics ("John Courtney Murray, S.J.: A Jewish Appraisal," in Novak, *Ethics*, pp. 67–83). Like Murray, Novak represents a community that has been outside the mainstream of American public life. Following Murray, Novak attempts to draw on natural law theory to open a way for Jewish involvement in the American public square. However, it must be acknowledged that Novak sees the danger of stepping outside one's tradition in order to make oneself relevant (in fact, he critiques Murray on this very point), and thus he seems able to maintain a critical distance from American politics that was quickly lost for both Niebuhr and Murray. In short, Novak's engagement in the public square always serves the more determinative end of Jewish life and faithfulness, and thus it is more clearly conditional and pragmatic than Murray's or Niebuhr's (see Novak, *Ethics*, p. 242, n. 42). Whether Novak will be able to sustain the voice of his tradition in a public sphere determined to make such traditions irrelevant will be of decisive importance. Given Novak's recent move to the University of Toronto, it will be interesting to see if the politics of Canada presents any different challenges for bringing a Jewish voice to the public conversation.

94. Wyschogrod, *Body*, p. 243. This conviction may have become harder to sustain in the wake of the 1995 assassination of Yitzhak Rabin by a fellow Jew.

95. Paul van Buren nicely summarizes the challenge that this no presents to the church: "In its argument with the church, Israel charges that the church has spiritualized and moralized God's election and promises to his people. Whereas God's Torah testifies to God's choice of an actual, physical people, and his promises to their biological descendants, the church has wanted to speak only of the spiritual descendants of Abraham and has turned his promises into spiritual gifts, as if God could not morally commit himself to anything so ambiguous as the contentious Jewish people. From Israel's point of view, the church has lacked the courage to confess God's genuine engagement with the creaturely world of physical birth and a people of flesh and blood. . . . Israel raises the question for the church whether it really knows this God" (Paul van Buren, *A Theology of the Jewish-Christian Reality*, vol. 2, pp. 228–229).

96. Wyschogrod, *Body*, pp. 6–7, 9, 68, 178–179.

97. Ibid., p. 56.

98. Ibid., pp. 178–179. In his discussion of Jesus, Wyschogrod mistakenly attributes the *Haustafeln* (household codes) of the pastoral epistles to Jesus himself as an example of

Jesus' disinterest in making material changes in the status quo. Despite this error, Wyschogrod's apolitical reading of Jesus is strongly attested in Christian tradition. Texts such as John Howard Yoder's *Politics of Jesus*, 2nd ed. (Grand Rapids, MI: Eerdmans, 1994) have helped call such readings into question.

99. Novak, *Election*, pp. 155–156.

100. David Novak, "When Jews Are Christians," *First Things* 17 (November 1991): 44.

101. Novak, *Election*, p. 67, citing Cohen's *Religion of Reason Out of the Sources of Judaism*, trans. S. Kaplan (New York, 1972), pp. 240, 249, 264.

Chapter Three

1. For further documentation and comment on this tradition, see Rosemary Ruether, *Faith and Fratricide: The Theological Roots of Anti-Semitism* (Minneapolis: Seabury Press, 1974), pp. 17–82; and Clark Williamson, *A Guest in the House of Israel: Post-Holocaust Church Theology* (Louisville, KY: Westminster/John Knox Press, 1993), pp. 107–117.

2. The following discussion is indebted to Richard Hays's insightful analysis of anti-Judaism in the New Testament in *The Moral Vision of the New Testament: Community, Cross, New Creation* (San Francisco: HarperSanFrancisco, 1996), pp. 407–443.

3. Ibid., p. 423.

4. Ibid., pp. 424–428.

5. Ibid., p. 427.

6. In Chapter 5 I argue for a reading of the New Testament in continuity with the Old Testament as a nonsupersessionist account of God's one plan for Jews and Gentiles within an economy of trinitarian election. This account is not a denial of the supersessionism present in the New Testament but a theological and hermeneutical decision to highlight certain canonical voices (such as Paul and Luke) that I believe present a stronger and more faithful witness to the overarching narrative integrity of the Christian canon.

7. *The Epistle of Barnabas*, in Alexander Roberts and James Donaldson, eds., *The Ante-Nicene Fathers*, vol. 1 (Grand Rapids, MI: Eerdmans, 1981), p. 138.

8. Isaac of Antioch, *Homilies Against the Jews*, cited in Ruether, *Faith and Fratricide*, p. 138.

9. R. Kendall Soulen, *The God of Israel and Christian Theology* (Minneapolis: Fortress Press, 1996), p. 29.

10. Ibid., p. 46.

11. George Lindbeck incisively sums up this shift: "The hardening of the opposition between synagogue and church led even Jewish Christians, as such documents as the Letter of Barnabas illustrate, to reject the notion that unbelieving Jews remained part of God's people. Faithfulness became the mark of election, and election, conversely, became conditional on faithfulness. The doctrines of predestination and of salvation *sola gratia*, insofar as they persisted, tended to be applied only to individuals and not to communities" (George Lindbeck, "The Church," in Geoffrey Wainwright, ed., *Keeping the Faith* [Philadelphia: Fortress Press, 1988], p. 186).

12. *Epistle of Barnabas*, p. 142.

13. See Augustine, "In Answer to the Jews (*Adversus Judaeos*)," in *Treatises on Marriage and Other Subjects*, vol. 27 of *The Fathers of the Church*, ed. Roy Joseph Defarrari (Washington: Catholic University of America Press, 1955), p. 398, cf. 402–409. Elsewhere, for instance in the *City of God*, Augustine gives more material content to election, church, and redemption. See n. 35 below.

14. Ruether, *Faith and Fratricide,* pp. 127–128, citing Ephrem, *Rhythm Against the Jews,* and John Damascene, "On the Sabbath."

15. Soulen, *The God of Israel,* p. 13.

16. Ibid., p. 16.

17. Ibid., p. 49.

18. Ibid., p. 16.

19. Ibid., p. 17.

20. Ibid., pp. 54–55.

21. This connection between a de-Judaized church and the rise of Constantine is noted also by Kendall Soulen, who writes, "Christendom names the church's theological and so-cial posture when it is triumphalistic toward Jews and gnostic toward God's engagement in history. The God of Israel, in contrast, names the God who is identified by fidelity to the Jewish people through time and therefore by engagement with human history in its public and corporate dimensions" (Soulen, *The God of Israel,* p. xi). Although the rela-tionship of supersessionism and Christendom is not developed in Soulen, the contrast he presents here corresponds closely to my own distinction between the politics of superses-sionism and the politics of election.

22. Robert Wilken notes that "the best-documented and most persistent eschatology in the first two Christian centuries was chiliasm, the belief that God would establish a future kingdom on earth centered in Jerusalem. The term *chiliasm* comes from the Greek word for 'thousand' (*chilias*) and refers to the belief, first stated in the book of Revelation, that Christ would one day return to rule on earth for a period of a thousand years before the heavenly Jerusalem comes down from the heavens (Rev. 21)" (Robert Wilken, *The Land Called Holy: Palestine in Christian History and Thought* [New Haven, CT: Yale University Press, 1992], p. 56).

23. Justin Martyr, *Dialogue with Trypho,* 80.5; cited in ibid., p. 57.

24. Tertullian, *Adversus Marcionem,* iii.24, in Henry Bettenson, ed. and trans., *The Early Christian Fathers* (New York: Oxford University Press, 1956), p. 164.

25. Irenaeus, *Adversus Haeresis,* V.xxxii.1, in Bettenson, *The Early Christian Fathers,* p. 99.

26. Wilken, *Land Called Holy,* p. 65.

27. Origen, *First Principles,* 2.11.2, cited in ibid., p. 77.

28. Ibid., pp. 69, 75.

29. Ibid., 4.2.1,, p. 77; emphasis in original.

30. Wilken, *Land Called Holy,* p. 77.

31. Eusebius, *Oration in Honor of Constantine on the Thirtieth Anniversary of His Reign,* in Maurice Wiles and Mark Santer, eds., *Documents in Early Christian Thought* (Cambridge: Cambridge University Press, 1975), p. 233.

32. Wilken, *Land Called Holy,* p. 79.

33. David Novak, *The Election of Israel: The Idea of the Chosen People* (Cambridge: Cambridge University Press, 1995), p. 67.

34. Ruether, *Faith and Fratricide,* p. 141.

35. Augustine, *City of God,* trans. Henry Bettenson (New York: Penguin, 1972), XIX, 12. Where exactly Augustine's *City of God* falls in relation to the above three answers is de-batable, and it would require a book of its own to work through the variant interpreta-tions of Augustine's politics. The heart of the question lies in whether Augustine's contrast between the *civitas Dei* and the *civitas terrena* is only between a heavenly and an earthly

reality (in a Neoplatonic sense) or whether the *civitas Dei* in its earthly pilgrim form, that is, as the church, actually functions for Augustine as a concrete political contrast society. The popular reading given by Reinhold Niebuhr that makes Augustine a political realist follows the first reading and turns the *civitas Dei* into a transcendent ideal. See Reinhold Niebuhr, "Augustine's Political Realism," in *The Essential Reinhold Niebuhr*, ed. Robert McAfee Brown (New Haven, CT: Yale University Press, 1986), pp. 123–141; and R. A. Markus, *Saeculum: History and Society in the Theology of St Augustine* (Cambridge: Cambridge University Press, 1970). For the alternative view, see Rowan Williams, "Politics and the Soul: A Reading of the *City of God*," *Milltown Studies* 19-20 (1987): 55–72. See also the comments of Gerhard Lohfink, who highlights the ambiguity in Augustine's ecclesiology in *Jesus and Community: The Social Dimension of Christian Faith*, trans. John P. Galvin (Philadelphia: Fortress Press, 1984), pp. 181–185.

36. This is not to say that Christendom can be understood only in Eusebian terms. In Chapter 4 I consider O'Donovan's non-Eusebian vision of the "Christendom idea." In addition, Lindbeck suggests that the conversion of the Roman Empire "might be compared, perhaps, to the Israelite monarchy which God consented to *contre coeur* (1 Sam. 8), and yet also mightily used to preserve his people and prepare for the Messiah (Jesus sprang from the Davidic line). In somewhat similar fashion, so one could argue, the imperial church preserved the faith amid barbarian chaos, converted Europe, and was the cradle of the first civilization to become worldwide (whether there is anything messianic about Western-spawned modernity is another question)" (Lindbeck, "The Church," p. 188). Lindbeck powerfully reminds us that even the church's least faithful moments are not finally outside of the providential direction of God's plan to consummate the covenant.

37. Milbank notes that "[sociology] interprets the theological transformation at the inception of modernity as a genuine 'reformation' which fulfills the destiny of Christianity to let the spiritual be the spiritual, without public interference, and the public be the secular, without private prejudice." Milbank challenges this reading of modernity, arguing that "this interpretation preposterously supposes that the new theology simply brought Christianity to its true essence by lifting some irksome and misplaced sacred ecclesial restrictions on the free market of the secular, whereas, in fact, it instituted an entirely different economy of power and knowledge and had to invent 'the political' and 'the state', just as much as it had to invent 'private religion'" (John Milbank, *Theology and Social Theory: Beyond Secular Reason* [Cambridge, MA: Blackwell, 1990], p. 10). I contend that the sociological interpretation of modernity that Milbank critiques is prefigured in the church's own supersessionistic teachings. Thus, although Milbank's claim that these new political forms are modern inventions is correct, it is also true that the split between the secular political realm and private religion did not arise ex nihilo in modernity but rather drew its intelligibility from the church's long-standing distinction between its own spiritual nature and the material form of Israel.

38. Novak, *Election*, pp. 46–47.

39. Thomas Hobbes, *Leviathan: or the Matter, Forme and Power of a Commonwealth Ecclesiasticall and Civil*, ed. Michael Oakeshott (New York: Macmillan, 1962), p. 354.

40. Benedict de Spinoza, *A Theologico-Political Treatise*, trans. R. H. M. Elwes (New York: Dover, 1951), pp. 54–55.

41. Ibid., p. 250.

42. Ibid., p. 55.

43. Novak, *Election*, pp. 46–47.

44. Spinoza, *Theologico-Political Treatise,* pp. 70–71, compare pp. 64–65.

45. Hobbes, *Leviathan,* p. 353.

46. Ibid., p. 362.

47. Ibid., p. 355.

48. Spinoza, *Theologico-Political Treatise,* p. 250.

49. Ibid., p. 245.

50. In this way Spinoza anticipates Thomas Jefferson's famous comment, "The legitimate powers of government extend to such acts only as are injurious to others. But it does me no injury for my neighbor to say there are twenty gods, or no god. It neither picks my pocket nor breaks my leg" ("Notes on the State of Virginia," in *Thomas Jefferson: Selected Writings* [Arlington Heights, IL: Harlan Davidson, 1979], p. 48). Jefferson states negatively what Spinoza states positively, that government is only concerned with actions and thus it may allow people to believe what they wish. It is significant to note the ease with which both writers divorce belief and piety from actions and practices.

51. For instance, Hobbes writes, "The *Kingdom of God* in the writings of divines, and specially in sermons and treatises of devotion, is taken most commonly for eternal felicity, after this life, in the highest heaven. . . . To the contrary, I find the KINGDOM OF GOD to signify, in most places of Scripture, a *kingdom properly so named,* constituted by the votes of the people of Israel" (*Leviathan,* p. 297).

52. Ibid., pp. 298–301, emphasis in original.

53. Joshua Mitchell, *Not by Reason Alone: Religion, History, and Identity in Early Modern Political Thought* (Chicago: University of Chicago Press, 1993), p. 12.

54. Hobbes, *Leviathan,* p. 297; Spinoza, *Theologico-Political Treatise,* pp. 220–221.

55. Novak, *Election,* pp. 23–26.

56. Spinoza, *Theologico-Political Treatise,* p. 44.

57. As Novak writes, "Even when Spinoza uses the term 'choice,' which we shall see is in fact a metaphor, he does not mean that God had any other option. God himself is only free *from* any outside influences because in truth there are none. But God is not free *for* anything other than ultimately immutable eternity" (*Election,* p. 24).

58. Spinoza, *Theologico-Political Treatise,* p. 45.

59. Yet even this proves to be a less than exact description for Spinoza, since human choice as well turns out to be an illusion created by lack of knowledge. On this see Novak, *Election,* pp. 27–30.

60. Spinoza, *Theologico-Political Treatise,* p. 203.

61. Ibid., p. 298.

62. As Spinoza puts it, "A compact is only made valid by its utility, without which it becomes null and void" (ibid., p. 204).

63. Hobbes, *Leviathan,* p. 110, emphasis in original.

64. Spinoza, *Theologico-Political Treatise,* pp. 74–75.

65. Ibid., p. 219.

66. William R. Hutchison, introduction to Hartmut Lehmann and William R. Hutchison, eds., *Many Are Chosen: Divine Election and Western Nationalism* (Minneapolis: Fortress Press, 1994), p. 23.

67. A. F. Walls, "Carrying the White Man's Burden: Some British Views of National Vocation in the Imperial Era," in Lehmann and Hutchison, *Many Are Chosen,* p. 40.

68. Conrad Cherry, "Response," in Lehmann and Hutchison, *Many Are Chosen,* pp. 110–111.

69. Thomas F. Gossett, *Race* (Dallas, TX: Southern Methodist University Press, 1963), p. 190, cited in Jon Levenson, "Exodus and Liberation," in *The Hebrew Bible, the Old Testament, and Historical Criticism* (Louisville, KY: Westminster/John Knox Press, 1993), p. 156.

70. Hartmut Lehmann, "'God Our Old Ally': The Chosen People Theme in Late Nineteenth- and Early Twentieth-Century German Nationalism," in Lehmann and Hutchison, *Many Are Chosen*, p. 104.

71. Bill Clinton, "A Vision for America: A New Covenant," speech delivered at the Democratic National Convention, July 16, 1992; "Address Before a Joint Session of the Congress on the State of the Union," *Weekly Compilation of Presidential Documents* 31, 4 (1995): 107.

72. See Alasdair MacIntyre, *After Virtue: A Study in Moral Theory*, 2nd ed. (Notre Dame, IN: University of Notre Dame Press, 1984), pp. 1–5.

73. Raymond Geuss, *The Idea of a Critical Theory* (Cambridge: Cambridge University Press, 1981), p. 15.

74. Cited in Hutchison, introduction to Lehmann and Hutchison, *Many Are Chosen*, p. 18.

75. Conrad Cherry, *God's New Israel: Religious Interpretations of American Destiny* (Englewood Cliffs, NJ: Prentice-Hall, 1971), p. 42.

76. Ibid., p. 114.

77. Herman Melville, *White Jacket*, chap. 36, cited in Robert Bellah, *The Broken Covenant: American Civil Religion in Time of Trial*, 2nd ed. (Chicago: University of Chicago Press, 1992).

78. *Congressional Record* 33 (Washington, DC: Government Printing Office, 1900), p. 711; cited in Bellah, *Broken Covenant*, p. 38.

79. Albert J. Beveridge, "The Star of Empire," cited in Cherry, *God's New Israel*, p. 153.

80. Bellah, *Broken Covenant*, p. xix.

81. Ibid., pp. 185–186.

82. Ibid., p. 60.

83. The powerful abolitionist spokesman William Lloyd Garrison pulled no punches when he invoked this psalm in judgment of America. Bellah tells us, "Ridiculing Washington's notion that the establishment of America was an 'experiment' on which the fate of the world depends, in 1837 Garrison wrote, 'As if God has suspended the fate of all nations, and hazarded the fulfilment of his glorious promises, upon the results of a wild and cruel 'experiment' by a land-stealing, blood-thirsty, man-slaying and slave-trading people in one corner of the globe! As if God could not easily dash this nation in pieces, as a potter's vessel is broken, and thereby vindicate his eternal justice'" (cited in ibid., p. 50).

84. Herman Melville, *Clarel*, cited in Bellah, *Broken Covenant*, p. 58.

85. John Howard Yoder, *The Priestly Kingdom: Social Ethics as Gospel* (Notre Dame, IN: University of Notre Dame Press, 1984), pp. 144–147.

Chapter Four

1. David Novak, *The Election of Israel: The Idea of the Chosen People* (Cambridge: Cambridge University Press, 1995), p. 117, n. 23.

2. John Calvin, *Institutes of the Christian Religion*, trans. Ford Lewis Battles (Philadelphia: Westminster, 1960), II.x.23. Further references to the *Institutes* in this chapter are noted parenthetically in the text by book, chapter, and section.

3. Irenaeus, *Against Heresies*, 4.9.2.; noted in R. Kendall Soulen, *The God of Israel and Christian Theology* (Minneapolis: Fortress Press, 1996), p. 46.

4. Thomas Aquinas, *Summa Theologica,* trans. Fathers of the English Dominican Province (Allen, TX: Christian Classics, 1948), I, 23, 27–43.

5. See Heinrich Heppe, *Reformed Dogmatics,* trans. G. T. Thomson (London: George Allen & Unwin, 1950), pp. 130–189. On the persons of Christ and the Holy Spirit as means or instruments of God the Father's election, see pp. 168–172.

6. Beza's famous flow chart, in which he presents "The Sum of all Christianity" as the outworkings of the eternal decrees of a God "whose ways are past finding out," can be found in ibid., 147–148. This chart makes very clear the sharp dualism that such a view builds into the entirety of one's theology.

7. Karl Barth, *Church Dogmatics,* ed. G. W. Bromiley and T. F. Torrance (Edinburgh: T. & T. Clark, 1962), IV/3.2, p. 877. All further references to the *Church Dogmatics* in this chapter are cited parenthetically in the text by volume, part, and page number.

8. For an account of this period, see Hartmut Lehmann, "'God Our Old Ally': The Chosen People Theme in Late Nineteenth- and Early Twentieth-Century German Nationalism," in Hartmut Lehmann and William R. Hutchison, eds., *Many Are Chosen: Divine Election and Western Nationalism* (Minneapolis: Fortress Press, 1994), pp. 85–107.

9. Ibid., pp. 106–107.

10. Letter to O. Weber, June 20, 1949, quoted in Eberhard Busch, *Karl Barth: His Life from Letters and Autobiographical Texts* (Philadelphia: Fortress Press, 1976), p. 301.

11. Barth's "individual," however, is to be understood as the correlate of God's oneness and thus in relation to God. Barth gives no ground to a modern secular "individualism," where the human person stands in self-assertion over against all others, including God (II/2, 313–316).

12. Karl Barth, "The Jewish Problem and the Christian Answer," in *Against the Stream* (New York: Philosophical Library, 1954), p. 200.

13. Michael Wyschogrod, "A Jewish Perspective on Karl Barth," in Donald K. McKim, ed., *How Karl Barth Changed My Mind* (Grand Rapids, MI: Eerdmans, 1986), p. 160.

14. Nicholas Healy, "The Logic of Karl Barth's Ecclesiology: Analysis, Assessment and Proposed Modifications," *Modern Theology* 10, 3 (1994): 265. He goes on to add, "Barth relativizes the visible institution [of the church] to the extent that it becomes in itself no more than one among a large number of other religious groups that compete for people's allegiance on the basis of a set of beliefs about the way things really are." Yoder, however, calls attention to the occasional concreteness of Barth's ecclesiology and the ways in which this provides a contrasting witness to Constantinianism. See John Howard Yoder, "Why Ecclesiology Is Social Ethics: Gospel Ethics Versus the Wider Wisdom," in Michael G. Cartwright, ed., *The Royal Priesthood: Essays Ecclesiological and Ecumenical* (Grand Rapids, MI: Eerdmans, 1994), pp. 102–126, and his essay "Karl Barth: How His Mind Kept Changing," in Donald K. McKim, ed., *How Karl Barth Changed My Mind* (Grand Rapids, MI: Eerdmans, 1986), pp. 166–171.

15. Robert Jenson, "The Holy Spirit," in Carl E. Braaten and Robert W. Jenson, eds., *Christian Dogmatics,* vol. 2. (Philadelphia: Fortress Press, 1984), p. 138. Jenson's argument for a pneumatological account of election is extremely helpful and has shaped my own thinking on this matter. See also his critique of Barth's doctrine of election in *Alpha and Omega: A Study in the Theology of Karl Barth* (New York: Thomas Nelson and Sons, 1963).

16. Rosemary Ruether, *Faith and Fratricide: The Theological Roots of Anti-Semitism* (Minneapolis: Seabury Press, 1974), p. 246.

17. John H. Leith, ed., *Creeds of the Churches*, 3rd ed. (Louisville, KY: John Knox Press, 1982), pp. 33, 35.

18. George Lindbeck, *The Nature of Doctrine: Religion and Theology in a Postliberal Age* (Philadelphia: Westminster, 1984), p. 16.

19. Ruether, *Faith and Fratricide*, pp. 248–257.

20. Ibid., p. 256.

21. Ibid., pp. 256–257.

22. Clark Williamson, *A Guest in the House of Israel: Post-Holocaust Church Theology* (Louisville, KY: Westminster/John Knox Press, 1993), pp. 194–195; Paul van Buren, *A Theology of the Jewish-Christian Reality*, vol. 3, *Christ in Context* (San Francisco: Harper and Row, 1988), pp. 44–45.

23. Paul van Buren, *A Theology of the Jewish-Christian Reality*, vol. 1, *Discerning the Way* (San Francisco: Harper and Row, 1980), p. 85; compare Williamson, *Guest in the House of Israel*, pp. 188, 197–200.

24. Williamson follows H. Richard Niebuhr and Paul Tillich in formulating his christological and trinitarian positions, and as such his Monarchianism appears to have the character of Niebuhrian "radical monotheism" (see Williamson, *Guest in the House of Israel*, pp. 188–201; van Buren, *Discerning the Way*, pp. 66–67; *Christ in Context*, xviii, pp. 284ff.). Williamson provides an almost humorous illustration of the pervasive Monarchianism in these works. As he begins to discuss the doctrine of the Trinity, he opts to set aside the question of relating three and one, saying that "the question at issue . . . has *nothing* to do with a numbers game. In this discussion, we will leave the numbers to one side" (p. 228). (Does this mean we could just as well talk about binitarianism or septarianism?) Yet very quickly Williamson seems to have forgotten this promise, as he goes on to refer to God as "one" twelve times in the following five pages. It turns out that only the number three gets set aside.

25. It is interesting to note that Marcellus of Ancyra, one of the signers of the creed formulated at Nicea in 325, later used the above passage from 1 Corinthians to argue a Sabellian position. It was precisely against this reading of the Scripture, which van Buren and Williamson share, that the phrase was inserted in the final form of the creed at Constantinople in 381: "of his [Christ's] reign there will be no end" (Jaroslav Pelikan, *The Christian Tradition*, vol. 1, *The Emergence of the Catholic Tradition [100–600]* [Chicago: University of Chicago Press, 1961], p. 208).

26. Williamson, *Guest in the House of Israel*, p. 231.

27. Van Buren, *Discerning the Way*, p. 88.

28. Ibid., p. 75.

29. One might have thought that van Buren's attention to Ludwig Wittgenstein would have made him careful not to assume a deeper level of common meaning underneath contrasting descriptions, which in turn arise from different linguistic communities (*Discerning the Way*, pp. 28, 87; *Christ in Context*, pp. 28–29).

30. Michael Wyschogrod, "Christology: The Immovable Object," *Religion and Intellectual Life* 3, 4 (1986): 77.

31. David Novak, *Jewish-Christian Dialogue: A Jewish Justification* (New York: Oxford University Press, 1989), pp. 77–80.

32. Kendall Soulen, "YHWH the Triune God," *Modern Theology* (forthcoming).

33. Soulen, *The God of Israel,* pp. 164–165. Further references to this work in this chapter are noted parenthetically.

34. Leander E. Keck, "Toward the Renewal of New Testament Christology," *New Testament Studies* 32 (1986): 364.

35. By "late-modern" and "late-modernity," O'Donovan means specifically life in the twentieth century, though he recognizes that the roots of this life lie in the ways modernity has developed over the past several centuries (Oliver O'Donovan, *The Desire of the Nations: An Outline for Political Theology* [Cambridge: Cambridge University Press, 1996], p. 271). All further references to this text in this chapter will be made parenthetically.

36. O'Donovan's use of "secular" is an attempted recovery of the original meaning of the term *saeculum* (age). The secular was, in medieval theology, not a space but a time—the time between the fall and the eschaton, when the world awaits final redemption. It is the time that is passing away now that Christ has come. O'Donovan writes, "Secular institutions have a role confined to this passing age (*saeculum*). They do not represent the arrival of the new age and the rule of God. . . . The corresponding term to 'secular' is not 'sacred', nor 'spiritual', but 'eternal'. Applied to the political authorities, the term 'secular' should tell us that they are not agents of Christ, but are marked for displacement when the rule of God in Christ is finally disclosed. They are Christ's conquered enemies; yet they have an indirect testimony to give, bearing the marks of his sovereignty imposed upon them, negating their pretensions and evoking their acknowledgment" (O'Donovan, *Desire of the Nations,* pp. 211–212). The transformation of the term "secular" from an age to a social space results from the demise of Christendom and the attempted creation of a neutral politics that no longer serves the church. On the creation of this secular domain, see Milbank's helpful discussion in *Theology and Social Theory: Beyond Secular Reason* (Cambridge, MA: Blackwell, 1990), pp. 1–6.

37. One of the problems with O'Donovan's reading of Romans 13 is that he assumes verses 1–7 refer equally well to Christian rulers as they do to the pagan empire of which Paul speaks (pp. 147ff.). Paul himself does not address the question of whether or not a Christian could be a ruler, yet given his description of the Christian life in Romans 12, which includes the call *not* to exact the vengeance the political authorities exact, it is hard to see that these are compatible callings. It may be that Paul would say a Christian could indeed be a ruler but that the role of ruler would have to be transformed to conform to the more determinative Christian calling. If this transformation did not take place in the structure of the rule, it is hard to see that, on Paul's terms, one could be a ruler and Christian at the same time.

38. "Structural supersessionism" is Soulen's term; see *The God of Israel,* pp. 28–33.

39. Ibid., pp. 49–52.

40. Oliver O'Donovan, *Resurrection and Moral Order,* 2nd ed. (Grand Rapids, MI: Eerdmans, 1994), p. 128.

41. Ibid.

42. By itself, the fact that O'Donovan largely came up with this political structure apart from the witness of Israel does not prove that it is unfaithful to or ultimately disconnected from Israel's witness. But I hope I have at least begun to show that these concepts do indeed float above Israel's life and witness, and thus they make the Jews, not the "idea" of Israel but the chosen people themselves, indecisive for God's politics.

43. In response to this critique, O'Donovan has asked me in what sense I really believe in the victory of Christ. The point at issue, it seems, is not the extent to which either of us

believes in this victory (for I am sure we both do) but rather where we might look to see its visible form in this time between the times. I argue in Chapter 5 that the visibility of Christ's victory is the visibility of Israel's redemption and can be seen in those places where the church's life witnesses to peace between Jew and Gentile, plentiful sharing of goods, and a cruciform pattern of obedience that, paradoxically, manifests Christ's triumph under the sign of the cross. Readily I would admit that this witness has not always been very visible, but I have no need to secure a structural location where Christ's victory will maintain a guaranteed presence. It seems to me that in God's decision to elect a chosen people through whom God's ways would be known to the world, God was willing to risk their failure. But God was never willing to bypass them in order to secure the visibility of God's victory without them.

44. Novak, *Election*, p. 67.

Chapter Five

1. Thanks to Gene Rogers for helping me conceptualize the trinitarian focus of this chapter.

2. N. T. Wright, *The Climax of the Covenant: Christ and the Law in Pauline Theology* (Minneapolis: Fortress Press, 1991), pp. 231–257.

3. Ibid., p. 243.

4. Ibid., p. 249.

5. Ibid., p. 256.

6. Paul van Buren, *A Theology of the Jewish-Christian Reality*, vol. 1, *Discerning the Way* (San Francisco: Harper and Row, 1980), p. 197.

7. Van Buren also makes clear that these are not the only two ways to walk in God's path—there are many "diverse paths" for walking in "the Way of the One" (ibid., pp. 3–4; cf. p. 197).

8. Ibid., p. 60.

9. I owe this language of the Gentiles' "overhearing" to Willie Jennings.

10. Richard Hays, *Echoes of Scripture in the Letters of Paul* (New Haven, CT: Yale University Press, 1989), p. 99.

11. David Novak, *The Election of Israel: The Idea of the Chosen People* (Cambridge: Cambridge University Press, 1995), p. 156.

12. Hays, *Echoes*, p. 134.

13. In reading Romans 9–11 as a justification of God's righteousness toward the Jews, I am indebted to Hays's reading in *Echoes*, pp. 34–84.

14. Hays notes that a similar conception of Gentile inclusion is at work in 1 Corinthians. In what might be an easily overlooked phrase, Paul addresses his readers, saying, "When you were Gentiles [ἔθνη] you were enticed and lead astray" (1 Cor. 12:2). His use of the imperfect tense suggests that Paul no longer thinks of the Corinthian Christians as Gentiles—they have been made a part of Israel. Hays writes, "It is no accident that Paul never uses expressions such as 'new Israel' or 'spiritual Israel.' There has been and always will be only one Israel. Into that one Israel Gentile Christians such as the Corinthians have now been absorbed" (Hays, *Echoes*, pp. 96–97).

15. For a wonderful analysis of Paul's use of Abraham to argue for Gentile inclusion, see Jeffrey Siker, *Disinheriting the Jews: Abraham in Early Christian Controversy* (Louisville, KY: Westminster/John Knox Press, 1991), pp. 28–76.

16. Richard Hays, *The Moral Vision of the New Testament: Community, Cross, New Creation* (San Francisco: HarperSanFrancisco, 1996), p. 432.

17. Catherine Mowry LaCugna, *God for Us: The Trinity and the Christian Life* (San Francisco: HarperSanFrancisco, 1991), p. 43.

18. For a welcome proposal to remedy this problem, see Kendall Soulen's "YHWH the Triune God," *Modern Theology* (forthcoming).

19. LaCugna, *God for Us*, p. ix. LaCugna's summary of God's economy is in no way uniquely problematic among Christian theologians. I only point to her because her work has been at the forefront of contemporary trinitarian theology.

20. I am aware that this at once helps and makes more difficult "Jewish-Christian dialogue." On the one hand, it explicitly seeks to overturn traditional supersessionism by affirming that the Christian God is and will always be Israel's God. On the other hand, however, by specifically naming this God as Trinity, I am highlighting a fundamental difference between us.

21. LaCugna cites precisely this passage from Ephesians as a summary of God's economy, "the shape of salvation history" (*God for Us*, p. 21). Yet reading through the Procrustean lens of the "standard canonical narrative," she never mentions, never even seems to notice, that God's economy, as presented here, is an economy of election grounded (as becomes clear in Eph. 2) in the choosing of Israel. Rather, she harmonizes the economy in Ephesians 1 with the standard narrative, thus continuing to reproduce a doctrine of the Trinity that makes Israel largely indecisive for God's identity and plan for creation.

22. The affirmation that Christ "has abolished [καταργήσας] the law [τὸν νόμον] of commandments and ordinances [τῶν ἐντολῶν ἐν δόγμασιν]" (2:15) seems hard to square with the kind of continuity I am arguing for between Israel and church. I would suggest that this passage needs to be read both in light of Paul's emphatic assertion in Romans 3:31 ("Do we then overthrow [καταργὸῦμεν] the law [νομον] by this faith? By no means! On the contrary, we uphold the law [νμόν]") and also his treatment of the same topic in 2 Corinthians 3 (as discussed earlier in the chapter).

23. John Hall Elliot sees election "permeating and determining of the thought of I P [1 Peter] as a whole" (John Hall Elliot, *The Elect and the Holy* [Leiden, Netherlands: E. J. Brill, 1966], p. 147).

24. Whether or not the presentation here of the church as Israel is supersessionistic is debatable. The Jews who did not believe and follow Christ are simply not mentioned in this epistle, so it would be unfruitful speculation to seek to assess the author's posture toward unbelieving Israel *post Christum*. Elliot argues against any anti-Jewish tendencies in the letter, noting that the attribution of Israel's titles to gentile Christians, such as, "you are a chosen race, a royal priesthood, a holy nation, God's own people" (v. 9, cf. vv. 5, 10), is not anti-Jewish polemic but rather a positive statement about God's eschatological fulfillment (Elliot, *The Elect*, pp. 47, 176). At one point he writes, "There is . . . no basis for the assumption that the use of ἱεράτευμα in vv. 5 and 9 implies a polemic against the Jewish cultic institution. . . . I P 2:4–10 does not present an anti-Judaic polemic. The ascription of the honorific predicates of Israel to the believing community represents the unfolding of an eschatological event and not an engagement in polemics" (p. 220). Conversely, Luke Timothy Johnson, noting that "one of the most distinctive aspects of this letter is its identification of *gentile* believers with Israel," hears in the epistle sheer supersessionism. "The gentile Christians inherit the attributes of Diaspora Judaism. . . . For the

first time in the NT, we can speak accurately of the consciousness of a 'new Israel'"
(Johnson, *The Writings of the New Testament: An Interpretation* [Philadelphia: Fortress
Press, 1986], p. 439). Of course, the actual words "new Israel" never occur in 1 Peter, thus
leaving open the question of whether, for Peter, the Gentiles are grafted into Israel's
covenant and story (as in Rom. 9–11) or whether the Gentiles displace Israel as God's people (as became the standard move in the church's theology). Given that this letter does not
conclusively lean one way or the other, and in light of the broader New Testament witness
(including especially Rom. 9–11 and Eph. 1–2), I follow Elliot in reading 1 Peter as an example of how the church might understand itself when seen rightly as those who have been
gathered into God's election of the Jews.

25. LaCugna, *God for Us*, p. 25.

26. I refer to the author of this epistle as "Peter" not to make a claim about the historical authorship of the book but rather to maintain continuity with the canon.

27. My use of the capital *S* here follows Elliot's argument (contra the NRSV) that what
is being referred to in this verse is not some general sense of "spiritual" but particularly the
things of the Holy Spirit. He writes, "πνευματικός does not mean 'spiritual' in the
metaphorical sense of 'immaterial,' 'non-external,' 'geistig' or 'geistlich,' or 'heavenly.'
Rather, "πνευματικός is meant in the non-metaphorical, real sense of 'Spiritual,' 'caused
by or filled with the Holy Spirit'" (Elliot, *The Elect*, p. 153). In giving this reading of
πνευματικός, Elliot follows Walter Bauer, William F. Arndt, and F. Wilbur Gingrich, *A
Greek Lexicon of the New Testament and Other Early Christian Literature*, 2nd ed. (Chicago:
University of Chicago Press, 1979), pp. 678–679. He goes on to note that not only is this
reference to the Holy Spirit the nearly ubiquitous meaning of πνευματικός in the NT, but
it coheres with the understanding of πνεῦμα elsewhere in this letter (1:2, 11, 12; 4:14).

28. Elliot, *The Elect*, p. 177.

29. Frank J. Matera, *New Testament Ethics: The Legacies of Jesus and Paul* (Louisville, KY:
Westminster/John Knox Press, 1996), p. 123.

30. One finds also in the Gospel of John, chapters 14–17, a similar summary of God's
activity in terms of trinitarian election. The disciples have been given to the Son by the
Father—chosen and gathered out of the world ("You did not choose me, but I chose you";
15:16, 19; 17:2, 6, 7). They have been called into friendship with Christ through their obedience to his cruciform love (15:10–14). With the ascension of Christ, the Holy Spirit, the
Advocate, will come and abide with them, guiding them into truth (14:16–17, 26) and
leading them toward unity with one another and eternal life in union with the Father and
the Son (17:2, 3, 20–22). Once again emerges the pattern of election, vocation to cruciform
obedience, sanctification in the Spirit, and final consummation.

Chapter Six

1. David Novak, *Jewish-Christian Dialogue: A Jewish Justification* (New York: Oxford
University Press, 1989), p. 9. Though it is true that there is a shared mission here, in what
follows I can speak only to and for the church. Though I have sought to listen carefully to
Jewish voices, I cannot speak for them or seek to name the form their political vocation
should take. I can hope, however, that my proposals here might be of some interest to Jews
seeking to live in faithfulness to the covenant.

2. Gerhard Lohfink, *Jesus and Community: The Social Dimension of Christian Faith*,
trans. John P. Galvin (Philadelphia: Fortress Press, 1984), pp. 122–123.

3. Peter Berger, *The Heretical Imperative: Contemporary Possibilities of Religious Affirmation* (Garden City, NY: Anchor Press, 1979), p. 17.

4. I borrow the term *bricoleur* from Jeffrey Stout, who uses it to discuss moral language, and not, as I am using it, to mean the cobbling together of a religion (though the two are not unrelated). Jeffrey Stout, *Ethics After Babel: The Language of Morals and Their Discontents* (Boston: Beacon Press, 1988), pp. 74–77.

5. Berger, *Heretical Imperative,* pp. 26–31.

6. Bruce Marshall, "What Is Truth?" *Pro Ecclesia* 4, 4 (Fall 1995): 413.

7. One might argue against me that this language of choosing God is just what we find in Deuteronomy where Moses calls the children of Israel to reaffirm the covenant God made with their ancestors. "I call heaven and earth to witness against you today that I have set before you life and death, blessings and curses. Choose life so that you and your descendants may live" (Deut. 30:19). Yet the choice that is called for here is not a choice of God. Rather, the very possibility of choosing blessing or curse, obedience or disobedience, arises out of the structure of covenant life that God has already chosen for Israel. The people are then called to make decisions about how, not whether, they will live the covenant. As Levenson puts it, "For all the language of choice that characterizes covenant texts, the Hebrew Bible never regards choice to decline covenant as legitimate. The fact that a choice is given does not make the alternative good or even acceptable, as a proponent of a purely contractual ethic might wish" (Jon Levenson, *Creation and the Persistence of Evil* [Princeton, NJ: Princeton University Press, 1988], p. 141).

8. On this debate as it was carried forward by Protestants after Luther and Calvin, see Karl Barth's insightful excursus in *Church Dogmatics,* ed. G. W. Bromiley and T. F. Torrance (Edinburgh: T. & T .Clark, 1957), II/2, pp. 55–76.

9. Pope John Paul II, *Veritatis Splendor* (Vatican City: Libreria Editrice Vaticana, 1993), sec. 86. All further citations are noted parenthetically in the text by section number.

10. Avery Dulles, "John Paul II and the Truth About Freedom," *First Things* 55 (August-September 1995): 36.

11. Robert W. Jenson, "The God-Wars," in Carl E. Braaten and Robert W. Jenson, eds., *Either/Or: The Gospel or Neopaganism* (Grand Rapids, MI: Eerdmans, 1996), p. 31.

12. Ibid., pp. 31–32.

13. Ibid., p. 35.

14. William Placher, *Narratives of a Vulnerable God: Christ, Theology, and Scripture* (Louisville, KY: Westminster/John Knox Press, 1994), p. 150.

15. Stanley Hauerwas, *The Peaceable Kingdom: A Primer in Christian Ethics* (Notre Dame, IN: University of Notre Dame Press, 1983), p. 8.

16. Quotations from Ellen Goodman, "Child's Choices Come Crashing Down," *Durham (North Carolina) Herald-Sun,* April 16, 1996.

17. Jaroslav Pelikan, *The Christian Tradition,* vol. 1, *The Emergence of the Catholic Tradition (100–600)* (Chicago: University of Chicago Press, 1961), pp. 21–22.

18. David Keck, interpreting Henri Bergson, puts this matter nicely: "The free person is one who is able to act within the totality of her memories. She acts in continuity with who she is, not in discontinuity or randomness. The dancer becomes more free by being able to utilize the total repertoire of movements she has learned throughout her life. For the Christian, freedom must be considered in the context of God's grace. Hence, this linking of freedom and memory suggests that we can understand the freedom of a Christian as being able to live within the total memory of God's work in Israel and the church" (David

Keck, *Forgetting Whose We Are: Alzheimer's Disease and the Love of God* [Nashville, TN: Abingdon Press, 1996], pp. 68–69).

19. On this passage and Israel's "failed autonomy," see Walter Brueggemann, "Texts That Linger, Words That Explode," *Theology Today* 54, 2 (1997): 180–199.

20. Jon Levenson, "Exodus and Liberation," in *The Hebrew Bible, the Old Testament, and Historical Criticism* (Louisville, KY: Westminster/John Knox Press, 1993), p. 145.

21. Cited in Paul van Buren, *A Theology of the Jewish-Christian Reality*, vol. 2, *A Christian Theology of the People Israel* (San Francisco: Harper and Row, 1983), p. 156.

22. Van Buren, *A Christian Theology*, p. 157.

23. John Calvin, *Institutes of the Christian Religion*, ed. John T. McNeill and trans. Ford Lewis Battles (Philadelphia: Westminster, 1960), III.xxi.1. Though Calvin was clearly influenced by Stoicism, his affirmation of unfailing election is not to be confused with determinism. Rather, it is his way of naming the theological correlate of his conviction that justification is through God's grace alone.

24. Dorothy Day, *Loaves and Fishes* (Maryknoll, NY: Orbis Books, 1997), p. 86.

25. Ibid., p. 92.

26. C. S. Lewis, *Reflections on the Psalms* (New York: Harcourt Brace Jovanovich, 1958), pp. 59–60.

27. Ibid., p. 62.

28. Presbyterian Church (USA), Theology and Worship Ministry Unit, *Book of Common Worship* (Louisville, KY: Westminster/John Knox Press, 1993), p. 19, compare p. 17.

29. George Matheson, "Make Me a Captive, Lord," in LindaJo McKim, ed., *The Presbyterian Hymnal: Hymns, Psalms, and Spiritual Songs* (Louisville, KY: Westminster/John Knox Press, 1990), p. 378.

30. Karl Barth, "The Gift of Freedom," in *The Humanity of God* (Atlanta, GA: John Knox Press, 1960), pp. 71–72.

31. Augustine, *City of God*, trans. Henry Bettenson (New York: Penguin, 1972), pp. 1088–1089.

32. Ibid., p. 1089.

33. Ibid.

34. Wayne Meeks, *The First Urban Christians* (New Haven, CT: Yale University Press, 1983), p. 152.

35. Presbyterian Church, *Book of Common Worship*, pp. 404–405.

36. Ibid., pp. 406–407.

37. Ibid., p. 407.

38. John Locke, *The Second Treatise of Government*, in *Political Writings of John Locke*, ed. David Wootton (New York: Penguin, 1993), p. 274.

39. Walter Williams, "'Right to Die' Tests Commitment to Liberty," *Durham (North Carolina) Herald-Sun*, November 13, 1996.

40. Stanley Hauerwas and Charles Pinches, *Christians Among the Virtues: Theological Conversations with Ancient and Modern Ethics* (Notre Dame, IN: University of Notre Dame Press, 1997), pp. 149–165.

41. Ibid., pp. 161–162, emphasis added.

Chapter Seven

1. Anthony Giddens, *The Nation-State and Violence* (Berkeley: University of California Press, 1987), p. 254.

2. The use of masculine language here reflects the historical context of the polis as well as the significant linguistic connection between *virtus* (power, excellence, virtue) and *vir* (male, man).

3. Here I follow Barth's rejection of the classical doctrine of an *apokatastasis,* or universal salvation. For as Barth writes, "Even though theological consistency might seem to lead our thoughts and utterances most clearly in this direction, we must not arrogate to ourselves that which can be given and received only as a free gift" (Karl Barth, *Church Dogmatics,* ed. G. W. Bromiley and T. F. Torrance [Edinburgh: T. & T. Clark, 1961], IV/3.1, p. 478).

4. Daniel Boyarin, *A Radical Jew: Paul and the Politics of Identity* (Berkeley: University of California Press, 1994), p. 229.

5. Ibid., p. 235.

6. Ibid., p. 241.

7. Ibid., p. 242.

8. Ibid., p. 250.

9. Ibid., p. 256.

10. Cited in Murray Polner and Naomi Goodman, eds., *The Challenge of Shalom: The Jewish Tradition of Peace and Justice* (Philadelphia: New Society Publishers, 1994), p. 2.

11. Michael Wyschogrod, *The Body of Faith: God in the People Israel* (San Francisco: Harper and Row, 1983), p. 243. Of course, the next logical question is: What about peace with Israel's neighbors? Is it enough to talk about peace within the chosen people, or is there also a calling, even prior to redemption, to extend this peace to relations with the Gentiles?

12. David Novak, *The Election of Israel: The Idea of the Chosen People* (Cambridge: Cambridge University Press, 1995), p. 162.

13. This humility, however salutary such a posture may seem, may in fact threaten Israel's critical witness to the nations. Milbank's critique of Christian theology applies equally here: "The pathos of modern theology is its false humility. For theology, this must be a fatal disease, because once theology surrenders its claim to be a metadiscourse, it cannot any longer articulate the word of the creator God, but is bound to turn into the oracular voice of some finite idol" (John Milbank, *Theology and Social Theory: Beyond Secular Reason* [Cambridge, MA: Blackwell, 1990], p. 1). A Christian or Jewish political theology that in humility refrains from positioning and challenging the secular political discourses through its own articulation of an alternative can all too easily be turned into a sanctioning of the dominant powers.

14. There are certainly other options for Jews as well, but I could not suggest for them what these might be. Clearly, though, they would have to be grounded in different theological convictions than the specifically Christian claims about redemption that I am putting forward here.

15. Michael Goldberg, *Why Should Jews Survive? Looking Past the Holocaust to a Jewish Future* (New York: Oxford University Press, 1995), p. 146.

16. Polner and Goodman, *The Challenge of Shalom,* p. 5. See also the other essays on Jewish nonviolence in this same volume.

17. Paul Wadell beautifully reminds us of the ways in which the Eucharist writes us into God's story by training us as disciples. "To be a disciple is to submit ourselves to being disciplined in the surprising, often confounding, ways of God. We encounter those ways in the Eucharist when we listen to the Word of God and take that Word to heart. . . . To cel-

ebrate the Eucharist is to step into a story that illumines the meaning and direction of our life. The saga of creation, covenant, redemption, and restoration is not a narrative we are to view from afar, but precisely the story that governs our understanding of reality and our sense of what our being in the world involves" (Paul J. Wadell, "What Do All Those Masses Do for Us? Reflections on the Christian Moral Life and the Eucharist," in Kathleen Hughes and Mark R. Francis, eds., *Living No Longer for Ourselves* [Collegeville, MN: Liturgical Press, 1991], pp. 158–159).

18. Aquinas writes, "The difference between corporeal and spiritual food lies in this, that the former is changed into the substance of the person nourished, and consequently it cannot avail for supporting life except it be partaken of; but spiritual food changes man into itself, according to that saying of Augustine (*Conf.* vii), that he heard the voice of Christ as it were saying to him: *Nor shalt thou change Me into thyself, as food of thy flesh, but thou shalt be changed into Me*" (Thomas Aquinas, *Summa Theologica*, trans. Fathers of the English Dominican Province [Allen, TX: Christian Classics, 1948], III, 73, 3).

19. William Placher, *Narratives of a Vulnerable God: Christ, Theology, and Scripture* (Louisville, KY: Westminster/John Knox Press, 1994), p. 155.

20. John Calvin, *Institutes of the Christian Religion*, ed. John T. McNeill and trans. Ford Lewis Battles (Philadelphia: Westminster, 1960), IV.xvii.38.

21. Ibid., IV.xvii.44; compare IV.xvii.46 and John Calvin, "Articles Concerning the Organization of the Church and of Worship at Geneva Proposed by the Ministers at the Council," January 16, 1537, in *Calvin: Theological Treatises*, ed. J. K. S. Reid (Philadelphia: Westminster, 1954), pp. 48–50.

22. Calvin, *Institutes*, IV.xvii.44.

23. Ronald J. Sider, "Sharing the Wealth: The Church as Biblical Model for Public Policy," *Christian Century* 94, 21 (1977): 562.

24. Augustine, *City of God*, trans. Henry Bettenson (New York: Penguin, 1972), I, 35.

25. Robert Wilken notes that this translation reflects the fact that for the New Testament translators "'possess the land' does not sound like the kind of thing Jesus or early Christians would have said. Hence the beatitude is translated with the anemic and opaque expression 'inherit the earth.' 'Land' is too particular, too territorial, too national, yes, too Jewish. If, however, one interprets Jesus within, rather than against, his Jewish world, the translation 'possess the land' merits consideration. As we have seen, it is a recurring refrain in Jewish history, and in Jesus' time it was one way of designating the messianic kingdom centered in Jerusalem. 'Inherit the earth' captures neither the spiritual nor the territorial overtones of the phrase" (Robert Wilken, *The Land Called Holy: Palestine in Christian History and Thought* [New Haven: Yale University Press, 1992], p. 48).

26. Dennis C. Duling, *HarperCollins Study Bible*, ed. Wayne A. Meeks (New York: HarperCollins, 1993), note to Matthew 11:29, p. 1878.

27. W. D. Davies, *The Gospel and the Land* (Berkeley: University of California Press, 1974), p. 217.

28. Ibid., p. 219.

29. Walter Brueggemann, *The Land* (Philadelphia: Fortress Press, 1977), pp. 180–181.

30. Despite their similarities, Davies remains more willing to read the New Testament as a "spiritualizing" of the land, whereas Brueggemann links the land more determinatively to history, politics, and the physical realm (see ibid., pp. 170–171, 181, n. 31). Brueggemann distinguishes his study in this way: "The present discussion owes much to

Davies's work. However, it is here urged that the land theme is more central than Davies believes and that it has not been so fully spiritualized as he concludes" (p. 170).

31. John Milbank, "Enclaves, or Where Is the Church?" *New Blackfriars* 73, 861 (June 1992): 341–342.

32. Barth, *Church Dogmatics,* IV/2, p. 721.

33. Van Buren continues to keep before us the witness of Israel on this matter. "Israel serves [the world] by being true to its God and its covenant, by being Israel, the people of God. Its service to the world is not something additional for it to carry out. The world is best served when Israel serves God in the covenant. . . . This witness, so far as I can see, is one that the church needs to hear and think about. If the church can hear this witness, it might better learn that its first service to the world is to be the church, to be faithful to its God and to the life to which it has been called" (Paul van Buren, *A Theology of the Jewish-Christian Reality,* vol. 2, *A Christian Theology of the People Israel* [San Francisco: Harper and Row, 1983], p. 207).

34. Karl Barth, "The Christian Community and the Civil Community," in *Community, State, and Church* (Gloucester, MA: Peter Smith, 1968), p. 170.

35. Ronald Beiner, *What's the Matter with Liberalism?* (Berkeley: University of California Press, 1992), pp. 160–161.

36. Ibid., p. 168.

37. Stephen Carter, *The Culture of Disbelief: How American Law and Politics Trivialize Religious Devotion* (New York: Doubleday, 1993), pp. 147ff.

38. Ibid., p. 152.

39. "We Are Not Tax-Exempt," *Catholic Worker* 65, 5 (August-September 1998).

Bibliography

Aquinas, Thomas. 1948. *Summa Theologica*. 5 vols. Translated by Fathers of the English Dominican Province. Allen, TX: Christian Classics.

Augustine. 1955. "In Answer to the Jews (*Adversus Judaeos*)." In *Treatises on Marriage and Other Subjects*, vol. 27, *The Fathers of the Church*. Edited by Roy Joseph Defarrari. Washington, DC: Catholic University of America Press.

_____. 1972. *City of God*. Translated by Henry Bettenson. New York: Penguin.

Barth, Karl. 1954. *Against the Stream*. New York: Philosophical Library.

_____. 1956–1975. *Church Dogmatics*. 4 vols. Edited by G. W. Bromiley and T. F. Torrance. Edinburgh: T. & T. Clark.

_____. 1960. *The Humanity of God*. Atlanta, GA: John Knox Press.

_____. 1968. *Community, State, and Church*. Gloucester, MA: Peter Smith.

Beiner, Ronald. 1992. *What's the Matter with Liberalism?* Berkeley: University of California Press.

Bellah, Robert. 1992. *The Broken Covenant: American Civil Religion in Time of Trial*. 2nd ed. Chicago: University of Chicago Press.

Bellah, Robert, Richard Madsen, William M. Sullivan, Ann Swidler, and Steven Tipton. 1985. *Habits of the Heart: Individualism and Commitment in American Life*. New York: Harper and Row.

Berger, Peter. 1979. *The Heretical Imperative: Contemporary Possibilities of Religious Affirmation*. Garden City, NY: Anchor Press.

Bettenson, Henry, ed. and trans. 1956. *The Early Christian Fathers*. New York: Oxford University Press.

Boyarin, Daniel. 1994. *A Radical Jew: Paul and the Politics of Identity*. Berkeley: University of California Press.

Brueggemann, Walter. 1977. *The Land*. Philadelphia: Fortress Press.

_____. 1997. "Texts That Linger, Words That Explode," *Theology Today* 54, 2, pp. 180–199.

Busch, Eberhard. 1976. *Karl Barth: His Life from Letters and Autobiographical Texts*. Philadelphia: Fortress Press.

Calvin, John. 1954. *Calvin: Theological Treatises*. Edited by J. K. S. Reid. Philadelphia: Westminster.

_____. 1960. *Institutes of the Christian Religion*. Edited by John T. McNeill and translated by Ford Lewis Battles. Philadelphia: Westminster.

Carter, Stephen. 1993. *The Culture of Disbelief: How American Law and Politics Trivialize Religious Devotion*. New York: Doubleday.

Cavanaugh, William T. 1995. "'A Fire Strong Enough to Consume the House': The Wars of Religion and the Rise of the State." *Modern Theology* 11, 4, pp. 397–420.

Cherry, Conrad. 1971. *God's New Israel: Religious Interpretations of American Destiny*. Englewood Cliffs, NJ: Prentice-Hall.

Clinton, Bill. 1992. "A Vision for America: A New Covenant." Speech delivered at the Democratic National Convention, July 16.

———. 1995. "Address Before a Joint Session of the Congress on the State of the Union." *Weekly Compilation of Presidential Documents* 31, 4.

Coles, Romand. 1992. "Storied Others and the Possibility of *Caritas:* Milbank and Neo-Nietzschean Ethics." *Modern Theology* 8, 4, pp. 331–351.

Croner, Helga, ed. 1977. *Stepping Stones to Further Jewish-Christian Relations: An Unabridged Collection of Christian Documents.* New York: Stimulus Foundation.

———, ed. 1985. *More Stepping Stones to Jewish-Christian Relations: An Unabridged Collection of Christian Documents, 1975–1983.* New York: Stimulus Foundation.

Davies, W. D. 1974. *The Gospel and the Land.* Los Angeles: University of California Press.

Day, Dorothy. 1997. *Loaves and Fishes.* Maryknoll, NY: Orbis Books.

Dulles, Avery. 1995. "John Paul II and the Truth About Freedom." *First Things* 55, August-September, pp. 36–41.

Elliot, John Hall. 1966. *The Elect and the Holy.* Leiden, Netherlands: E. J. Brill.

The Epistle of Barnabas. 1981. In Alexander Roberts and James Donaldson, eds., *The Ante-Nicene Fathers,* vol. 1. Grand Rapids, MI: Eerdmans.

Flannery, Austin, ed. 1992. *Vatican Council II: The Conciliar and Post Conciliar Documents.* New rev. ed. Collegeville, MN: Liturgical Press.

Forde, Gerhard O. 1984. "The Work of Christ." In Carl E. Braaten and Robert W. Jenson, eds., *Christian Dogmatics,* vol. 2. Philadelphia: Fortress Press.

Freedman, Sarah. 1992. "Some Views of the Jews in the Fiction of Walker Percy." M.T.S. thesis, Duke University.

General Assembly of the Presbyterian Church (USA). 1988. "A Theological Understanding of the Relationship Between Christians and Jews." In World Council of Churches, ed., *The Theology of the Churches and the Jewish People.* Geneva: WCC Publications.

Geuss, Raymond. 1981. *The Idea of a Critical Theory.* Cambridge: Cambridge University Press.

Giddens, Anthony. 1987. *The Nation-State and Violence.* Berkeley: University of California Press.

Goldberg, Michael. 1995. *Why Should Jews Survive? Looking Past the Holocaust to a Jewish Future.* New York: Oxford University Press.

Goodman, Ellen. 1996. "Child's Choices Come Crashing Down." *Durham (North Carolina) Herald-Sun,* April 16.

Gustafson, James. 1981. *Ethics from a Theocentric Perspective.* Vol. 1, *Theology and Ethics.* Chicago: University of Chicago Press.

Hall, Douglas John. 1996. *Confessing the Faith.* Minneapolis: Fortress Press.

Hauerwas, Stanley. 1981. *A Community of Character: Toward a Constructive Christian Social Ethic.* Notre Dame, IN: University of Notre Dame Press.

———. 1982. *Vision and Virtue: Essays in Christian Ethical Reflection.* Notre Dame, IN: University of Notre Dame Press.

———. 1983. *The Peaceable Kingdom: A Primer in Christian Ethics.* Notre Dame, IN: University of Notre Dame Press.

———. 1988. *Christian Existence Today: Essays on Church, World and Living in Between.* Durham, NC: Labyrinth Press.

———. 1991. *After Christendom? How the Church Is to Behave if Freedom, Justice, and a Christian Nation Are Bad Ideas.* Nashville, TN: Abingdon Press.

_____. 1992. *Against the Nations: War and Survival in a Liberal Society.* Notre Dame, IN: University of Notre Dame Press.

_____. 1994. *Dispatches from the Front: Theological Engagements with the Secular.* Durham, NC: Duke University Press.

_____. 1995. *In Good Company: The Church as Polis.* Notre Dame, IN: University of Notre Dame Press.

Hauerwas, Stanley, and Charles Pinches. 1997. *Christians Among the Virtues: Theological Conversations with Ancient and Modern Ethics.* Notre Dame, IN: University of Notre Dame Press.

Hauerwas, Stanley, and Paul Wadell. 1982. "Book Review: *After Virtue." Thomist* 46, 2, pp. 313–322.

Hauerwas, Stanley, and William H. Willimon. 1989. *Resident Aliens.* Nashville, TN: Abingdon Press.

Hays, Richard B. 1989. *Echoes of Scripture in the Letters of Paul.* New Haven, CT: Yale University Press.

_____. 1996. *The Moral Vision of the New Testament: Community, Cross, New Creation.* San Francisco: HarperSanFrancisco.

Healy, Nicholas. 1994. "The Logic of Karl Barth's Ecclesiology: Analysis, Assessment and Proposed Modifications." *Modern Theology* 10, 3, pp. 253–270.

Heppe, Heinrich. 1950. *Reformed Dogmatics.* Translated by G. T. Thomson. London: George Allen & Unwin.

Hobbes, Thomas. 1962. *Leviathan: or the Matter, Forme and Power of a Commonwealth Ecclesiasticall and Civil.* Edited by Michael Oakeshott. New York: Macmillan.

Jacobs, Louis. 1995. *The Jewish Religion: A Companion.* New York: Oxford University Press.

Jefferson, Thomas. 1979. *Thomas Jefferson: Selected Writings.* Arlington Heights, IL: Harlan Davidson.

Jenson, Robert W. 1963. *Alpha and Omega: A Study in the Theology of Karl Barth.* New York: Thomas Nelson and Sons.

_____. 1984. "The Holy Spirit." In Carl E. Braaten and Robert W. Jenson, eds., *Christian Dogmatics,* vol. 2. Philadelphia: Fortress Press.

_____. 1996. "The God-Wars." In Carl E. Braaten and Robert W. Jenson, eds., *Either/Or: The Gospel or Neopaganism.* Grand Rapids, MI: Eerdmans.

Jewish Publication Society. 5748/1988. *Tanakh: The Holy Scriptures.* Philadelphia: Jewish Publication Society.

John Paul II. 1993. *Veritatis Splendor.* Vatican City: Libreria Editrice Vaticana.

Johnson, Luke Timothy. 1986. *The Writings of the New Testament: An Interpretation.* Philadelphia: Fortress Press.

Jones, L. Gregory. 1987. "Alasdair MacIntyre on Narrative, Community, and the Moral Life." *Modern Theology* 4, 1, pp. 52–69.

_____. 1990. *Transformed Judgment: Toward a Trinitarian Account of the Moral Life.* Notre Dame, IN: University of Notre Dame Press.

_____. 1995. *Embodying Forgiveness: A Theological Analysis.* Grand Rapids, MI: Eerdmans.

Jospe, Raphael. 1994. "The Concept of the Chosen People." *Judaism* 43, 2, pp. 127–148.

Keck, David. 1996. *Forgetting Whose We Are: Alzheimer's Disease and the Love of God.* Nashville, TN: Abingdon Press.

Keck, Leander E. 1986. "Toward the Renewal of New Testament Christology." *New Testament Studies* 32, pp. 362–377.

Kenneson, Philip D. 1993. "Selling [Out] the Church in the Marketplace of Desire." *Modern Theology* 9, 4, pp. 319–348.

LaCugna, Catherine Mowry. 1991. *God for Us: The Trinity and the Christian Life*. San Francisco: HarperSanFrancisco.

Lamm, Julia A. 1996. *The Living God: Schleiermacher's Theological Appropriation of Spinoza*. University Park: Pennsylvania State University Press.

Lehmann, Hartmut, and William R. Hutchison, eds. 1994. *Many Are Chosen: Divine Election and Western Nationalism*. Minneapolis: Fortress Press.

Leith, John H., ed. 1982. *Creeds of the Churches*. 3rd ed. Louisville, KY: John Knox Press.

Levenson, Jon. 1988. *Creation and the Persistence of Evil*. Princeton, NJ: Princeton University Press.

_____. 1993. *The Hebrew Bible, the Old Testament, and Historical Criticism*. Louisville, KY: Westminster/John Knox Press.

Lewis, C. S. 1958. *Reflections on the Psalms*. New York: Harcourt Brace Jovanovich.

Lindbeck, George. 1984. *The Nature of Doctrine: Religion and Theology in a Postliberal Age*. Philadelphia: Westminster.

_____. 1988. "The Church." In Geoffrey Wainwright, ed., *Keeping the Faith*. Philadelphia: Fortress Press.

Locke, John. 1993. *Political Writings of John Locke*. Edited by David Wootton. New York: Penguin.

Lohfink, Gerhard. 1984. *Jesus and Community: The Social Dimension of Christian Faith*. Translated by John P. Galvin. Philadelphia: Fortress Press.

Lohfink, Norbert. 1991. *The Covenant Never Revoked: Biblical Reflections on Jewish-Christian Dialogue*. New York: Paulist Press.

MacIntyre, Alasdair. 1984. *After Virtue: A Study in Moral Theory*. 2nd ed. Notre Dame, IN: University of Notre Dame Press.

_____. 1988. *Whose Justice? Which Rationality?* Notre Dame, IN: University of Notre Dame Press.

_____. 1990. *Three Rival Versions of Moral Enquiry*. Notre Dame, IN: University of Notre Dame Press.

Markus, R. A. 1970. *Saeculum: History and Society in the Theology of St Augustine*. Cambridge: Cambridge University Press.

Marshall, Bruce. 1995. "What Is Truth?" *Pro Ecclesia* 4, 4, pp. 404–430.

Matera, Frank J. 1996. *New Testament Ethics: The Legacies of Jesus and Paul*. Louisville, KY: Westminster/John Knox Press.

McKim, LindaJo, ed. *The Presbyterian Hymnal: Hymns, Psalms, and Spiritual Songs*. 1990. Louisville, KY: Westminster/John Knox Press.

Meeks, Wayne. 1983. *The First Urban Christians*. New Haven, CT: Yale University Press.

_____, ed. 1993. *HarperCollins Study Bible*. New York: HarperCollins.

Migliore, Daniel. 1991. *Faith Seeking Understanding*. Grand Rapids, MI: Eerdmans.

Milbank, John. 1990. *Theology and Social Theory: Beyond Secular Reason*. Cambridge, MA: Blackwell.

_____. 1992. "Enclaves, or Where Is the Church?" *New Blackfriars* 73, 861, pp. 341–352.

_____. 1997. *The Word Made Strange: Theology, Language, and Culture*. Cambridge, MA: Blackwell.

Mitchell, Joshua. 1993. *Not by Reason Alone: Religion, History, and Identity in Early Modern Political Thought.* Chicago: University of Chicago Press.

Montefiore, C. G., and H. Loewe. 1974. *A Rabbinic Anthology.* New York: Schocken Books.

Neusner, Jacob. 1991. *Jews and Christians: The Myth of a Common Tradition.* Philadelphia: Trinity Press International.

Niebuhr, Reinhold. 1963. *An Interpretation of Christian Ethics.* San Francisco: Harper and Row.

_____. 1986. *The Essential Reinhold Niebuhr.* Edited by Robert McAfee Brown. New Haven, CT: Yale University.

Nietzsche, Friedrich. 1968. *Basic Writings of Nietzsche.* Edited and translated by Walter Kaufmann. New York: Random House.

Novak, David. 1989. *Jewish-Christian Dialogue: A Jewish Justification.* New York: Oxford University Press.

_____. 1990. "Jewish Theology." *Modern Judaism* 10, pp. 311–323.

_____. 1991. "When Jews Are Christians." *First Things* 17, November, pp. 42–46.

_____. 1992. *Jewish Social Ethics.* New York: Oxford University Press.

_____. 1995. *The Election of Israel: The Idea of the Chosen People.* Cambridge: Cambridge University Press.

Nussbaum, Martha C. 1986. *The Fragility of Goodness: Luck and Ethics in Greek Tragedy and Philosophy.* Cambridge: Cambridge University Press.

_____. 1994. *The Therapy of Desire: Theory and Practice in Hellenistic Ethics.* Princeton, NJ: Princeton University Press.

Ochs, Peter. 1990. "A Rabbinic Pragmatism." In Bruce D. Marshall, ed., *Theology and Dialogue: Essays in Conversation with George Lindbeck.* Notre Dame, IN: University of Notre Dame Press.

O'Donovan, Oliver. 1994. *Resurrection and Moral Order: An Outline for Evangelical Ethics.* 2nd ed. Grand Rapids, MI: Eerdmans.

_____. 1996. *The Desire of the Nations: Rediscovering the Roots of Political Theology.* Cambridge: Cambridge University Press.

Pelikan, Jaroslav. 1961. *The Christian Tradition.* Vol. 1, *The Emergence of the Catholic Tradition (100–600).* Chicago: University of Chicago Press.

Percy, Walker. 1971. *Love in the Ruins: The Adventures of a Bad Catholic at a Time Near the End of the World.* New York: Ballantine Books.

_____. 1987. *The Thanatos Syndrome.* London: Andre Deutsch.

Pinches, Charles, and Jay B. MacDaniel. 1993. *Good News for Animals? Christian Approaches to Animal Well-Being.* Maryknoll, NY: Orbis Books.

Placher, William. 1994. *Narratives of a Vulnerable God: Christ, Theology, and Scripture.* Louisville, KY: Westminster/John Knox Press.

Polner, Murray, and Naomi Goodman, eds. 1994. *The Challenge of Shalom: The Jewish Tradition of Peace and Justice.* Philadelphia: New Society Publishers.

Presbyterian Church (USA). Theology and Worship Ministry Unit. 1993. *Book of Common Worship.* Louisville, KY: Westminster/John Knox Press.

Ritschl, Dietrich. 1987. *The Logic of Theology.* Philadelphia: Fortress Press.

Ruether, Rosemary. 1974. *Faith and Fratricide: The Theological Roots of Anti-Semitism.* Minneapolis: Seabury Press.

Schleiermacher, Friedrich. 1989. *The Christian Faith.* Edinburgh: T. & T. Clark.

Sider, Ronald J. 1977. "Sharing the Wealth: The Church as Biblical Model for Public Policy." *Christian Century* 94, 21, pp. 560–565.

Siker, Jeffrey. 1991. *Disinheriting the Jews: Abraham in Early Christian Controversy.* Louisville, KY: Westminster/John Knox Press.

Soulen, R. Kendall. 1996. *The God of Israel and Christian Theology.* Minneapolis: Fortress Press.

_____. Forthcoming. "YHWH the Triune God." *Modern Theology.*

Spinoza, Benedict de. 1951. *A Theologico-Political Treatise.* Translated by R. H. M. Elwes. New York: Dover.

Stout, Jeffrey. 1988. *Ethics After Babel: The Language of Morals and Their Discontents.* Boston: Beacon Press.

van Buren, Paul. 1980–1988. *A Theology of the Jewish-Christian Reality.* 3 vols. San Francisco: Harper and Row.

Wadell, Paul J. 1991. "What Do All Those Masses Do for Us? Reflections on the Christian Moral Life and the Eucharist." In Kathleen Hughes and Mark R. Francis, eds., *Living No Longer for Ourselves.* Collegeville, MN: Liturgical Press.

West, Cornel. 1982. *Prophesy Deliverance!* Philadelphia: Westminster.

Wiles, Maurice, and Mark Santer, eds. 1975. *Documents in Early Christian Thought.* Cambridge: Cambridge University Press.

Wilken, Robert. 1992. *The Land Called Holy: Palestine in Christian History and Thought.* New Haven, CT: Yale University Press.

Williams, Bernard. 1993. *Shame and Necessity.* Berkeley: University of California Press.

Williams, Rowan. 1987. "Politics and the Soul: A Reading of the *City of God.*" *Milltown Studies* 19-20, pp. 55–72.

Williams, Walter. 1996. "'Right to Die' Tests Commitment to Liberty." *Durham (North Carolina) Herald-Sun,* November 13.

Williamson, Clark. 1993. *A Guest in the House of Israel: Post-Holocaust Church Theology.* Louisville, KY: Westminster/John Knox Press.

Wright, N. T. 1991. *The Climax of the Covenant: Christ and the Law in Pauline Theology.* Minneapolis: Fortress Press.

Wyschogrod, Michael. 1970. "Israel, Church, and Election." In John M. Oesterreicher, ed., *Brothers in Hope.* New York: Herder and Herder.

_____. 1983. *The Body of Faith: God in the People Israel.* San Francisco: Harper and Row.

_____. 1986. "Christology: The Immovable Object." *Religion and Intellectual Life* 3, 4, pp. 77–80.

_____. 1986. "A Jewish Perspective on Karl Barth." In Donald K. McKim, ed., *How Karl Barth Changed My Mind.* Grand Rapids, MI: Eerdmans.

Yoder, John Howard. 1986. "Karl Barth: How His Mind Kept Changing." In Donald K. McKim, ed., *How Karl Barth Changed My Mind.* Grand Rapids, MI: Eerdmans.

_____. 1984. *The Priestly Kingdom: Social Ethics as Gospel.* Notre Dame, IN: University of Notre Dame Press.

_____. 1994. *The Politics of Jesus.* 2nd ed. Grand Rapids, MI: Eerdmans.

_____. 1994. "Why Ecclesiology Is Social Ethics: Gospel Ethics Versus the Wider Wisdom" In Michael G. Cartwright, ed., *The Royal Priesthood: Essays Ecclesiological and Ecumenical.* Grand Rapids, MI: Eerdmans.

Index

and freedom, 118, 123–125
with Israel, 19, 22, 24, 31, 37–44, 54,
    70–71, 82, 95–103
new, 48, 95–103, 107, 139–140, 143
and politics, 88, 94
See also Election; Israel

Davies, W. D., 144, 179–180(n30)
Day, Dorothy, 127–128. *See also* Catholic
    Worker
Death, 132–134
Dualism
    in election, 54–55
    Gnostic, 54

Election
    in Barth, 73–77
    in Calvin, 70–73
    and church, 2–3, 94
    de-Judaized, 52–57
    and freedom, 117–134
    Gnosticized, 54–55, 139
    of the individual, 71–77
    of Israel, 2–3, 28–51, 70, 94
    and Jesus Christ, 2, 73–77, 95–97,
        99–107, 110–116, 125, 127
    materiality of, 32, 46, 54–55, 71, 76,
        137–138, 140, 164(n95)
    national, 59–69, 74, 77
    and peace, 135–148
    politics of, 72, 94, 117–148
    recent discussions of, 150(n9)
    in Spinoza, 3, 19, 60–65, 160(n33)
    trinitarian, 3, 73, 77, 95–116
    and the USA, 65–69, 135
    and violence, 135–137
    See also Covenant; Politics;
        Redemption
Emotivism, 7, 11
Enlightenment, 3, 8, 60
Eschatology. *See* Redemption
Eucharist, 24, 86, 139–145, 148
Eusebius, 58–59

Euthanasia, 132–134

Freedom
    as autonomy, 3, 11, 28, 38, 123
    as choice, 7, 118–123, 132–135
    as consumerism, 7–8
    of election, 38–40, 43, 117–134,
        160(n45), 161(n53)
    and grace, 120, 123
    as isolation, 8
    of the will, 84, 120, 161(n53)
    See also Covenant; Election; Liberalism;
        Politics

Giddens, Anthony, 135
Gnosticism, 54–55, 57
God
    and baptism, 130–131
    as Being, 17
    as choice, 119–120, 176(n7)
    and christendom, 92–94
    and election, 18–19, 22, 30–37, 52–55,
        63, 70–77, 95–116
    and freedom, 117–134, 161(n53)
    and Israel, 22–52, 70, 78–90, 94–116,
        159(n25)
    and the nations, 60–69, 85–90,
        92–94
    nature of, 18, 20, 154–155(n56)
    and peace, 136–148
    and violence, 135
    See also Church; Holy Spirit; Israel;
        Jesus Christ; Trinity
Goldberg, Michael, 139
Gustafson, James, 154–155(n56)

Hauerwas, Stanley, 6, 15–16, 21–24, 87,
    122, 133, 156(n70), 156(n74),
    157(n84)
Hays, Richard, 22, 26, 53, 97, 173(n14)
Healy, Nicholas, 77, 170(n14)
Hegel, G.W.F., 16–17
Hobbes, Thomas, 9, 60–65